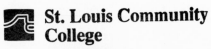

St. Louis Community College

Forest Park
Florissant Valley
Meramec

Instructional Resources
St. Louis, Missouri

GAYLORD

MALE MYTHS AND ICONS

Also by Roger Horrocks

MASCULINITY IN CRISIS: Myths, Fantasies and Realities

Male Myths and Icons

Masculinity in Popular Culture

Roger Horrocks

St. Martin's Press   New York

St. Martin's Press, Scholarly and Reference Division,
175 Fifth Avenue, New York, N.Y. 10010

Printed and bound in Great Britain

ISBN 0–312–12622–0 (cloth)
ISBN 0–312–12623–9 (paper)

Library of Congress Cataloging-in-Publication Data
Horrocks, Roger, 1946–
Male myths and icons : masculinity in popular culture / Roger
Horrocks.
p.   cm.
Includes bibliographical references and index.
ISBN 0–312–12622–0. — ISBN 0–312–12623–9 (pbk.)
1. Men in popular culture.   2. Masculinity (Psychology)
I. Title.
HQ1090.H67   1995
305.32—dc20   95–7737
                                                         CIP

For Adam

'Signs are small measurable things, but their interpretation is illimitable.'

George Eliot, *Middlemarch*

Contents

Acknowledgements

Warm thanks go to Jo Campling, who helped me to give shape to this book; and also to Annabelle Buckley, my editor, who has been unfailingly helpful. I am indebted to the anonymous reviewer, who helped me improve many sections.

Since I am not an academic, I am particularly reliant on various institutions and libraries for supplying me with material: in particular, I thank staff of the British Film Institute; the Independent Television Commission; the Sports Council, London; the Central Music Library, Westminster; the Samaritans; and the Library, University College London.

Several people have listened to me tirelessly, as I struggled to articulate the ideas in this book: specifically, I am very grateful to Sybilla Madigan and Judith Hemming. My friend Victoria Zinovieff has been just that, and has helped me enormously.

I can never thank Rachel enough for being there, and for helping me grasp concretely how men and women can live together in a spirit of equality and harmony.

A special thanks to my son Adam for all the hockey games we've played, the horror films we watched together, and the Metallica tapes he lent me.

ROGER HORROCKS

1 Introduction

This book sets out to analyze some images of men, and some images used by men, in popular culture. I have chosen to look at popular culture in the belief that such forms as the horror film, the western novel and film, rock and pop music, and sport, give interesting insights into the themes and contradictions in the masculine gender.

I see popular culture to some extent as dream-like, naive, not censored by a more sophisticated intellectual understanding. It is full of images that seem archetypal, primitive, welling up from the depths of the psyche. For example the horror film exists because people want to see images that frighten them and horrify them, yet also permit them some cathartic relief from their nightmarish fantasies. The horror film maker may develop very sophisticated ideas about his craft, but unless he sticks to the images that touch a chord in people, he will fail.

Thus, just as dreams can be used to gain insight into areas of the psyche that we are unwilling or unable to penetrate consciously, so popular images can be used to investigate collective unconscious attitudes and feelings.

At the same time, popular culture seems to relay political ideas very quickly, and can be seen as an arena where certain political struggles are contested. Hollywood, for example, has portrayed the rising self-confidence of women, the male backlash against this, and at times the 'gender war' that results.[1]

Thus, popular culture can be analyzed psychologically or politically. I shall endeavour to do both, since one without the other strikes me as quite imbalanced.

Popular art forms are also interesting in themselves, because they have a high degree of energy, an aesthetic quality that may lack finesse but provides something satisfying in its own way. There is something valuable and pleasurable in 'reclaiming' areas of culture that were formerly disdained or simply ignored.

One might superficially assume that popular images of masculinity would be unfailingly of the Rambo type – giving us a picture of ultra-machismo – but this is far from the truth. Indeed popular art is filled with contradictory images that reflect the tensions and ambivalences of masculinity. In fact, Rambo himself may not be as coherent an image of manliness as some critics have assumed.[2]

1

And we also find images of terrible damage being done to men. An outstanding example is the film *Born on the Fourth of July*, which describes how a young man is trained in gung-ho patriotism, goes to Vietnam, where he is badly injured and paralyzed. Such a film can be seen not only as a lament or protest about the war in Vietnam itself, but as a metaphor for the condition of American men generally.

The basic thrust of my analysis is a psychological one, deriving from my work as a psychotherapist. But a purely psychological theory of gender is quite inadequate, and I have therefore brought into play other theories and methods of analysis, particularly those derived from feminism, sociology and Marxism. In particular, from the political point of view, the various masculinities can be seen as part of the structure of patriarchy, as ideological constructions that create and consolidate male power over women.

In the first part of the book, I shall set out an approach to gender, and particularly masculinity, that accepts elements from both psychology and the feminist/sociological account of gender. However, my account of masculinity has quite a different flavour from some, since I do not see masculine identities as coherent. To my mind, gender studies has neglected the sheer scale of damage done to men under patriarchy, and the way in which masculine identities require a considerable shrinkage and curtailment of life for men.

This obviously affects my analysis of popular culture: for if the Terminator, for example, is in one sense an image of male brutality and carnage, it is also an image of the male robotized, and, quite literally in the film *The Terminator*, torn apart and 'terminated'. Thus, I find some accounts of male identity superficial and too monolithic. For example, it strikes me that 'male violence' is not simply a facet of patriarchal domination over women, but often arises from the abuse that men have themselves received.

THE SELECTION OF GENRES AND TEXTS

In a study such as this, the actual texts selected help determine the nature of the project. On what basis have I made this selection?

I have naturally chosen genres and texts which mean something to me, which have influenced me in different ways. To paraphrase Dylan Thomas, I would be a fool if I didn't![3] But one cannot simply pick and mix one's own personal choice of texts: my aim is to give a reasonably coherent view of certain areas of popular culture which depict men and masculinities.

In the first place, I need to choose at least one myth or set of myths concerning masculinity that has been prominent in popular culture, and in this light, the western seems to select itself. No other genre has so consistently, repetitively, addressed a set of issues and narratives concerning men. It has also been the chief mythic construction in Hollywood, and that again argues for a close examination of it, since Hollywood is one of the most important 'myth-making' institutions in Western culture. But the western is not simply an American genre: its appeal and influence have been world-wide.

Secondly, I have devoted a chapter to horror films, for two main reasons. This is a genre that seems to appeal mainly to young male audiences – this in itself makes it interesting to students of gender. Also horror films and novels form a very important body of material exploring notions of insanity, science, religion, sexuality, perversity, and so on. And gender (along with sexuality) runs through horror like the San Andreas fault. We might even say that gender *is* the horror.

My third choice – pornography – might seem to lie outside the ambit of 'popular culture', but there are several reasons why I have included it. First, it is precisely its threshold status, lying on the boundaries of good/bad taste, that makes it interesting. Secondly, it has been one of the great topics in feminism for the last two decades, and some of the arguments put forward in feminist discussion, concerning the nature of representation, the nature of male desire, and so on, are very important in any overall consideration of masculinity. Thirdly, it strikes me that the obsession with images of the female body – found *par excellence* in pornography – must be addressed in any overall discussion of 'male culture'. Indeed, the female body has probably been the chief icon of Western culture, and porn can be seen as a subset of a massive set of such representations.[4]

Cinema and pornography have been fairly extensively discussed in cultural studies, feminism and film studies. One might say they have been, and are being, 'theorized'. It therefore seems important to choose several other cultural areas that are more opaque, mystified, unconscious. I see both popular music and sport in this light, and it seems worthwhile to tackle such areas of culture and attempt to 'unpack' them.

Music has seen a contemporary explosion of energy in all the various genres of pop music, and young males have been heavily involved since the beginning of rock 'n' roll. And pop music has also been associated with various 'subcultures', which themselves seem to provide insights into various masculinities – for example, mods, punks, skinheads, 'headbangers', and so on.

Sport has until recently been remarkably resistant to academic enquiry, but the research now being done by historians and sociologists shows how important male sport is in the consolidation of various masculine images and life-styles.

I am all too conscious of the many omissions from this book. For example, I have ignored the popular press, advertising, television, popular fiction, computer games, children's toys, clothing and fashion, shopping and its associated culture. There is no sense in which any of these topics deserves to be excluded: but I believe the ones included are important in any consideration of the 'cultures of masculinity'.

A further point is that I have tried to present a wide cross-section of genres and media: in particular, I have utilized an ambiguity in the phrase 'male myths' in the title of this book. This can either mean 'myths about men' or 'myths for men'. Thus there are genres which present a male spectacle to a male audience – the western, male sport; there is one genre with a mainly male audience, but with both male and female 'objects' – horror; and another with a mainly female spectacle – pornography. Rock/pop music is quite heterogeneous, and contains many genres which have different audiences and performers. Thus there are genres in which males perform to males (heavy metal); and genres in which males perform mainly to females (boy groups).

Clearly this issue of gendered audiences and spectacles is itself an important one, and will be discussed throughout the book.

THE ATLANTIC

One issue that I have dealt with only sketchily is the mutual influence of British and American popular culture. At times this seems to be uni-directional, sweeping like a great gale from West to East: I am thinking of Hollywood, which has obviously dominated contemporary cinema. And so many films about men are from Hollywood, and therefore may not sit at all neatly within a British context. For example, the obsession with the 'buddy' movie in Hollywood does not have an exact equivalent in British culture. Indeed, one can argue that the 'buddy' theme is the central theme in American culture as a whole, and has replaced the themes of romantic love and adultery which are so prevalent in European culture (see Chapter 5).

Rock music shows fascinating to-and-fro shifts of influence – the first great impetus coming from America in the shape of black blues and rhythm 'n' blues, and white country music. But in the 60s, British pop music added its own qualities of energy and lyricism to produce groups such as the Beatles and the Rolling Stones.

Sport has been less porous: British and American sport have historically taken separate courses – until recently. One can see in the 80s and 90s some penetration of American sport into British culture.

The 'Americanness' of various cultural forms has itself provided for British audiences a symbol of the exotic, the glamorous and the hedonistic. For example, the figure of Elvis Presley had an unfamiliar quality for British fans which made him even more fantastic and outrageous as a symbol of sexuality, aggression and counter-culture.

Equally, many critics have bewailed the increasing amount of American culture found in Britain, and have seen in it signs of barbarism and anti-culture.[5]

ORGANIZATION OF THE BOOK

The book falls into two parts: the first part (Chapters 2 to 4) outlines some of the theoretical background to the study of gender, and the study of popular culture. The second part (Chapters 5 to 9) presents an empirical sketch of certain cultural forms that present interesting images of masculinity.

First, then, we need to look briefly at how masculinity can be studied. In Chapter 2 I shall discuss five approaches to gender which I have found useful: feminism, gay studies, Marxism, a specific psychological approach, and the treatment of gender as myth.

In Chapter 3 I consider the new approaches to popular culture found in cultural studies, particularly the influence of structuralism, certain Marxist ideas, and the notions of pleasure and aesthetics.

In Chapter 4 I shall outline various psychological approaches to the study of culture. I have focused on the issue of the reader's/viewer's identification with elements in the 'text'. This has been extensively discussed in cultural studies, and in specific disciplines such as film studies, and is also central to psychological theory in psychotherapy.

In Chapters 5–9 I examine a number of popular cultural forms: the western film and novel; horror in film and novel; pornography; rock music; and sport as a mass masculine spectacle.

2 Approaches to Gender

The study of gender is in ferment today. Feminists, sociologists, political analysts, psychologists and psychoanalysts, literary critics, film critics – many scholars are taking part in the 'discovery' of gender. Previously, the relations of power between men and women, the hidden political structures of heterosexuality and the family, the way gender permeates many cultural areas such as sport, film, music, literature – these aspects of social existence had been relatively ignored. One could argue that they were simply unconscious; alternatively one might suggest that they were 'mystified', in the semi-conscious wish to keep injustice hidden. But certainly there has been an explosion of work in the last two decades: work on gender can be found in many areas where it had been unknown, for example in the sociology of sport, or in film studies.

From this contemporary ferment I need to extract some analytical tools, with which I can examine the structure and content of masculine images in popular culture. Out of this vast field, I have found five main areas particularly useful, and I would like briefly to summarize them here.

FEMINISM

Feminism has carried out an invaluable task in the last thirty years: it has uncovered the political nature of gender. Instead of seeing gender relations as somehow 'natural' or trivial, feminists have been able to show that they embody relationships of power, and form an integral part of patriarchal rule. Thus, both 'masculinity' and 'femininity' are socially constructed, and function as ideological placements. Men have generally been exalted and women demeaned under patriarchy; but this is not simply a question of 'attitudes' between the sexes. Gender embodies concrete structures of male domination and female subordination.[1]

Let me cite as a specific example the different ways in which men's and women's bodies have been treated in the nineteenth and twentieth centuries. In the Victorian age, whereas men were encouraged to take exercise and practise sport, women were told that their bodies were inherently frail and vulnerable. This had the effect of imprisoning women in static positions in the home, and in cumbersome restrictive clothing, such as the whalebone corset.[2] Indeed this distinction continued into the twentieth century, and can still be found today.

This example shows how feminism has been able to demystify phenomena which were previously taken for granted, or seen as 'natural'. However, having accepted the explanatory power of the feminist treatment of gender, I want to utter a note of caution. I don't think masculinity is simply politically 'hegemonic': it has other complex functions and meanings. At times feminism falls into a kind of pessimistic philosophical idealism: 'men' and 'women' are portrayed as eternal forces forever doomed to struggle against each other, with women the perennial victims of male power.

Let me give as an example of this tendency, Beatrix Campbell's book, *Goliath: Britain's Dangerous Places*.[3] This strikes me as a schizophrenic book. On the one hand, it gives a stunning portrayal of inner-city riots in the 1990s in Britain, and shows how New Right policies in the 1980s had decimated working-class housing estates, leaving a trail of unemployment, reduced social services, and urban areas abandoned by politicians and police.

But in discussing the gangs of male rioters, Campbell posits a 'lawless masculinity', which wages war on its own community. It is at this point that Campbell falls into essentialism – ironically, since feminism has done so much to deconstruct essentialist concepts in many disciplines. 'Lawless masculinity' simply exists *sui generis*: destructive, aggressive, wreaking havoc on its own communities. This is her conclusion in the final chapter: 'Crime and coercion are sustained by men. Solidarity and self-help are sustained by women. It is as stark as that'.[4]

This prospect stretches out into the next century as an eternal blight on society. The end of her book strikes a note of doom:

> It is hard to imagine anything in *fin de siècle* Britain that will change the conditions of existence among the poor people. By the end of the century the children who entered society when they started school during the riots will be entering their dangerous years when they become teenagers. Among them will be these five-year olds, who talk about their life and times in Meadowell with an enlightening realism. They reveal how far their identities as boys and girls are assigned to the tasks taking *from* and taking *care*. Their futures are already ancient history. When asked what she wanted to be, a girl insisted: 'I want to be a mam'. Her playmates agreed, they wanted to be mams and dads. Then a boy dissented: 'I don't want to be a dad, I want to be a robber'. [original emphasis][5]

'Their futures are already ancient history'. There speaks a helplessness and hopelessness that is painful to hear. Campbell is tuning in to one of the great moral panics of the 1980s and 90s, seen for example in Britain in the furore aroused by the James Bulger murder trial in 1993. How could ten-year-old boys commit murder? Commentators threw numerous theories in the air: social deprivation, single mothers, video nasties. But hovering over much of the comment was the spectre of male criminality, often ripped out of its social context and treated as a kind of *deus ex machina*. The violent male, the male rapist, *homo terribilis*, haunts many books by radical feminists such as Mary Daly, Robin Morgan and Andrea Dworkin. Strangely enough, this view is supported by some right-wing politicians, who periodically make use of 'thugs on the street' rhetoric to whip up moral panics over law and order.

I find it significant that Campbell devotes very little space to the anti-poll tax struggles of the late 80s, for in this struggle men and women, young and old, black and white, worked together. Indeed, the movement against the poll tax is surely one of the most significant political struggles in Britain since the war. It was massive and implacable. For example, large areas of urban Scotland simply refused to pay the poll tax, and when the bailiffs came to claim goods in lieu, communities turned out *en masse* to resist them. And the government were forced to retreat on the poll tax issue, and substituted the less contentious council tax. I see the poll tax struggle as directly contradicting Campbell's pessimism and idealism: such categories as 'lawless men' are not fixed for all time.

But feminism is not homogeneous. Socialist feminists have protested at the picture presented by the radical feminist thinkers. Writers such as Lynne Segal have been able to make a critique of traditional masculinities, without falling into the trap of eternalizing them or reifying them. In her books *Is the Future Female?* and *Slow Motion*, Segal argues that radical feminism has produced a new form of essentialism: 'The belief that men will never change, that male dominance is inevitable and incurable, has become a dominant view, at least within radical feminism.'[6] And she argues fiercely against this position, from a socialist feminist position:

> Social realities are not static. Future relations between men and women remain open, battles are continuously fought, lost and won; and change, whether the intended outcome of emancipatory activity or the unintended consequence of other agencies, is inevitable. Much of the recent feminist writing on men has seemed to suggest that nothing has changed. But it is more interesting, and certainly more useful, to see how things do in fact change.[7]

This also suggests to me that men cannot simply be seen as beatified supreme rulers: patriarchy constricts and damages them considerably.

Something else that Campbell ignores in her book is the contemporary epidemic of suicides among young men.[8] If we take this along with alcoholism and drug addiction – also much commoner among men – we get some insight into the profound despair amongst men in Britain's wastelands. So far from revealing an eternal savage masculinity, concerned above all to keep women down, these social indices present a picture of men in despair, broken, without meaning.

There are clearly profound divisions within feminism concerning the nature of patriarchy and the roots of male oppression. Similar divisions can be found in the feminist analysis of culture. 1960s and early 1970s feminism tended to see patriarchal culture as ideologically *coherent*. For example, while Kate Millett's *Sexual Politics* (1970) brilliantly demonstrates the supremacism and misogyny in writers such as D. H. Lawrence, Henry Miller and Norman Mailer, I think she underestimates the considerable fear of women in these writers. They are not simply arrogant, but also confused, terrified, in awe of women. Millett detects this fragility, but seems to see it as fantasy. Thus, in speaking of Norman Mailer's obsession with machismo, she states: 'he has gone so far as to conceive of masculinity as a precarious spiritual capital, in endless need of replenishment and threatened on every side'.[9]

I am not defending Mailer's peculiar mixture of romanticized violence and homophobia. What interests me here is Millett's phrase 'he has gone so far as to ...'. This suggests that the idea of a fragile masculinity is absurd. But it is clear to me, from my therapy work with men, that many of them do see women as very powerful, and see their own masculinity as indeed 'precarious' and 'threatened'.[10] My own view of Lawrence's misogyny, for example, is that he lived in mortal terror of women, and experienced himself as powerless and without a true centre. In fact he had a massively ambivalent view of women. In a novel such as *Women in Love*, women are at times seen in almost religious terms ('Mother and substance of all life she was'), while at other times Birkin (a very Lawrence-like character) is horrified by them ('He had a horror of the Magna Mater, she was detestable').[11]

However, during the 1980s and 90s, feminist cultural analysis has broken up the apparent surface coherence of patriarchy, and has explored in greater depth the contradictions of masculinity. Such books as Carol Clover's *Men, Women and Chainsaws* (on the 'slasher' film), Jane Tompkins' *West of Everything* (on the western), Linda Williams' *Hard Core* (about pornography) and Tania Modleski's *The Women Who Knew Too Much* (on Alfred Hitchcock) have investigated the 'deep structure' of masculinity, and have noticed its friability, its ambivalences and its defensive qualities. I shall be returning to such studies later in the book.

GAY AND LESBIAN STUDIES

No area of study and research has contributed more energy and verve to the study of gender and sexuality than gay and lesbian studies, which have swept cobwebs out of many areas too long dominated by the aridities of psychoanalysis and sexology. Gay studies has become a virtual explosion since the mid-1980s, and its contribution has become so wide and varied that I can only mention a few topics here.

First, such concepts as heterosexuality and homosexuality have been deconstructed and historicized. Instead of being seen as absolute (even innate) categories, gay studies has been able to demonstrate their relativity. Thus, the concept of 'homosexuality' and the 'homosexual' is a comparatively recent one, as is the concept of heterosexuality itself.[12] In particular, one can cite the monumental achievement of Foucault, who in his *History of Sexuality* has provided the most significant theoretical account of sexuality since Freud's. Foucault argues that

> Sexuality must not be seen as a stubborn drive ... It appears rather as an especially dense transfer point for relations of power: between men and women, young people and old people, parents and offspring, teachers and students.[13]

Thus, Foucault carried on the great shift away from biological and behaviourist ways of approaching gender and sexuality, which was begun by psychoanalysis. If Freud had shown the *psychic* foundations of sexuality, Foucault went a stage further by *politicizing* and *historicizing* sex and gender. He also dissolved sexuality into a 'multiplicity of sexual discourses', although this aspect of his work has tended to alienate some Anglo-Saxon scholars.[14]

Secondly, gay studies has been able to deconstruct straight culture and straight images of men and women, and show that in fact a considerable degree of homoerotic and homosexual imagery and feeling exist within them. This idea was anticipated by Leslie Fiedler's astonishing critical work, *Love and Death in the American Novel* (1966), which pointed out, much to the scandal of some scholars, that American literature was full of intense male relationships: men who strove to avoid heterosexuality at all costs, and escaped into the wilderness in order to be with each other.[15] This theme has now been taken up and amplified by later writers, who have demonstrated how both high and low culture are shot through with 'queer' images and ideas. One can mention here books such as Wayne Studer's on 'gay' rock 'n' roll, *Rock on the Wild Side*, Mark Simpson's

Male Impersonators, and Marjorie Garber's book on transvestism, *Vested Interests*.[16]

What is perhaps more problematical is to account for the large amount of homoerotic material in male culture. Politically, one can refer to the notion, put forward by scholars such as Eve Sedgwick, that patriarchy requires intense male homosocial bonding.[17] This also explains why certain cultural areas, such as male sport, are both homoerotic and homophobic, since patriarchy has simultaneously to bring men together but disbar an overt mutual sexuality. Sedgwick describes this pithily as the '*pre*scription of the most intimate male bonding and the *pro*scription of the (remarkably cognate) "homosexuality"'.[18]

In fact, this is a rather gloomy perspective, since it suggests that patriarchal society requires the manufacture of large amounts of homosocial/homoerotic culture, which is then policed by fierce homophobic prejudices and laws. This might indicate, pessimistically, that an increase in homoerotic images – described with great enthusiasm by Mark Simpson, in *Male Impersonators*, as a liberatory explosion, and a virtual disintegration of traditional heterosexuality[19] – might in fact function as a reinforcement of patriarchal masculinism, and a backlash against feminism.

But one can also point to other possible motivations for a widespread homoeroticism: the classical psychoanalytic view is that homosexuality exists covertly in everyone, and it is not surprising therefore that it periodically erupts into consciousness. In 1915 Freud added the famous footnote to his *Three Essays on Sexuality*, so often cited subsequently as an argument for an innate human bisexuality:

> All human beings are capable of making a homosexual object-choice, and have in fact made one in their unconscious ... from the point of view of psychoanalysis the exclusive sexual interest felt by men for women is also a problem that needs elucidating and is not a self-evident fact.[20]

One can also suggest that the growth of homoerotic imagery is part of a general crisis in masculine identity. Old boundaries of gender and sexuality are being blurred and transcended: if you like, there is a 'leakage' between categories. I also see in it a yearning for maleness and masculinity, which may seem odd in a 'masculinist' culture, but which shows perhaps how many men feel both insecure about, and dissatisfied with, their identity.

This leads me to a third major contribution of gay and lesbian studies: the traditional categories and boundaries in gender and sexuality have been blurred and melted, indeed sabotaged, not just theoretically but in practical life. One can cite here the playing with gender that both gay men and lesbians have undertaken, breaking down the old stereotypes, for example, that gays are camp and lesbians are butch. Notions of active and passive, phallic and vaginal, sadism and masochism, fathering and mothering, seem much more fluid as a result of the great wave of gay liberation and research.

Fourthly, and really acting as an umbrella idea, gay studies has intensely politicized gender and sexuality. Gay men and lesbians had no choice in this matter, since the state had politicized their own identity, but one of the spin-offs has been that heterosexuality itself can be analyzed politically, not as a 'natural' choice, or a biologically driven appetite, but as an identity that locks into the gears of a patriarchal capitalist culture that fetishizes the family, and uses heterosexuality to punish other identities (and also, to punish heterosexuals!).

One need only point to the persecution of gay people in Nazi Germany and in contemporary Iran to see the clear connection between dictatorship and sexual tyranny. But it has also become possible for heterosexual people to investigate how much their own gender and sexuality is imprisoned by hide-bound stereotypes which serve reactionary ends. It is clear therefore that heterosexuality is no bed of roses, but for many people involves intense suffering and self-distortion. But the interesting point is that heterosexuality can itself be deconstructed.[21]

Fifthly, gay culture has had a huge impact in certain areas of popular culture, particularly music, dance and fashion, and has again caused a generalized loosening of inhibitions and constrictions.

In short, the explosion of gay studies and gay culture has opened up the whole area of gender and sexuality, by subverting unconscious assumptions that certain genders and sexualities were 'normal' and others were 'perverse'. This is reminiscent of Freud's comments about the 'unbroken chain' that exists between the normal and the perverse, but that insight, and its radical implications, have been (not surprisingly) neglected subsequently in psychoanalysis.[22]

Very profound issues to do with identity, meaning and political power have been raised by gay studies, and many other disciplines can be interrogated using its insights. For example, is the psychoanalytic notion of the 'perverse' a viable one, or is it in fact a means of establishing, consolidating and comforting those who define themselves as non-perverse? Is Marxism correct in its economic explanation of the family? How does this square with the great importance of sexuality in some cultures?[23] The whole gamut of left-wing thought has been challenged by gay research, since the left has traditionally been shot through with homophobic and sexist ideology.

I have glossed over some of the undoubted difficulties found in a gay-inspired model of gender and sexuality. For example, it has sometimes led to an understandable but unhelpful 'heterophobia' – this issue is discussed at length in Lynne Segal's book *Straight Sex*.

I also sometimes see gay studies as too optimistic and too voluntaristic in its assumptions: as if (in caricature) all we have to do is *choose* our orientation! Or, in the words of Jeffrey Weeks: 'what is needed today is a politics around desire which is a politics of choice, which clarifies the criteria by which as sexual subjects we can *choose* our social and sexual commitments' [original emphasis].[24] This ignores the profound insight of both psychoanalysis and Marxism that 'freedom is the recognition of necessity'. We can't simply sidestep or dissolve the identities imposed on us by family and society: that is a fantastic utopia that quickly breaks down in any confrontation with the personal unconscious or the social unconscious.

Despite such problems, the overall contribution of gay studies has been so positive and energetic, that it can now be seen, after psychoanalysis and feminism, as a third great impetus in the study of gender and sexuality.

MARXISM

The first Marxist theory of gender was provided by Engels in his work *The Family, Private Property and the State*. Briefly, Engels derives male dominance from the male ownership of land, cattle, tools, and so on. It is fundamentally an economic thesis: gender is underpinned by the relations of production.

Engels' original model has been heavily criticized by some post-war Marxists for positing such a one-to-one relationship between economics and 'superstructural' factors such as gender. 'Critical' Marxists such as Althusser have suggested that the relationship between economic, political and cultural formations is much more subtle than this, and that each area has a quasi-autonomy.[25]

Thus, Bob Connell has commented that the position of men in the modern state cannot be simply related to their economic power: 'sexual politics brought to light patterns of power, interest and conflict which made little sense in terms of socialist class analysis'. And Caroline Ramazanoglu states baldly: 'marxist analysis could not explain women's oppression by men.'[26] Certainly gender has been a massive lacuna in classical Marxism, many writers simply paying lip-service to Engels' original formulations, but ignoring any closer analysis of the family, or hegemonic heterosexuality. Marxism has also been vulnerable to the criticism that it is itself a patriarchal body of knowledge, and that Marxist parties have been notoriously 'masculinist' in their organization and political activity.[27]

A rather different kind of materialist theory is provided in social anthropology by those investigators who see masculinity as derived from the social and economic demands of patriarchy.[28] This can be related to the feminist position, but it has important differences. For here, we are concerned not only with men's domination of women, but with all the tasks that men are called upon to do. Men are required to carry out onerous and dangerous tasks, for example, obtaining food through hunting, protecting the tribe against other warring tribes, propagating many children, providing for them, and so on. In this sense, manhood has economic and social functions. David Gilmore therefore goes to some lengths, in his book *Manhood in the Making*, to demonstrate that masculine identity is not fixed or unchanging, but can be shown to vary according to the requirements of particular societies.[29]

This view also suggests that men are themselves exploited and objectified by capitalism. This point is quite important in political struggles against traditional gender, since it suggests that men are prisoners of gender and not simply beneficiaries of it.

SYMBIOSIS

I would now like briefly to consider the psychological approach to gender, and in particular, one hypothesis that has great importance: that for the male infant, masculinity is a defence against femininity. In this view the acquisition of masculinity consists of an emergence from a female world into a male world. How does this proceed?

Every human infant goes through a trajectory of growing separation. At first it exists inside a woman's body. Separate existence is actually physically impossible. We might imagine ideally, that for the growing foetus, life is intra-uterine bliss. Everything is done for it – feeding, excretion, oxygenation – these are all taken care of automatically.

After birth mother provides the infant with a degree of continuity. She is still there as a provider and container. Nonetheless there has already been a huge act of physical separation.

Then the growing infant desires to separate from mother, within certain limits. He wants both to be separate and to be able to reunite with her, and mothering has to deal with these conflicting needs in the infant. This need for separation is found in both male and female children, and in adult psychotherapy many people are found to be suffering from some trauma derived from this stage: some people never managed to separate and therefore find it difficult to find their own way in life; others became permanently alienated and unable to be intimate.

But the male infant has to make a further separation – he must become a different gender. He has to become a not-woman, and unlike his mother in various ways. Here the role of father is often seen as crucial in inducting his son into this other world – but behind father stands the patriarchal world, with its demand on the boy: become a man.

There has been much speculation in psychology that the male severance from the maternal symbiosis causes deep and permanent trauma. Hudson and Jacot, in their book *The Way Men Think*, describe the separation from mother as the male 'wound', and describe the considerable advantages and disadvantages that flow from this wound:

> The more 'male' the male, the greater the imaginative gulf separating him from his sources of primitive comfort; and the greater that gulf, we would predict, the greater his underlying existential insecurity is bound to be. He is perfectly poised, nevertheless, to heal his wound at one symbolic remove; to use the anxiety his separation provokes in him to create systems of ideas which can stand in the place of the lost intimacy, and within which he can strive for coherence and harmony.[30]

The idea of compensatory activity in men – activity which 'stands in the place of the lost intimacy' – strikes me as a very powerful idea, which partially explains the intense drive that many men possess in the business world, in science, and in the professions. We can express it metaphorically: men are cast out from the maternal Paradise, and struggle to find ways of getting back there, or set out to create a new phallic Paradise from their own ideas and actions. It is certainly not a new idea – psychoanalysts such as Karen Horney discussed it forty years ago – but it acquires new significance today within gender studies.

My chief quarrel with the psychological notion of the male wound, and the symbolic attempts to heal it, is that it tends to isolate the production of men and masculinity from the socio-political context. Thus, Hudson and Jacot focus on the 'family nexus' as the arena within which masculinities are founded, as do other psychologists and analysts working on gender, for example Robert Stoller.[31] But I think one has to widen the arena: the removal of boys from the maternal symbiosis is *a demand made by patriarchy*, which requires the production of 'men' to carry out the various duties outlined in the previous section. In British culture, this traumatic rupture has been expressed most vividly in the removal of boys to boarding schools at very young ages.

Thus, we are able to bring together the political and psychological analysis of gender: the demand for certain kinds of masculinity, promoted initially in the family, flows from patriarchal rule. In this sense the family acts as an executive organ of society, and a conduit for the channelling of ideological messages, a point made by Erich Fromm in his critique of psychoanalysis:

> The family is the medium through which the society or the social class stamps its specific structure upon the child, and hence on the adult. *The family is the psychological agency of society.* [original emphasis][32]

This may seem a rather obvious point to make, yet it represents a most fruitful bringing together of psychological and political ideas about gender. Psychology has tended to focus on the family as the source of gender identity, whereas sociology and political analysis have focused on larger-scale structures, for example work practices. But as Fromm says again: 'the thesis that psychology only deals with the individual, while sociology only deals with "society" is false'.[33]

GENDER AS MYTH

Clearly the young male infant is confronted with a gendered world: he learns that he is, or ought to be, 'different' from his mother and sisters, and 'the same' as his father and brothers. But what importance does cultural activity have in the induction and maintenance of gender stability? If we consider the training of children in gender, it is clear that they are not taught abstractly or intellectually, but concretely. All the time, children are presented with imaginative constructs which tell 'stories' about gender: narratives of all kinds, including fairy-stories, toys, games, TV, music, newspapers and magazines, books, and so on. All of this forms a battery of 'propaganda', which informs the child how men and women differ. And of course his interactions with family members, and his perceptions of their interactions, can also be seen as 'stories' containing information about gender.

In this light I want to claim that part of our education in, and knowledge of, gender involves the absorption of a set of very complex interlocking unconscious myths about men and women, how they should behave, think, feel, dress, work, make love, speak, and so on.

I am not saying gender is 'untrue' or unreal, when I say that it contains a set of myths. It is certainly real, and most of the time for most of us it just seems to be true that men are 'masculine', and women are 'feminine', so much so that people are often tempted to say that these things are innately given.

The nature of myth is highly complex, and cannot be fully dealt with here.[34] Let me say briefly that myths flow from the social unconscious: they are an important part of the socially constructed reality in every culture. I shall define myths quite simply as *collective fantasies*, that give substance and structure to a society's political, social, economic and cultural existence, and also help structure the individual's existence.

The word 'fantasy' here should not be taken as a pejorative term, denoting perhaps a world of make-believe and unreality. That is one way in which the word is used today, but within psychotherapy it has been used to describe the way that mental life itself functions – through fantasy, we construct narratives, scenarios, collections of images. Thus, for example, one might argue that everyone's sense of personal identity, or notions of nationhood and patriotism, are powerful collective myths.

Within mythical narratives, 'icons' are fashioned, that is, key figures or exemplars, who have somehow lost their everyday reality and have become legendary figures, who seem to contain within themselves a whole résumé of emblematic meanings. Thus, if we say that Clint Eastwood has become an icon of the post-war western, we are referring to the strange fact that it is Eastwood himself who has become a focus of attention in the films he directs and acts in. This gives his presence in a western an odd dual quality, for as spectators we watch the character played by Eastwood (say William Munny in *Unforgiven*), and we also watch Eastwood *qua* Eastwood. Thus, Eastwood's own career itself becomes a narrative that fascinates both his fans and detractors, and interacts with the fictive narratives he plays in.[35]

Myths and icons can be both fictive and non-fictive. Eastwood is an example of a non-fictive icon, but the character he plays in *Unforgiven* – the retired gunfighter who comes back for one last fling – is an icon within the standard western set of symbols, in other words, western 'iconography'.

The term 'icon' also has the further connotation of religious worship, which provides an interesting reflection on the way that 'stars' of cinema and pop music seem to become semi-religious figures.[36]

Clearly myths have to be inculcated and maintained. For example, Christianity has always taken great pains to educate children in its teachings, and to punish those who dissent. The severity of punishments can also be related to the insecurity with which the myths are held.

Thus, for men the slippery nature of gender seems to be particularly frightening: many aspects of masculinity myths are concerned with the assertion of toughness, stoicism, courage, and the distinguishing of this from a 'soft' femininity that belongs to women. Thus, the Hollywood western endlessly repeats certain attributes of manhood, and excises women and femininity to a large degree. But there is also an unconscious betrayal here: some of the men become male 'heroines' within the male couple. The feminine slips in the back door, as the repressed always will.

It is always possible then to cross over the boundary between one gender and another. Masculinity has to be maintained, or like the male erection itself, it threatens to topple. Thus, myths of masculinity must promise both rewards for conformity, and punishment for transgression. For example, within male sport there is tremendous pressure to be 'one of the boys'; there is also fierce homophobia and misogyny, which threaten any man who diverges from the accepted norm. I recall, for example, at my secondary school, how those boys who didn't enjoy physical sport were mocked by other boys, and by certain PE teachers. The fat boy, the boy with spectacles, the more feminine boy, the introverted boy – they all had to run a gauntlet of disapproval or worse. 'You play like a bunch of girls' – that taunt still echoes in my mind. Its misogyny was used to punish boys who weren't 'man enough'.

Something else must be pointed out: the maintenance and reinforcement of gender myths does not cease as childhood ends. Throughout our adult lives there is an endless stream of messages about gender which tend to keep us to the primrose path of rectitude. It has been observed by commentators in different disciplines, such as anthropology and psychoanalysis, that the strenuousness of the masculine identities is a pointer, not to their solidity, but their fragility: to be *mucho hombre* is not a birthright, but an accomplishment won and maintained with pain and difficulty. Puberty in many cultures is marked by agonizing rituals which test young boys for their entry into manhood; later in life, men are constantly tested against a ferocious set of myths and rituals. I recall a client of mine who queried the necessity for him to have a painful examination in hospital – his doctor rounded on him with these words: 'Am I to tell the consultant that my patient is a coward?'

MYTH AND LIFE

Any discussion of myth and fantasy must consider the relationship between myths and the lives of individuals and societies. To what extent are our lives guided by such collective narratives? Are we coerced by them, merely entertained by them, or even created by them? Are they surface decorations or 'deep structural' features which help to generate culture and social existence itself? Do myths symbolize an objective non-symbolic reality? Are we ourselves walking myths, or collections of myths?[37]

There are no instant answers to these questions. In other words, myth is not a homogeneous phenomenon: its functions are diverse. There are very deep-going mythical structures which help create our perceptions of reality – a classic example being our grasp of time and space, or our notions of 'history' and 'science' and 'literature'. There are myths which carry a heavy weight in the social arena – for example, the incest taboo. And there are fantasies which seem much lighter, more on the surface, for example the Superman stories.

None the less, researchers have established that even apparently 'leisure-oriented' rituals and games may encode very important features of particular societies. For example, the anthropologist Clifford Geertz found, in his examination of cock-fighting in Bali, that these ritual contests expressed many of the important features of Balinese society. The historian T. H. Breen has carried out a similar analysis of horse-racing in late seventeenth century Virginia.[38]

We can relate these ideas to football in Britain. When people say 'It's only a game', perhaps they miss the point that a game can function as the repository of very important social and psychological meanings. Men have used football to construct images of their own existence – a struggle, a display of brutish strength and graceful skill, a combination of an 'us' against a 'them', a consolidation of masculine solidarity against women, a display of male flesh, and so on.

There appear to be no simplistic formulae which will help us determine the importance and meaning of myths in any culture. One can only arrive at their meanings by studying their place in social existence, and the way in which they work for people, and one may well arrive at contradictory conclusions. Thus, in relation to the Hollywood western, one could argue that this is a fairly ephemeral set of narratives, designed largely to fit the bottom of the bill in double showings – most westerns are B-films. On the other hand, one could argue that the western is in fact one of the major myths of American history and certainly of American masculinity, and that it has entwined with American political life to a remarkable extent. One only has to think of Theodore Roosevelt, who led his 'Rough Riders' in the Spanish–American war, and wrote books extolling the manly virtues found in the west, or Ronald Reagan, who exploited his connections with western iconography.[39]

Deep structure or surface structure? One partial solution to this conundrum concerns the question of universals. It is clear in the study of language that the 'deeper' a particular feature is reckoned to be, the more universal it is likely to be – that is, found in many different languages and language groups – and the more 'superficial' it is, the more localized it is.[40]

This interesting correlation can be applied to codes of masculinity, since certain features of them appear to be astonishingly widespread, lending weight to the notion that patriarchy is a universal social structure on earth. Some anthropologists have made quite extraordinary comparisons in this respect: Thomas Gregor, for example, compared Amazonian Indians with contemporary Americans, and claimed that many similarities exist between the codes of masculinity in the two societies.[41]

Such claims are fascinating, if speculative, but certainly the notion of a 'deep' and 'surface' structure to gender is a fertile one. Going back to the western, it is pertinent that although the actual narratives concern a very restricted set of geographical areas and a restricted set of characters, western films have had appeal throughout the world, suggesting that western myths play on quasi-universal themes.

AN INTERDISCIPLINARY THEORY OF GENDER

Is it possible to draw together these different approaches to gender? To some extent I have already done this by showing how the political demands of patriarchy are translated into the psychological training of children in the family.

Thus, gender forms an intersection between political, psychological and symbolic systems in human existence. *Politically*, gender embodies relations of power between men and women, and the divisions of labour under patriarchy. Crudely, men have been identified with the public world, and with occupations; women have been identified with the domestic world, and particularly with child-rearing. Furthermore, certain identities to do with gender and sexuality are designated as 'perverse' and others 'non-perverse'. *Psychologically*, these divisions have massive implications for the structure of families, and the raising of children, who must be trained to conform to gender requirements. Of great importance here is the identification that boys make with their fathers, and the turning away from mother. *Symbolically*, gender is embodied in various myths, which teach, warn, punish and reward.

Overall, and very simplistically, one can argue that patriarchal society has demanded and constructed a fearsome male narcissism, a culture of aggrandizement and inflation, a phallic omnipotence, which young boys are inducted into. At the same time, I shall argue in Chapter 4 that boys also absorb more unconscious messages about the nature of female power, against which male power shrinks and sometimes seems to disappear.

In relation to popular culture, one of my tasks is to see to what degree this male narcissism is portrayed, and to what degree we find its opposite, its collapse, even its nemesis.

I am not claiming that this is a comprehensive account of gender! For example, the whole issue of innate factors, genetic or hormonal, in the acquisition of gender, deserves more space than I can give it here. One problem with biological theories of gender is that they are at present tremendously complex, confused, and shot through with ideological struggle, since innateness is generally abhorred within radical social science.[42]

But I am positing a notion of gender that is interdisciplinary, since gender acts as the node-point for so many human activities and beliefs. In particular, I shall argue throughout this book that political and psychological accounts of gender ignore each other at their peril.

This brief examination of different approaches has shown clearly how complex and fluid gender and sexuality are. It is useful to create some landmarks amidst this complexity, and I find it particularly helpful to make a distinction between sex identity – the male/female distinction; gender – which relates to the categories of masculinity and femininity; and sexual orientation.

But two further comments can be made about these parameters: they operate independently of each other, and they are not monolithic concepts. This is clearly true of gender and sexuality: there are many masculinities, and one individual male is able to 'put on' a variety of masculine and feminine personae, which can also be blended; and there are many sexualities – people are not simply heterosexual or homosexual. But even the male/female distinction – which appears biologically fairly clear – can be easily blurred in human behaviour and fantasy. Take a man who wears women's clothes: is he male or female? He might feel that he is both. Or during sexual intercourse, it seems pretty clear that men and women not only have fantasies of being feminine and masculine respectively, but also of being female and male. Some people have a very powerful desire physically to become the opposite sex.[43]

Thus, the distinction between conscious and unconscious identities adds a further complication to an already complex picture: human beings do not simply 'act' their gender and sexuality in a definitive and clearly delineated manner. They also 'play with', or put on, or unconsciously act out, identities that may be quite contradictory to their normal outward persona.[44]

3 Studying Popular Culture

Just as one cannot approach gender without some theoretical preparation, so any study of popular culture must begin by briefly considering the scholarly background to it.

The study of popular culture today is expanding rapidly. Academic courses cover it; many books are written on it; research projects monitor the effect of TV and videos and other popular forms. Cultural studies, from its modest beginnings in the 1950s, has become an important area of academic study, embracing as it does a wide range of cultural forms and employing a variety of approaches. And within cultural studies, the examination of popular culture has been important as part of the reaction against the elitist types of criticism formerly prevalent. We also see the 'deconstruction' of the literature syllabuses (the 'canon') in universities and colleges: the elitist study of 'the best literature' is giving way, particularly in America, to a study of 'low' culture. In fact it is preferable to say that the 'high'/'low' distinction is beginning to be eroded.[1]

One must also point out that studying popular culture offers great enjoyment, since it is full of energy, colour and flamboyance. I trace my own fascination with popular culture back through my entire life. When I was 17, I was studying Shakespeare, Goethe and Racine at school – intellectual heavyweights with a vengeance – but at week-ends feasted myself on films at local cinemas – films such as *The Masque of the Red Death*, *The Incredible Shrinking Man*, *Psycho*, *The Man Who Shot Liberty Valance*. I also went to coffee bars every week-end where there was live pop music.

But music at school was quite different: in music lessons, we were placed in a classroom and had classical music played at us. I use the phrase 'at us' because that's what it felt like. What is remarkable in hindsight is that the music we actually liked and played at home – various kinds of rock 'n' roll, country music, and so on – was studiously ignored.

Thus the week-end entertainment offered relief from all that high culture at school, but also provided pleasures that seemed quite different in kind. Cinema and pop music are extraordinarily sensuous media. I still find when I go into a cinema, sit down, and watch the first advertisements, that the sheer physical immediacy of the images on the screen are ravishing, almost overpowering. The same is true of rock music. A live rock concert is a remarkable experience, that involves the body as well as the mind. Indeed rock music is an astonishing art form, since it is inherently participatory, closely linked with dance. Legend or not, the story that early audiences for *Rock Around the Clock* ripped up cinema seats feels emotionally right. Here is an art that goes beyond contemplation.

Indeed the ravishing nature of certain popular art forms presents a fundamental paradox. One can be seduced into a chain of ideas or images that would normally seem alien. An example from TV: the yuppy soap series *thirtysomething* was filmed in a very sensuous manner, particularly the central couple, Michael and Hope. Thus, although at times one wanted to object that we were being presented with a kind of dream couple, with no connection with ordinary life, the sheer beauty of the spectacle being offered (and Michael and Hope were very beautiful) could dissolve that objection. Similarly, Ien Ang studied people's reactions to the American soap *Dallas*, and found that disapproval and enjoyment could easily coexist.[2]

Many people have the same split reaction with Italian westerns, which at times appear quite sadistic, semi-psychotic. Nonetheless one can be pulled into them through the sheer visual delirium that is presented (for example in *Django*). How can 'bad taste' appear so delicious?

Of course psychologically one can immediately answer: because we are being offered *forbidden pleasures*. It is the bad taste that we secretly (unconsciously) crave, as an outlet for those feelings and desires that we disapprove of but that still persist inside us. Pornography is the supreme example of this phenomenon: in my experience many men who buy and use pornography feel ashamed. Yet the pleasure and the shame are inextricably linked: it is because this kind of looking is so 'bad', that it can seem so pleasurable and exciting.

But many popular cultural forms seem associated with the pleasures of the taboo: surely one of the values of 'junk' food for children is precisely that it is disapproved of by adults.[3] The same has been true of pop music: the songs 'your mother wouldn't like' are exciting because she wouldn't like them. I assume that part of the attraction of genres such as heavy metal and punk is that they excite disapproval. Dick Hebdige describes this in his book *Subculture* as 'style as a form of Refusal'.[4]

This indicates also that 'tastelessness' in popular culture is a political, and not simply a psychological presence. In a sense, 'tasteless' or 'trash' culture unconsciously or consciously mounts an attack on the bourgeois concept of art, and lifts up from repression feelings, actions, representations, which are excluded in such art. Thus rock 'n' roll can be seen as reinstating in Western music some of the riotousness and orgiastic energy that classical music silenced. The horror film presents to us material that is disapproved of: whether it be dismembered bodies, vomiting little girls, or sadistic violence. Or pornography arguably mounts a fierce assault on the bourgeois notion of the female body – tasteful, glossy, euphemized – and instead reveals to us a vulgar body, with gaping orifices, blemished skin, and so on.

And even within particular cultural forms, movements develop to over-throw 'correctness' and good taste: thus punk rock mounted a furious assault on the perceived pomposity of 'progressive' rock. But in its turn, punk began to be perceived as conservative, and the New Romantics – Culture Club, Duran Duran, Adam Ant, Spandau Ballet – mounted a counter-revolution.[5]

CULTURAL STUDIES

If it is possible today to make a serious study of such areas of culture, it is partly because cultural studies has effected a revolution in the way in which culture is studied, certainly in Britain. If we go back only 30 years, the influence of F. R. Leavis, T. S. Eliot and other critics was still power-ful, and this school firmly believed in the distinction between 'high' and 'low' culture, and in the superiority of the former in propagating the moral vision which they saw as essential in education.

Cultural studies has partly evolved in revulsion from the Leavisites, and has tended to seek out the 'lower' forms of culture which had been so dis-dained, for example cinema, popular music, sport and so on. But cultural studies has also developed completely different methods of study. In par-ticular, texts are studied within political contexts, and are seen as con-structing political meanings themselves. Influences from European thought have been important: Marxism, structuralism, psychoanalysis. These have brought an unusually sophisticated theoretical apparatus to what had largely been an empiricist field of study in Britain.

Cultural studies has become such a rich and variegated collection of approaches that it is impossible to do it justice in a short space. Instead I shall briefly outline certain key ideas that I have found useful.

1   Signifying systems

Perhaps the most important influence on cultural studies has been struc-turalism, and particularly Saussure's theory of the linguistic sign, which has subsequently been adapted to the study of non-linguistic symbolic systems, for example by Barthes in his studies of 'myths'.

The kernel of Saussurean structuralism is the role of the sign within a system. In itself, an individual sign has no meaning, but acquires this by virtue of its relationship to other signs. Saussure states: 'In language there are only differences *without positive terms*' [original emphasis].[6] The example that is often given is the system of colour terms: red, blue, green, and so on. These terms divide up the colour spectrum, so that the meanings 'red', 'blue', 'green' are created by the words themselves and their interrelations, and are not pre-existent.[7]

The implications of this idea are enormous, for signs are seen to be entirely 'non-natural' and relational. This view shattered the traditional view of meaning as the relation between 'name' and 'thing', and demonstrated conclusively that 'meaning' is a cultural construction: in Saussure's own terminology, 'the social fact alone can create a linguistic system'.[8]

2 The social production of art

Structuralism has enabled cultural studies to escape the cul-de-sac created by neo-Kantian theories of art, which tended to emphasize the pure transcendental qualities of the work of art, or the charismatic nature of the artist. Such theories tend to isolate both the work and the artist, so that both float free from the social world, and become in that sense utterly mysterious and enigmatic.

Instead, sociologists such as Pierre Bourdieu have pointed to the social institutions, within which both 'works' and 'artists' are produced:

One must replace the ontological question ['What is art?'] with the historical question of the creation of the universe, that is, the artistic field, within which, through a veritable continuous creation, the value of the work of art is produced and reproduced.[9]

And Bourdieu cites the example of a urinal signed by Duchamp – what makes it a work of art? One can wrestle endlessly with notions of the 'genius' or 'charisma' of the artist without being able to find a satisfactory answer, unless one turns to the institutions that consecrate the work and the artist. Thus Duchamp's urinal is nominated as 'art', and Duchamp is nominated as 'artist', within a set of social conditions, including museums, art galleries, collectors, art historians, critics, art colleges, and so on.[10]

Such an approach turns away from the Romantic fascination with individual artists towards a more social grasp of the function of art and its creation. There are possible dangers in this sociological turn – particularly that aesthetic questions will be discarded. I shall discuss this issue in section 6 below.

3   Ideology and Hegemony

In her book *Celluloid Sisters*, Janet Thumim describes how for centuries culture has been used as a controlling, propagandist force: 'it is necessary for the dominant group, in the struggle to maintain its hegemony, to demonstrate its ability to control potentially subversive elements'.[11] This can be seen clearly enough with Hollywood, which has often functioned as a 'dream factory', pumping out the reassuring message that American society is the best in the world, that every American can become rich and powerful if they want to, that things like poverty, crime, homosexuality and feminism will all evaporate. A film such as *Pretty Woman* (1990) shows this perfectly: a ruthless and soulless business man meets a sassy hooker, and they are transformed by each other. The zombie-like man is enlivened by the woman, and becomes a good capitalist; the energetic hooker becomes a Barbie doll with a credit card on Rodeo Drive, Beverley Hills. All ills are healed and smoothed over.

This is a true fairy-tale, and perhaps one shouldn't cavil at Hollywood's undoubted talent for producing Cinderella-like myths. However one does want to cavil if it seems that overall Hollywood stresses the romantic, sentimental side of life, and underplays a realistic grasp of life as it is. Hollywood does periodically turn to social protest if it seems to be doing well at the box-office, but it has mainly been the purveyor of conservative dreams. Thus after briefly espousing certain films in the 70s which were loosely 'feminist', Hollywood has played its full part in the 'backlash' against feminism – and *Pretty Woman* is surely part of that backlash.[12]

But the whole notion of art 'justifying' the society in which it exists is a complex one. Popular culture does not simply reflect conservative ideology, or the dominant socio-economic relations. That is a Stalinist idea – an extremely crude relation between economic 'base' and cultural 'superstructure'. In relation to masculinity, it might lead us to expect that the pervasive images of men would be of dominance, arrogance, and power. There are many such images, but there are also images of men as victim, as zombie, as lost soul. Indeed *Pretty Woman* contains such an image in the Richard Gere character: beneath the surface charm this is a rather devastating portrayal of the 'hollow man'. Thus the 'patriarchal' text may well contain points of fracture or weakness that reveal a different, more unconscious message, just as our conscious behaviour often contains moments of self-revelation that surprise us. Although this idea has been extensively developed in cultural studies, it is clearly not a new one. Freud's work on jokes showed the same phenomenon.[13]

This argument has been particularly important in critiques of Marxist theories of ideology. The notion of the economic 'base' and the cultural 'superstructure' has been heavily criticized, since it tends to view people as passive dupes of culture, anaesthetized by an efficient bourgeois propaganda machine. British cultural studies discovered the work of Althusser and Gramsci, which challenged the 'top-down' crudities of Stalinism: 'Critical Marxism ... [insisted] that culture was not merely a reflection of its economic base but produced its own effects'. And Gramsci's notion of 'hegemony' implies a cultural field that is shot through with struggle and negotiation.[14]

However, the whole history of the base–superstructure relationship in Marxism is confused, since Stalinism considerably deformed and vulgarized it. It is likely that pre- and non-Stalinist Marxists did not have such a crude view of culture: for example, in 1919 Trotsky published an article in *Izvestia*, which describes the development of ideology as a very complex process:

> While Marxism ... teaches that all forms of ideology and first and foremost politics, correspond to class relations, this does not at all mean that between politics, class groupings and production there exist simple mechanical relations, calculable by the four rules of arithmetic. On the contrary, the reciprocal relations are extremely complex.[15]

Later in his life, Trotsky was to pour scorn on the crudeness of analysis carried out by Stalinist theoreticians. Unfortunately, in the West such work was often taken as genuine Marxist theorisation.

Similarly the Gramscian notion of hegemony is rather more subtle than one of 'class domination' or 'false consciousness', for hegemony has to be fought for and won. This suggests that popular culture has a contradictory nature – it contains 'dominant', 'negotiated' and 'oppositional' meanings, often blended in the same text. I find this idea very useful in the study of masculine images, since mainstream culture can simultaneously present an image of machismo and something more subversive. The film actor Arnold Schwarzenegger provides an excellent example of this. Although often touted as the supreme icon of muscular masculinity, it is interesting that some of his films portray men who are shattered. Thus *Total Recall* describes a man who has been totally destroyed and recreated by a totalitarian regime. In addition, Schwarzenegger's enormous, inflated body simultaneously acts as a hypermasculine emblem, but also mimics women's bodies.[16]

The terms used by Lucy Fischer in the title of her book on women's cinema, *Shot/Countershot*, strike me as very useful in this discussion.[17] As against the masculinist 'shot' in mainstream culture, which could be summarised crudely as the depiction of heroic male subjects dominating inert female objects, is there also a 'countershot', that is, are there fractures, weak points, rebellious images in the texts?

We can also bring into play psychological language here. Does the conscious surface of the popular text reveal any unconscious slips, counter-statements, that indicate another, subversive sub-text, that is in fact a 'counter-text'?

In other words, is popular culture monolithic? If it is not, what cracks do we see in the monolith, and what do they signify? Are they mere pinpricks in the side of the patriarchal elephant, which remains unmoved by them, or are they deeper wounds, which betoken perhaps a deep crisis at its heart?

It would be unlikely that any cultural form is an absolute monolith, no more than any human individual is. There is clear evidence for 'cracks' in popular culture: for example, the development of *film noir* in the 1940s showed a darkening of the ethical climate in American films, perhaps even a failure of nerve. In the western the ethical certainties of the B-film gave way to a darker understanding of human beings, shown very clearly in *The Ox-Bow Incident* (1943). The 'heroes' of that film collude with a lynching which turns out to have killed innocent men. The 'hero' is on his way to becoming an 'anti-hero'.

A crucial question arises at this point: how far do such 'counter-shots' go? Are they simply moments of doubt in an otherwise imperturbable and complacent patriarchy? Or even worse, are they the permitted rebellions of a licensed set of fools? On the other hand, are they signs of a general decay in values, a loss of self-faith, conditions which may precede major socio-political shifts?

Are there cracks in the facade of patriarchy, or huge splits?

These questions are of great moment in the study of masculinities, since patriarchal capitalism has needed the masculine gender as one of its main buttresses. Therefore cracks or splits in traditional 'virile' masculinity, and representations of it, may well indicate at least a weakening, and possibly a disintegration, in patriarchy and capitalism themselves.

4   Text and audience

The relation between text and reader has been one of the foci for research in cultural studies, but there has been a wide spectrum of views on this issue.

At one extreme, film studies in the late 70s and early 80s adopted a rather determinist view, derived partly from the French psychoanalyst

Lacan, that texts construct or 'interpellate' the subject. Thus feminist film studies argued that mainstream Hollywood cinema not only principally catered for the male viewer, but through its structuring devices actually constructed a 'male position', which all viewers, willy-nilly, must occupy. Thus the female viewer was perforce 'masculinized'.[18]

This view was contested by some researchers within cultural studies, who argued that the audience had a much greater creativity than this, and could actively subvert or oppose the text's dominant reading. Thus in relation to TV soap operas, a number of writers have pointed out that the viewers of soaps are not passive idiots, but have a lively and interactive relation with the programme, maybe ridiculing it, or in other ways refusing to take it at face value.[19] Some critics have also argued that gay audiences may obtain very different reactions and pleasures from say, macho action films, from other audiences. And gay audiences for heavy metal music are presumably interpreting the music and the performance in a different way from heterosexual audiences.[20] Thus in principle every audience (and every individual) may derive quite different, even opposed, interpretations of a text from other audiences (and individuals).

I shall return to this debate in Chapter 4, since it is one of the most important topics in the psychological approach to culture, but let me say briefly here that my sympathies lie more towards the latter view. To my mind, the Lacanian view of the text (and the unconscious) as structuring the subject is unduly pessimistic in its attitude towards human agency. As a psychotherapist, I spend my working life with people who are locked in struggle with their own unconscious, and it is a cornerstone of this work that we are not the victims of the unconscious. In the same way, I doubt that we are simply the victims of texts, coerced into an interpretation or a subject position which is alien to us.

5 Pleasure

In the late 80s, cultural studies began to perceive that the ideological analysis of culture left out something important: popular culture provides great enjoyment and pleasure for people. But pleasure can itself be seen as a political force, for arguably it flouts the spirit of bourgeois puritanism. Thus amongst the youth of today, the pleasures of music, dance, fashion, drugs and so on can partly be seen as a refusal to be cowed by the dole-queue or the sanctimonious injunctions of politicians that we must all be economically efficient and morally correct.[21]

The 'return' of the idea of pleasure has focused attention on hitherto-neglected topics. For, example, the split between body and intellect seems important. The Leavisite analysis of culture had focused in an intellectual way on literary texts – whereas popular culture moves away from written texts towards the visual image, and above all towards the body.

Pop music seems important here, for it could be argued that post-war youth looked for and constructed a cultural form that was non-cerebral, hedonistic and body oriented. Pop music has always been music to dance to – in this sense it is participatory. This is quite different from the contemplative atmosphere of the art gallery or the concert hall, and perhaps increased the fear and disdain felt towards pop by many Leavisite intellectuals.

One of the memories I have of my first degree, which was in English, is relevant here. We received outstanding lectures from Professor L. C. Knights, who was associated with Leavis and *Scrutiny* magazine. Students were spell-bound by Knights, sensing the presence of a great mind, amazingly sensitive to textual nuances.[22] Yet at the same time there was something missing. There was a kind of fracture in this way of teaching 'English'.

This fracture operated both in terms of *what* we studied – for the notion of 'great literature' excluded many of the things students used for their own pleasure (for example, the Beatles' album *Sgt. Pepper*) – and *how* it was studied, for somehow Shakespeare – the summit of the mountain of Eng. Lit. – seemed best studied in the cloistered quiet of the library. The schizophrenic world I have already alluded to, which divided high and low culture, assumed extraordinary proportions at times. One could write an essay on *Hamlet*, then put *Sgt. Pepper* on the record-player, and the two activities, the two texts, seemed entirely disconnected. One was respectable within the academy, one wasn't. One was the focus of much hard work, the other the focus of pleasure. One was imposed, the other chosen. Of course the idea that *Sgt. Pepper* might be studied within a university course was at that time simply unthinkable, as were alternative ways of studying *Hamlet* – for example, through improvised acting.

The reinstatement of pleasure within cultural studies brings to mind the concept of play that was developed by the psychoanalyst D. W. Winnicott in his book *Playing and Reality*. Winnicott defined psychoanalysis as a 'play area' where the patient was ideally free to play with his thoughts, feelings and verbalizations, in an unconstrained manner.[23] Thus therapy should progress to a point where for both therapist and client it is a form of play. For many people this is not an easy thing to make use of, as many of us have been severely constrained in our ability to play – education takes care of that.

It is significant also how wit has been given importance in psychoanalysis – a patient who possesses wit has a good therapeutic prognosis.[24]

From this standpoint, it strikes me that popular culture can be looked at very usefully as a huge play area. This does not mean we have to depoliticize culture: play is in fact highly politicized. We only have to think of the Puritan concern to restrict it to realize that play has vast economic importance. One of the chief duties of bourgeois ideology is to discipline people in the severe work practices that are required for capitalism to be productive and efficient. Play therefore has potential 'oppositional' value, and children's play is full of attacks on adult values.

But why does play begin so early in life? Why is it such a core part of childhood? Psychologically, play can be seen as a primary expression of creativity, which Winnicott describes as the 'search for the self'. It is in 'playful' activity that we are able to move between states of relaxed formlessness and the creation of form, which enables us to experience the self actually coming into being.[25] Within this view, play assumes a massive importance in human development.

But play does not stop with childhood: many occupations and spare time activities are grown-up forms of play. For example, writing this book is a very pleasurable adult play activity.

However, the reinstatement of pleasure and play as important analytical categories should not lead us into a naive and apolitical idealization of popular culture. For capitalism has turned 'leisure' into a billion pound and dollar industry, and spends a fortune creating new tastes and new trends. For example, it is clear that developments in pop music do not simply happen from the 'bottom' up, but also 'top down', that is, music companies actively seek to marshal and direct people's musical tastes.[26]

6 Aesthetics

The study of popular culture has set the cat among the pigeons in relation to theories of aesthetics. Whereas 'high' culture critics had often assumed that their particular cultural form or genre had some kind of autonomy from society, and could therefore be examined in a self-contained manner, pop culture critics have tended to take a much more sociological and political stance. But this in turn has spurred debate about the 'autonomy' stance of high culture critics: is this really valid?

Thus classical musicologists and critics have tended to dismiss popular music – Allan Moore describes the 'intransigence of the academic musical community in refusing to negotiate with [rock]'. And he cites the common belief that classical music is 'somehow autonomous with respect to the society in which it appears, a belief that has become an intrinsic aspect of most analytic musicology'.[27]

Such views can be connected with the pessimistic and elitist views that used to pervade discussion of high/low culture. Thus Adorno contrasted the autonomy of classical music, which, he claimed, has been 'replaced by a mere socio-psychological function' in popular music.[28] And in his famous essay 'On Popular Music' he makes the interesting statement that 'most listeners of popular music do not understand music as a language in itself'.[29] By implication this seems to invalidate their enjoyment of music!

By contrast, those studying popular music point out that a purely formal aesthetics simply cannot deal with its true significance. In their essay 'Start Making Sense! Musicology Wrestles with Rock', McClary and Walser make the incisive point that country blues and urban blues come off badly in a formalist musicology, since they are harmonically very limited. Does this mean that the blues are therefore not worthy of study? The question is rhetorical, and simply exposes the limitations of a formal aesthetics. In this sense, studies of popular music threaten the whole basis of formal musicology: 'to admit to the social mediation of music is to undermine the illusion of the transcendence of social interests musicology so values in it'.[30]

It seems clear that classical music is in fact just as rooted in a socio-political context as the blues, just as much a 'signifying practice' for particular groups of people. The musicologist Robert Walser calls it 'a constructed category that reflects the priorities of a historical moment and that serves certain social interests at the expense of others'.[31]

In his book *Sound Effects*, Simon Frith makes this illuminating comparison between the two approaches to music:

> High art critics often write as if their terms of evaluation were purely aesthetic, but mass culture critics can't escape the fact that the bases for cultural evaluation are always social: what is at issue is the *effect* of a cultural product. Is it repressive or liberating? Corrupting or uplifting? Escapist or instructive? The aesthetic question – how does it achieve its effects – is secondary.[32]

However, Frith's discussion brings up other problems – for example, is he saying that an 'escapist' genre or style is therefore poor? How do we determine whether something is 'repressive'? To speak of the 'corrupting' effects of a genre or style sounds like the early reactions to rock 'n' roll: one person's 'corruption' is another's liberation.

The problem here, particularly with critics on the left, is that they can take the reverse stance to the 'aesthetic' approach: that is, they can start to treat cultural works purely as political texts, ignoring the pleasure that is created, and ignoring aesthetic questions completely. McClary and Walser make this comment:

> Part of the problem is one that chronically plagues the Left: a desire to find explicit political agendas and intellectual complexity in the art it wants to claim and a distrust of those dimensions of art that appeal to the senses, and to physical pleasure.[33]

This strikes me as a very important point. One reason that punk rock has been discussed so much by critics is that it professed a kind of political radicalism.[34] By contrast dance music, which is relatively apolitical, has attracted much less attention. But as McClary and Walser point out: 'pleasure frequently is the politics of music'.[35] Furthermore, dance music strikes me as technically much more interesting than punk rock. For example, house/techno music has deconstructed the 'musician as hero', the 'rock star'. At a club playing house music, the audience does not revere a charismatic performer, but totally enters into the music, so that the distinction between 'audience' and 'performance' is dissolved.[36]

The political analysis of culture also runs the danger of assuming a kind of psychic/political homogeneity on the part of the reader/viewer. What I mean is that human beings are full of contradictions: to put it crudely, the unconscious is not politically correct! Thus, while sadistic scenes in films or books might be condemned on political grounds, the same person may secretly enjoy them. This whole area is a minefield, since we are all loath to confess to our 'dark desires', yet it seems unlikely that any of us lacks them.

Let me give a personal example. I have always enjoyed watching Clint Eastwood on the screen, for a variety of reasons, for example, his sheer physical presence. At times, if I read a critique of him from a feminist point of view,[37] I feel guilty or ashamed of my enjoyment. Yet, on reflection, my guilt is omnipotent: it claims that I can 'choose' whether to enjoy Eastwood or not. This strikes me as fantastic: I can no more choose this than I can choose which people I get on with, and which I don't. Furthermore, my guilt tells me that my reasons for liking Eastwood are 'bad', when of course this is open to question. Perhaps this kind of debate explains why much feminist criticism has since the mid-80s rejected simplistic judgments on figures such as Alfred Hitchcock or Eastwood, and has produced much more complex and dialectical analysis.[38]

We are confronted with a Scylla and Charybdis: on the one hand, a purely formal aesthetics that ignores the socio-political nature of cultural works; on the other hand, an overly socio-political critique that ignores the sensuous and pleasurable aspects of the work. The first approach will tend to dismiss pop music out of hand as musically rudimentary, but the second will tend to select from pop those areas that are particularly politicized, for example punk or reggae. Both stances ignore massive areas of culture. What is required is an interactive approach, that takes into account the political dimension, questions of aesthetic form and the pleasures that texts engender.

Above all, popular culture must be approached in terms of the *uses* to which it is put. It cannot be seen simply as an object of contemplation. For example, pop music is used in a wide range of contexts: as background in the home, in TV advertising, in the stadium as a mass spectacle and ritual, as a focus of solitary concentrated listening, to dance to in the club, in the car while driving, and so on. Another example that springs to mind concerns the use made by some men of 'action films'. Over the years, I have noticed in my work as a therapist, that some men who are avid fans of such films derive from them, not a sense of male dominance or predation, but a much needed reinforcement for their own faltering sense of male identity.

In a sense I am issuing a warning about reductionism. It is very tempting to use texts to illustrate one's own theoretical and political position. This is not necessarily wrong, but it becomes an abuse of the text if one's interpretation is said to be definitive. I am reminded of the epigraph to this book: like dreams, texts are able to offer an infinite number of meanings to different readers.

4 Psychological Approaches to Culture

I have devoted a whole chapter to psychological approaches to culture, since it is the approach which interests me most, and because in the last twenty years the use of psychoanalytic ideas, and to some extent ideas from Jungian psychology, has increased enormously in literary criticism, film criticism and cultural studies.

The true profundity of depth psychology is that it does not accept the human individual as a coherent entity. The concepts of the unconscious, the ego and the superego in psychoanalysis formalize the idea that we are made up of contradictory parts, each of which may 'speak' at different times, or simultaneously. This notion of 'incoherence' has been described in many other ways in different schools of therapy – in terms of sub-personalities, archetypes, and so on – but the underlying principle is that of a radical 'deconstruction' of the unitary self. This is one of the key motifs of modern psychological thinking: heterogeneity instead of homogeneity; contradiction instead of consistency; both/and instead of either/or.

This is a post-rationalist view of human beings, and in some ways a Romantic view, in the sense that the view of human existence as rational, well-ordered and progressive is contradicted by a more fragmentary and contradictory view.

Texts can be approached in the same way. One can speak of the 'conscious' and 'unconscious' aspects of a text, or its 'surface' and 'depth'. The apparent coherence of a text is subverted by positing different 'voices' within it. In his influential essay 'Freud and Literature', Lionel Trilling drew a direct parallel between persons and texts:

> Criticism has derived from the Freudian system much that is of great value, most notably the license and the injunction to read the work of literature as if it were, as indeed it is, a being no less alive and contradictory than the man who created it.[1]

However, the early application of psychoanalysis to art criticism also saw a rather naive attitude towards literary or artistic works, as if somehow texts could be explained as fascinating stockpiles of neurotic symptoms. For example, Ernest Jones's famous book on *Hamlet* falls into this trap.[2] Jones gives us many fascinating ideas about Hamlet's delay in taking revenge for his father, but he almost seems to suggest that *Hamlet* is a great and famous play because of its oedipal hero. This reduces the play enormously. *Hamlet* is more than a study in oedipal conflict! For one thing, it is one of the great modern dissertations on identity. Hamlet is pre-occupied above all with himself, and constantly interrogates himself, explores his own consciousness. And this self-interrogation is expressed in the subtle and complex texture of Shakespeare's language. Thus Jones's book is highly reductive, and crucially, ignores textual and aesthetic questions.

However, the psychoanalytic approach has enabled certain critics to discern rich subtleties and ambiguities in texts. Freud showed that artistic creativity is not some aberrant mental psychosis, but closely connected to the fundamental workings of the mind. Lionel Trilling argues that 'the Freudian psychology is the one which makes poetry indigenous to the very constitution of the mind'.[3]

Psychoanalysis has also been well placed to investigate aspects of art which previous generations found unsalubrious. The notion of uncon-scious motivations for behaviour, when used within art criticism, has produced some fascinating studies of 'latent' meanings. One can cite here for example D. W. Harding's famous essay on Jane Austen, 'Regulated Hatred', in which he suggests that Austen, far from being the well-mannered chronicler portrayed by genteel critics, allows an 'erup-tion of fear and hatred' into her work.[4] A rather similar work is Norman O. Brown's essay 'The Excremental Vision', which demonstrates how many critics have been unable to deal with Jonathan Swift's use of anal imagery.[5]

LACAN

While the orthodox Freudian stance has often produced too reductive a view of art, Lacanian psychology has caused a heady ferment within cul-tural studies, and particularly film criticism. Lacan provides a radical deconstruction of the traditional subject–object relationship, and hence the relation between subject and text. Instead of a prior subject calmly perus-ing a text, or creating a text, the Lacanian text is 'prior', and the subject is trying to discover who he/she is by means of the text. The subject is not even sure of its own existence, and only gets a glimpse of itself through a series of 'alienating identifications'.[6] Thus in some senses, the text creates the subject.

The Lacanian view of ego and text projects a most radical approach to culture. Quite simply the distinction between self and culture collapses, since the unconscious (matrix of identity) is itself a discourse. Language is seen not as an 'expression' of the human subject, but as a pre-existent order by means of which the subject must define itself.

If we take the cinema as an example, one of the interesting questions provided within a Lacanian framework is: 'Who is watching the film?'. For in the immersion in the film-watching experience, I may be quite unsure who I am, since the cinematic experience consists of numerous identifications which take me out of myself. Thus identification is the means whereby the ego discovers itself – particularly in Lacan's mirror-stage, where the subject is able to identify with a visual body-image.[7] But in cinema, as in the mirror-stage, we also discover that we have just lost ourselves – that is part of the pleasure of film, a kind of surrender to the text.

In this framework, identification is not some luxurious hobby that human beings indulge in, but the means whereby they come to know that they exist at all. But identification is also a cross, for the ego is trapped in an equation of itself with another. It can never know itself except through other objects, and this produces that homelessness and hunger that Lacan argues is part and parcel of ego identity. Lacan refers to this as the human being's 'original splitting' and he gives us the brilliant image that 'at every moment he constitutes his world by his suicide'.[8] Aesthetic pleasure is therefore a kind of blissful suicide: 'I' get lost in the experience of the art object. This may appear to satisfy some longing in me, but curiously also creates further longing, for I need the object so desperately, in order to know that I am me. Without it, who am I? The object comes to exert a tyranny over the subject.

There are all kinds of criticisms one can make of Lacanian psychology at this point – for one thing it leads to a very sceptical view of the possibility of human contact, whereas my view is that contact is the key force that makes psychotherapy work – but I think the most important issue here is that Lacan turns the relation of subject and text round by 180°. We are hungry for culture, not out of boredom, but because culture constantly tells us who we are, and perhaps allows us to forget who we think we are, or allows us to reconstitute ourselves or drown ourselves out. It is through various texts (including the text of my unconscious) that I know that I exist, and can give myself various familiar identifications.

If we take television, and the habit many people have of leaving it on as background, it could be argued that this provides a real comfort: at least when I glance at the TV screen I know that I am a TV watcher. The TV as 'other' enables me to construct myself as 'self'. Indeed, I recall various clients of mine in therapy who on returning home from work, would immediately put on the TV out of a fear of their own non-existence.

Watching TV constructed a 'viewer', and that was some kind of consoling identity. Of course it also acts narcotically, and prevents me from feeling certain things about myself, for example my emptiness.

The Lacanian view of the text also gives us a radical insight into creating texts, for whereas 'common sense' psychology tells us that 'I' create the text, we can reverse this and suggest that the text appears out of the Other, and creates my sense of me. For example, at the moment, who is writing these words? Actually I am not quite sure, for quite often the words appear to come 'from nowhere', that is, from a mysterious Other (which can be defined as the discourse of the unconscious). Then I take up a certain stance towards these words, and they become 'mine'. Similarly, who is reading these words? Of course, in one sense you are, but who and what is that 'you' at the moment of reading? Perhaps you have become simply 'the reader' and that is your consolation?

Curiously enough, Lacan has brought into the heart of Western psychology some of the central concerns of Buddhist psychology, which has likewise been highly sceptical as to the existence of the permanent I.[9]

If we turn to gender, its fragility becomes even more apparent within a Lacanian paradigm, since my own gender consists of a set of identifications. Furthermore, at times culture or art permit us to realign our gender identity, at least unconsciously or temporarily, by means of entering into different gender fantasies. This is my view of pornography: one of its (secret) functions is to permit the male viewer to lose himself in the female object, so that he becomes a female subject.

Lacanian psychology has had considerable impact on feminism, which has been attracted to its deconstruction of the traditional subject (the Cartesian *cogito*), and its explanation of male supremacy as not simply a socio-economic one, but one rooted in sexuality and language itself. In other words, men are constructed as *speaking subjects* within the patriarchal order, because only they have access to 'the phallus', that is, the signifier that betokens power and privilege. Thus, in Hollywood cinema, it is arguable that men have been the 'I', and women have been 'the other', used by men to define themselves. Thus, men desire, but women are desired.[10]

There are many difficulties here as to the nature of this phallic order – for example, is the phallus a purely arbitrary signifier, or does it connect with social conditions? What exactly is the relation between phallus and penis?[11] Certainly Lacan's explanation of phallic power goes beyond Freud's biological theory (although at times Lacan still flirts with this), and shows us how the actual discourses of culture construct the male position of power.

PHALLIC AND MATERNAL PSYCHOLOGY

There is a more serious objection to the Lacanian position: both Lacanian and Freudian psychology are masculinist paradigms, in the sense that they interpret the world as a coherent masculine order, and in particular view women as castrated men. Of course, many feminists have argued that Freud and Lacan have accurately described the reality of a patriarchy which subordinates women socially, politically and psychologically – this is broadly speaking Juliet Mitchell's thesis in her influential book *Feminism and Psychoanalysis*.

Particularly within film studies, certain Freudian concepts such as the Oedipus complex, castration anxiety, and so on, have been adopted wholesale. Thus in her introduction to the book *Feminism and Film Theory*, Constance Penley makes this comment:

> The image of the woman on the screen, while erotic, constantly threatens to reveal the fact of castration through the exposure of her own lack of a penis. The representation of woman as signifier of castration thus induces in the spectator's unconscious the mechanisms of voyeurism and fetishism ... as a defence against that threat.[12]

The problem I have with this kind of psychological analysis is that it seems both old-fashioned and monolithic. This does not of course invalidate it, but its psychoanalytical base does seem rather impoverished, neglecting as it does the considerable developments made in post-Freudian psychoanalysis, particularly the shift towards the study of the mother/child relation. The same accusation can be levelled at Lacanian psychology as a whole: although it produces a dazzling 'superstructure' of psychological theory, its 'base' still assumes the inevitable subjectivity of men and objectification of women. But post-Freudian psychology has discovered other relations between males and females.

Let me make a crude distinction between phallic and maternal psychology. The first argues that masculinity is primary and dominant, and that femininity is a kind of castrated masculinity, and exists in its own right only under the shadow of the male, or in Freud's phrase, 'the premiss of the universal presence of the penis'.[13] The second argues that the female has a primacy at a certain stage of life, and that masculinity is in part a defence against it, and an emergence from it.

Both Freud and Lacan see femininity as a shadow of masculinity, but analysts such as Karen Horney give plenty of evidence both as to the existence of female power, and men's dread of it. For example, Horney points out that castration anxiety in men can often be referred to an unconscious *wish to be castrated*, in other words, the wish to be a woman.[14] This argument is itself a beautiful example of Freudian methodology being applied to Freud himself: he was loath to acknowledge female power and male envy of it. Karen Horney points out rather sardonically that Freudian psychoanalysis is itself a excellent example of male defensive narcissism![15]

In relation to Constance Penley's argument, cited above, which posits the 'woman on the screen', as 'signifier of castration', we can now argue that this screen image may also represent for the male viewer something he wants to be. To put it bluntly, this 'woman' may symbolize, not something that she lacks, but something he lacks.

In many ways, the history of psychoanalytic thought of the last forty years has seen a shift towards a preoedipal and maternal psychology. Great analysts, such as Melanie Klein, Winnicott, Margaret Mahler and others, have pointed to the awesome power of the mother–child relation, and its considerable effects on adult life. In this sense, the masculine paradigm of Freud can now be seen as incomplete.

However, the application of preoedipal psychology to the analysis of culture is in its infancy, compared with the application of classical Freudian theory or Lacanian theory. But one can point to at least one outstanding work that has turned upside down the 'woman as victim' approach. Barbara Creed's book on the horror film, *The Monstrous-Feminine*, demonstrates with abundant evidence that the female monster in horror films is not horrific because she is castrated, but because she threatens to castrate. In other words, horror films take us back in fantasy to a time when the 'archaic mother' was all-powerful and threatening.[16] One outstanding film text in relation to this theme is *Alien*, in which the nightmarish interiors of the spaceship recall the fantasized interiors of mother's body, and the monster itself is a startling rendition of a phallic/vaginal fantasy.[17]

One can also relate these ideas to various political interpretations: for example, Amy Taubin connects the monster in *Alien*[3] with the myth of the 'black woman on welfare', who breeds incessantly and sucks the lifeblood from upright (white) citizens.[18] Furthermore, it is likely that feminism itself has increased the 'phallic panic' felt amongst men, and has therefore given the image of the 'monstrous feminine' an even sharper resonance for many men.

'Maternal' theory has a tremendous amount to offer to the analysis of popular culture. Let me just cite its relevance to the Frankenstein narrative. Frankenstein is a very complex symbol – for one thing, he is part of the long line of 'mad scientists' who populate horror and sci-fi texts. But it is also clear that Frankenstein has a 'womb complex': he has a burning desire to create life. He wants *to be like a woman*. And the figure of Dracula – that other evocative figure of horror from the nineteenth century – has many feminine features.[19] I shall devote more attention to Frankenstein and Dracula in Chapter 7.

I shall also suggest in my chapter on pornography that at least one facet of porn imagery is a fantasy of the long lost mother's body, with its ample breasts, its openness, its eternal receptivity.

Barbara Creed concludes her book with this succint comment on psychoanalytic thought:

> Psychoanalytic writings which argue that the symbolic is an order represented by the father alone can only do so by repressing and distorting the crucial role played by the mother in relation to the constitution of society and culture – albeit at this stage a patriarchal culture.[20]

JUNGIAN CRITICISM

It is ironic that while many feminists have become interested in psychoanalysis as a description of phallic power, Jung, who was fascinated by maternal power, and established the 'Great Mother' as one of the key archetypes in his system, has been relatively ignored in cultural studies.

There are other important differences between Jungian thought and psychoanalytic thought: whereas all psychoanalytical schools see the unconscious as infantile, Jungians see it very differently, as a creative mental organ which continually strives towards wholeness. The ego emerges from it, and then the relation between ego and Self (the unconscious centre of the whole psyche) is the pivotal axis in the individual. Damage done to the individual is often seen as damage done to the ego-Self relationship.[21]

Jung also posited a collective unconscious, that is, a part of the psyche not determined by personal experience. In the collective psyche, archetypes exist as universal templates, waiting to be filled in by an infinite possibility of contents. Jungian cultural analysis therefore leads to cross-cultural comparison.[22]

If we take the example of the James Bond films, a Jungian approach might see Bond as a variation of the universal hero motif, found in all cultures, the man who has to pass through many obstacles to find the truth or find a great prize. The hero figure can also be seen as an image of the ego, struggling with the forces of the unconscious. The hero slays the dragon – Bond sets out to neutralize figures such as Goldfinger or Dr No, who are likewise archetypal figures of evil. Note that under this interpretation Bond is not so much an image of *men* per se, but of that part of all human beings that leads us out into the world, overcomes obstacles, achieves things, and so on. The 'hero' pertains as much to women as men.

At the same time Bond is not really a conventional hero, but contains elements of the anti-hero, or the 'trickster', the figure who sets out to upset the apple-cart. Bond's cynicism and sadism shows the hero contaminated by other, darker psychic forces. In fact the trickster – found in Native American cultures – is described by Jung as a primitive form of the hero, who is concerned purely with his own physical appetites.[23]

As I have already mentioned, perhaps the most important distinction between Freudian and Jungian analysis, from the point of view of the study of gender, is that Freud's is a paternal and phallic psychology, and Jung's is a maternal, non-phallic one. Not that Jung studied the mother–child relationship in depth, but he emphasized the importance of the maternal archetype, and suggested that for every individual, one of the great questions posed by life was whether or not he/she could separate from Mother, which can be seen as an internal force as much as an external one. Crucially, the unconscious itself can be seen as maternal, from which the ego rises as a new-born son, and to which it will one day return. Thus, the Christ myth can be interpreted psychologically as an image of an idealized ego-Self relationship. Indeed many mythological systems can be related to this relationship of ego and unconscious – for example many fairy stories can be interpreted along these lines.[24]

Jung also stressed the importance of religion as a mythical system that enables human beings to work through various unconscious structures and processes. The symbols of a particular religion correspond to various psychic complexes and provide each individual, and the whole society, with a healthy means of relating to such complexes. The image of God itself can be related to the archetype of the Self, which is both the totality of the psyche and its centre.

Jung saw great dangers in the modern age, with its rejection of God: that we would lose touch with our own unconscious, and therefore, paradoxically, would become overwhelmed by it. He saw the rise of fanaticism – as in fascism and communism – as the eruption of repressed collective unconscious forces, obliterating the individual.

Jung's ideas are very useful when we look at the myths and icons of contemporary culture. Take for example the extraordinary posthumous legends that have arisen around Elvis Presley. I don't think it is an exaggeration to say that this is a rudimentary religious cult. For example, there are rumours that Elvis is still alive; there are memorabilia that can be bought commemorating him – for example, phials of his sweat are offered on sale; there are Elvis impersonators, who are like earthly representatives of the heavenly figure. And people have a relationship with Elvis that is similar to intercession with a saint.[25]

These phenomena might strike us simply as indications of how exotic and bizarre contemporary culture can be. But within a Jungian understanding, they are perfectly explicable: that need for mythical systems, which has been so starved by the decay of Christianity, must find (or create) new idols, new gods. The dying and reborn Man–God – one of the truly ancient myths, predating Christianity – finds a bizarre but unmistakable refraction in Presley. Thus my use of the word 'icon' in this book is peculiarly apt, since one of its meanings is an image that itself acquires religious value.[26] The creation of 'stars' in cinema, pop music and elsewhere partially satisfies our deep need for transpersonal images, which take us beyond the ordinariness of everyday life.

Jung's notion of the collective psyche also provides an interesting view of individuals: that they not only fulfil their own destiny, but also a fragment of the collective destiny. In relation to society, this means that we all express things for each other. Thus the tramp sleeping rough in the streets is actually expressing something that belongs to us all. Similarly the mad person, the violent person, the very successful person, is not simply pursuing an individual path, but is in some way representative of the collective.

The application of this method of analysis to culture offers this illumination: what is unconscious for some people will be expressed by others.

Perhaps the chief drawback of Jungian psychology is that although it posits a psychological collectivity – something which is surely a lack within Freudian thought – it is a militantly apolitical collective. Jung was hostile to political movements and ideologies: he saw them as fanatical and obsessive. In this sense perhaps, he failed to see that all the great collective myth systems, such as Christianity, modern science, our notions of 'literature' and 'history', gender itself, are political constructions.

WHO WHOM?

I now want to move from this brief consideration of the Freudian and Jungian approaches to cultural criticism, to some more specific issues, particularly concerning the relations between text and reader (or viewer).

'Who whom?' was a phrase used by Lenin to unlock the power relations in any situation: who was doing what to whom, who was oppressing whom, and so on. I have borrowed it as a succint reminder that in any kind of art criticism or cultural analysis, the question of the relationship between reader (or viewer) and the text is vital.

This topic has caused much interest in recent years in film criticism – does the male viewer identify with the male character in a film? Is film intrinsically predicated on the notion of the male viewer/hero? Is the camera's viewpoint itself a male voyeuristic or sadistic one? Is narrative itself patriarchal? Obviously the same issues arise in other media – novel, play, TV soap, children's comic.

Laura Mulvey, in her famous article 'Visual Pleasure and Narrative Cinema', posited the male subject/female object dyad as the basis of Western classical narrative cinema: 'Psychoanalytic theory is thus appropriated here as a political weapon, demonstrating *the way the unconscious of patriarchal society has structured film form*' [my emphasis].[27] However, since this article was published in 1975, considerable modifications have been made to both sides of the nexus of male subject/female object. I shall mention only three points here, since the whole debate has become very complex.[28]

First, Mulvey herself has modified her position in a later article which discussed the position of the female spectator. She argues that such a spectator may well enjoy narrative cinema, but at the price of accepting a 'masculinization' that is psychologically infantile, if we accept Freud's notion that girls originally have a masculine identity: 'the female spectator's phantasy of masculinization [is] at cross purposes with itself, restless in its transvestite clothes'.[29]

Secondly, I shall argue below that identification is much more complex than Mulvey's rigid schema: for example, the male viewer may well identify with the female body, and the female viewer with the male body. In general, identification is an extremely fluid and shifting process.

Thirdly, on the other side of the equation (male gaze/female object), the spectacle being offered in film does not simply consist of women. Men have been considerably 'spectacularized'. We only have to think of Rudolf Valentino, Fred Astaire, Rock Hudson, Marlon Brando, and so on, to see that the male body is considerably fetishized in cinema. People watch films partly to watch men.[30] And moving out of cinema, it is striking how in popular music and sport the male body has been considerably foregrounded as a spectacle.[31]

IDENTIFICATION

The development of object relations in psychotherapy has broken down any monolithic notion of the human subject. The individual psyche is said to consist of a number of elements ('internal objects') which come into conflict with each other, and sometimes into harmony, but which cannot be described as a unitary 'I'. Indeed one of the great problems faced by all human beings is how to deal with all the different components of their own psyche, particularly those that are disowned. 'The return of the repressed' often means that disowned psychic elements lead to compulsive behaviour. For example a man who disowns his own feminine side may find himself obsessed with women. People who deny their need for others may displace this need on to addictive behaviours, for example drug addiction, eating disorders and so on.

The unconscious can be defined as those parts of myself that I have never met: I can displace them or project them on to others, where they become desirable or hateful. This is the foundation for romantic love, and for scape-goating, to mention only two massive cultural forces in Western culture. In romantic love, I seek the delightful other, who represents parts of myself I have lost and wish to be reunited with; in scape-goating I punish the hated other, who represents part of myself that I wish to destroy, since I find it so distasteful. A classic example here is the persecution of witches: the witch represents my own sexuality, which I abhor and which torments me. A very disturbing cinematic illustration of this theme can be found in Michael Reeves' *Witchfinder General*.

In psychotherapy there are many areas of work where the 'plural psyche' becomes very important. For example in dream analysis, therapists generally do not assume any simple identity between dreamer and dream. It is common to find dreams interpreted as complex symbolic reflections of the dreamer's psyche, so that an element in the dream is symbolic of an element in the dreamer, and a set of dream elements represents a set of elements in the psyche.

I remember doing Gestalt dream workshops where this approach was taken, and led to surprising insights. For example, I recall a relatively simple dream I brought to such a group: I was walking along a canal, accompanied by a cat.

In the workshop, the leader helped me to enact the role of the cat, and then to my surprise, asked me if I could imagine being the canal and the road. The cat-role was easy to get into – and evoked in me all kinds of pleasure about being lithe, ferocious, playful, and so on. But being the canal and the road were no less insightful. As a road, I felt fed up with being walked on, but I also felt solid, long-lasting, almost eternal!

This approach is particularly interesting if the dreamer dreams of a person of the opposite sex. A woman client dreams of a man exploring Africa, and finding long-lost treasure belonging to an ancient tribe. A man dreams of a crowd of naked women playing darts in a pub.

In such cases, it is likely again that the character in the dream represents some element in the dreamer. In the above examples, the woman may be dreaming of a part of herself that wants to explore unknown areas (darkest Africa) which may contain things of value. The man dreams of his own feminine side doing something typically masculine – a blend of genders.

But dreams are not the only place where multiple identification goes on. People's lives are arenas where very complex dramas are played out. Let me give a simple example.

Jim had had quite abusive parents – a father who physically assaulted him, and a mother who undermined him, especially his sense of his own masculinity. When he started therapy he complained that over twenty years he had had a large number of relationships with women, but they always 'went wrong'.

When he began to look more closely at his relationships, it became apparent that there were broadly two kinds – those where he got hurt, and those where he hurt the other one. He tended to be hurt by rather cool, remote women, and he tended to hurt warmer, more loving women. And he had alternated between these two types of relationship.

From Jim's relationships, we can abstract two basic characters. There is a cool remote person who is rather disdainful, and a more emotional affectionate person who feels neglected. But Jim alternated between both roles in his relationships, and his partners took the other role. In a sense, it didn't matter who took which role, as long as the whole sado-masochistic relationship was played out. In particular, it was important that someone got hurt, for here Jim was 'remembering' his own tormented childhood. Jim continually recreated this drama in an unconscious attempt both to remember his childhood, and to forget it. And the addictive sexuality helped narcotize his secret pain.

But what concerns me is the *fluidity of identification* that is revealed here. Jim could either play out the role of the hurt child, victimized by the cruel parent, or he could project the hurt child on to his partner, and then he could play the cruel parent figure. It is also worth noting that the same drama got enacted between me and him – at times he was very scornful of me, but at other times he became sad and mournful, and thought I was unhelpful and remote – I became the 'cruel one'.

It has often been said that there are no pure sadists or masochists – there are only sado-masochists. The person who 'specializes' in being sadistic in relationships finds his masochistic side gratified by his partner.

In a more benign way, everyone who has raised children will know that part of the pleasure in being a parent is that it also gives one permission to be a child. I bought my son a Megadrive games computer – but Christmas

Eve saw me furiously bashing the joystick! The same is true in sexual relationships – one can be both oneself, and the other. In male/female relationships, both partners get to be both male and female.

When we turn to works of art, it seems immediately clear that the same fluidity of identity applies. Just as the dream is a complex symbolization of many elements in the dreamer's psyche, so is the painting or novel or play or song. When we watch *Othello*, we are able to enjoy being Desdemona, injured innocence, and Othello, blind jealous rage, and we take part in the sadistic manipulations of Iago. In other words the whole drama connects with an internal psychic drama. It is clear that Shakespeare had a profound grasp of such shifting points of view – in plays such as *Richard III*, he helps us first to identify with Richard, who is such an attractive villain, and later to identify with his killers.

In the cinema, Alfred Hitchcock had a brilliant grasp of the audience's shifting sympathies. A famous example occurs in *Psycho*, when psychotic killer Norman Bates is watching the car containing the dead Marion sink into a swamp. Momentarily the car stops sinking, and the audience holds its breath, and prays that it will sink! We don't want Norman to be caught, because we're enjoying the sadistic rampage of 'mother'. We identify with Norman, who has identified with his mother – a rather witty comment by Hitchcock on the nature of identification! Similarly in *Rear Window*, Hitchcock gradually draws us into the voyeuristic world of James Stewart.

Thus, object relations psychology helps us see the relation between reader and text in a fresh way. The question becomes very complex: what is the relation between which elements in the reader's psyche and which elements in the text?

Thus if a film contains a sadistic scene – say a man torturing a woman – it is rather simplistic to argue that the male viewer identifies with the screen male. Rather we can suggest that the inner sadist in the viewer identifies with the screen sadist, and the inner victim with the screen victim. Furthermore, it is also likely that the film scene 'assaults' the viewer: the sadist/masochist relationship is established between film (or director) and spectator.

Just as the text is broken down into different elements, which can be quite disparate and contradictory, so is the reader/viewer. To put it more abstractly, the relation between various elements in the particular text acts as a symbolic correlative for the interrelations in the reader's psyche. In the above case, the sado-masochistic relation in the film touches on the inner sado-masochistic relation in the viewer.

Indeed, just as Jung argued that religious symbolism arose in human cultures so that adherents of the cult could explore their own unconscious, one of the functions of art is to help the viewer explore his/her own psyche. The religious symbol or the artistic symbol gives access to otherwise inaccessible regions of the psyche.

This is the force of Carol Clover's thesis in her book *Men, Women and Chainsaws*, particularly her aptly titled chapter 'Her Body Himself': that the female body, tortured, maimed, destroyed in so many 'slasher' films, and opened up in the occult horror film (as in *The Exorcist*), is precisely that which the male viewer seeks out as a symbol *of himself*.[32] In the voluptuous Mario Bava film *Black Sunday* (also known as *The Mask of Satan*), the first scene shows the witch (played by Barbara Steele) being killed by an iron maiden placed over her face. When she comes back to life, her whole face shows a number of holes: female orificial sexuality (normally invisible) is made visible. But this is not simply a sadistic male fantasy, it may also represent for the male viewer a deep and repressed wish to be 'opened up' and to have female orifices. He sees on the screen 'the return of the repressed', in particular his own desire to be female and to be penetrated.

In many horror films, a woman represents sexuality and desire *within the male himself* – desire which has been considerably repressed, and therefore emerges with potent and often bizarre results, as in the female vampire. Thus in *Psycho*, sexual vitality – personified in Marion (Janet Leigh), who at the beginning of the film has just made love to her boyfriend – is destroyed by a poisonous familial relation, in the shape of Norman Bates and his internalized mother. But who does the male viewer identify with in *Psycho*? Simply with Norman Bates, peering impotently through his spy-hole at Marion undressing? And does the female viewer inexorably identify with Marion and her suffering in the shower scene?

I would argue that both male and female viewers are able to identify with either or both Bates and with Marion. Marion represents an energetic desire that is persecuted by the 'dark family' personified in Bates. Thus the viewer identifies with the film as a whole as a correlative for the psyche as a whole and society as a whole. The 'pleasure' in watching the famous shower scene in *Psycho* is thus very complex: there is the sadistic pleasure in being the attacker, and there is the masochistic pleasure in being attacked, the latter reinforced for all viewers since the scene is a ferocious filmic assault. As Hitchcock said, the film itself is torn to shreds. For this scene he demanded: 'An impression of a knife slashing, as if tearing at the very screen, ripping the film'.[33]

Horror in particular seems to be a strikingly masochistic genre for the spectator: we watch horror in order to be terrified, disgusted, and so on.

Normally the end of the film allows us to re-establish mastery, but in the middle of the film we may feel very vulnerable and wounded by the film. Thus the text opens up the subject, who becomes his own text.

We can take this argument into the controversy over pornography. The male viewer can simultaneously identify with the position of voyeur, devouring the female object with his gaze, and also with the female object, being devoured. Does this not partly explain the marginalized shameful aura around porn – that men secretly enjoy a most hidden pleasure: that of being a woman and being opened up to male penetration?

One interesting fact about soft porn photographs is that men are mainly absent. One could of course argue that this is because the key male subject is the viewer, but perhaps also porn gets rid of the male since the female is the primary target of identification. One can trace this back to oedipal conflicts: if I get rid of father, I get to enjoy mother on my own. But this position easily turns into a symbiotic one: I enjoy mother so much I become one with her: I become a woman like her. This is simultaneously blissful and shameful, and must be hidden, especially from oneself. Thus, identification shows a most primitive shift from 'having' to 'being', since in the young infant it is doubtful if these two processes are clearly distinguished, and indeed in many adults are not distinguished at all well. In fact, sexual orgasm could be described as an experience where there is a dissolution between having and being, between subject and object: this is what causes ecstasy for some, and terror in others, blocking orgasm or any sexual contact at all.

No-one can make hard and fast predicative generalizations about identification in such areas. It is fluid, shifting, paradoxical. Commentators have pointed out how the largely male audience for the slasher film cheer on the male assailant, but redouble their cheering as the female hero takes revenge.[34]

Yet one still finds in contemporary film analysis evidence that identification is taken in a linear fashion: men identify with screen males, and that's that. For example in Janet Thumim's book, *Celluloid Sisters*, she makes this assertion, in a discussion about rape in films:

> Male readers may deplore such assaults, *but they cannot identify with the victim*, neither can they draw on personal extra-diegetic experience in considering the connotative resonances of such representations. [my emphasis][35]

I would disagree with both these claims. Indeed Carol Clover's book is based on the opposite claim: that the slasher film in the 1980s (for example *Halloween, Slumber Party Massacre, Nightmare on Elm St, Friday the*

Thirteenth, and so on) got rid of the male saviour, traditional rescuer of the 'damsel in distress', precisely so that the victim role and the rescuer role could both be played by women, and *identified with by men*. Thumim's second point assumes that men are not raped. However, this seems a rather flimsy assumption, especially within an American context, where prison rapes appear to be numerous.[36] In addition, I am sure many men can identify with the rape experience, since they feel 'raped' by patriarchal culture.

One might as well argue that men never dream of women, or if they do, the dream woman cannot be part of the male psyche, or that if a woman dreams of an erect penis, she is dreaming of something alien, something that cannot be part of herself. Not so! I have had many women clients in whom such a dream has marked a most significant step in their own development. The dream penis was their own, and the dream permitted them to own it, enjoy it and use it powerfully in their life.

I would maintain that cross-gender identification is rife in many cultural forms, and is part of the theatre of gender and sexuality. This gives us a huge pay-off of excitement and pleasure, but also leads us into deep, dangerous and painful waters: as we search for the other, we search for ourselves.

Gender is one of the prime means in human existence of constructing an image of oneself in another. It is partly a game: subject and object are split, and then the object becomes infinitely desirable, because in the object is concealed certain aspects of myself that I pine for – a kind of hide and seek on a massive scale. However, it is also not a game: the human being is compelled to fracture him/herself in order to acquire knowledge and to become an 'I', but in the process the fractured self yearns for images that will restore itself to itself, and take it back to Paradise, where all things are one. This is deadly serious, and has tragic consequences, in the form of people who are so entranced with the other that they lose themselves, and also people who are so afraid of the other that they must build a fortress to repel him/her.

The notion of 'internal objects' leads us to this provocative claim: each individual has internalized a set of social relations and social conditions. Therefore the opposition between the 'individual' and 'society' is misleading, since the individual is made up of a set of social interrelations. The psyche is therefore not a 'reflection' of society: it simply is society in its most concrete and immediately apprehended form. The individual is intrinsically a collectivity; his/her conscious and unconscious are collective strata; even the sense of being an individual is a societal acquisition.

THE PATRIARCHAL UNCONSCIOUS

At this point let me return to the psychoanalytic background to this debate. Some feminists have argued that in Hollywood films, women are inevitably downgraded and subjugated, but this strikes me as a monolithic interpretation, which actually denies the existence of the unconscious.

According to this argument, film – and indeed any cultural form – therefore can have no contradictory depths, no paradox. This is an extraordinary claim about film, and about art and culture in general, and is reminiscent of some feminists' interpretations of pornography, where again the representations of women have only one meaning: that of degradation and masochism.

Thus when Mulvey refers to the 'unconscious of patriarchal society [which] has structured film form', she is saying something rather startling about the unconscious: that it is the same as the conscious. But surely the unconscious tends to contain contradictions to the conscious: for example, rather simplistically, the pacifist unconsciously enjoys war, the anti-pornographer is excited by porn, the meek man is furious, and so on. The notion of 'passive aggression', so valuable within a psychotherapeutic context, expresses the contradictions existing between the outer personality and the inner rather more profoundly. In many relationships, for example, one finds apparent 'victims' wielding great power.

To put it bluntly, if we can speak of patriarchal society having an unconscious, one would predict that it would not be entirely 'masculinist', but would contain images of female power and male degradation.[37] One would also predict that popular culture would reflect these hidden images. These images may be repressed, but they are not obliterated. They 'speak', as the unconscious must speak, whether or not we listen.

This debate is rather reminiscent of a debate within French film criticism in the 1950s and 1960s over the meaning of film. In an essay published in 1956, Jean Domarchi argued against the Stalinist argument that works of art were to be judged simply by their manifest social content. Domarchi advocates a dialectical approach, and suggests that Hollywood mainstream films (condemned by French Communists simply because they are glossy capitalist productions) are interesting precisely because they contain so many contradictions to the bourgeois order. Thus, speaking of Hitchcock's fascination with criminality, he says: 'the criminal can only affirm himself through a negation of the other, because he cannot realize himself within *universal values, which no longer exist since the system has long since destroyed them*' [original emphasis].[38]

To put it simplistically, *Psycho* and *The Birds* give us images of a society eaten up by repressed and disowned forces. The bourgeois order turns upon itself and devours itself – in the shape of Norman Bates and the attacking seagulls respectively. The spectator is bombarded with images, attacked by the frenetic editing, shocked by bizarre and startling events.

Of course in 1956 Domarchi did not express this in terms of patriarchal and anti-patriarchal ideology, but his argument still stands. This is why in this book I have set out to look at mainstream popular culture and not the avant-garde. That is where we will find unconscious or contradictory messages, if they exist. In my view they do exist, in plenitude. For example, the image of the macho male in 'action films' is not simply an over-the-top assertion of male white might: it is also a roar of despair, hysteria and panic. One only has to look at the Mel Gibson character in *Lethal Weapon* and *Lethal Weapon II* – here is a man 'on the verge of a nervous breakdown'; Gibson has a particular talent in portraying hysterical males. It seemed entirely logical that he went to play the title role in Zeffirelli's *Hamlet*.

It is not surprising therefore that a number of feminist critics have begun to perceive some of the contradictions within the Freudian/Lacanian position, for example Carol Clover, Jackie Byars in her book *All that Hollywood Allows*, Barbara Creed in *The Monstrous Feminine* and Yvonne Tasker in *Spectacular Bodies*.

Domarchi's argument is brought into more contemporary terminology by Jackie Byars:

> Mainstream film texts cannot be removed from the material conditions in which they are produced and consumed nor separated from the ideological struggles of which they are a part. They are not simple texts; they not only are not necessarily ideologically coherent but also are not monolithically repressive. They are participants in an ongoing ideological process; real ideological struggle goes on in and with mainstream entertainment texts.[39]

Going back to Hitchcock, should we simply say that his films show the male sadist attacking the female victim, both with his gaze and his physical assault? There is no doubt that women are the victims in Hitchcock's films: Marion is attacked by Bates in *Psycho*, Melanie is attacked by the birds in *The Birds*, 'Judy' is built up by Scottie in *Vertigo* to look like a dead woman. But what about the men in these films? Are they simply romantic heroes? The question is ludicrous – indeed one could argue that Hitchcock's primary interest is in *male perversity*. Voyeurism is rife in his films – it forms the main structure of *Rear Window* – but he also deals with necrophilia (*Vertigo*), rape (*Frenzy*), psychosis (*Psycho*). Hitchcock is also fascinated by male victims: in *The Paradine Case*, men are totally demolished by the central female character (Mrs Paradine), who has killed her husband, whose lover commits suicide out of unrequited love, and whose barrister is professionally ruined by his infatuation with her.

It would therefore be farcical to suggest that Hitchcock simply permits, or encourages in the male spectator, an uncomplicated identification with his male protagonists. Equally we cannot say that he mounts a conscious critical assault on patriarchy – but surely he subverts it? The film *Marnie* shows this clearly, for in that film patriarchal ideology is both bolstered – in the idea that the female kleptomaniac, suffering from sexual frigidity, can only be saved by the male rescuer, played by Sean Connery – and also subverted, in the portrayal of the fetishism of the male, who is attracted to Marnie because she is a 'professional thief and liar'. And this was the aspect of *Marnie* that interested Hitchcock, as he says in his interview with Truffaut:

Truffaut: It's taken from a Winston Graham novel, and I'd like to know which aspect of the book made you decide to do the film.

Hitchcock: The fetish idea. A man wants to go to bed with a thief because she is a thief … Unfortunately this concept doesn't come across on the screen. It's not as effective as *Vertigo*, where Jimmy Stewart's feeling for Kim Novak was clearly a fetishist love. To put it bluntly, we'd have to have Sean Connery catching the girl robbing the safe and show that he felt like jumping at her and raping her on the spot.[40]

If you like, Hitchcock tore away some of the veils of hypocrisy surrounding male desire and possessiveness in our society, and delighted in trying to prove, through the construction of cinematic identifications, that men are all voyeurs, fetishists, necrophiliacs, and so on. To call him a misogynist strikes me as rather limited: better call him an out and out misanthropist![41]

THE MALE OBJECT

Having discussed the issue of identification at some length, since it is of crucial importance in any consideration of high or low culture, let me move now to the claim that the male gaze is directed at woman as object. In her original article, 'Visual Pleasure and Narrative Cinema', Laura Mulvey expresses this idea as follows:

According to the principle of the ruling ideology and the physical structures that back it up, the male figure cannot bear the burden of sexual
objectification. Man is reluctant to gaze at his exhibitionist like.[42]

However, subsequent research has tended to contradict this view. For
example, Steve Neale, in his article 'Masculinity as Spectacle: Reflections
on Men and Mainstream Cinema', argues that men are frequently the
objects of voyeuristic looking, both by the spectator and by other characters in the film.[43] This is taken to an extreme in certain Italian westerns,
where men look at each other intensely, and we are invited to look at
them. But other essays in the Cohan and Hark collection, *Screening the
Male*, point out that throughout twentieth-century cinema men have quite
clearly been 'objectified' – the glaring prewar example being Valentino.
And returning to the 1980s, surely part of the appeal of the action film is
the exposure of the male body? And the buddy film shows a dual exposure: men are exposed to each other and to the viewer.[44]

The western directly contradicts Mulvey's thesis: for in many western
films, men are constantly looking out for each other, staring each other
down, before penetrating each other with bullets. Indeed, as Neale points
out, one of the problems for the western and other genres such as the
gangster film, is that if the viewer is male, and the film presents a male
object, then we have a homoerotic male/male nexus. This is troublesome
for Hollywood, and therefore male/male looking and loving has to be dis-
placed, for example into violence. Men can't literally ravish each other in
mainstream cinema: instead they kill each other. The final frame of *Butch
Cassidy and the Sundance Kid* demonstrates this to perfection: Butch and
Sundance are frozen for eternity, together, caught in a hail of bullets,
joking to the end, but surely also in love with each other.

Shifting outside cinema, part of the furore aroused in the early career of
Elvis Presley was precisely over his body, which was considered too
sexual. Hence the famous Ed Sullivan show where Presley was filmed
from the waist up, and the Steve Allen show where Presley was humiliated
by being made to sing the song 'Hound Dog' to a dog.[45] Later in his life,
in his stage shows in Las Vegas, Presley adopted a variety of exotic cos-
tumes that leave no doubt that his body is very much on display.

Particular fury was aroused in Presley's case, since a white working-
class man dared to stand up and be openly sexual, energetic and beautiful
– traits that have tended to be projected on to black men. My own view is
that Presley also initially aroused considerable fear about the combativity
and rebelliousness of the white working class, who have so often been
called on to support the American status quo against radicals.

The same approach can be taken towards male sport: the male body is openly exhibited as a locus of beauty, grace, brutality, and so on. It is interesting that male sport tends to dominate television, and attracts bigger sponsorship fees, bigger prizes and so on than women's sport. Why do male audiences want to watch male sport? One can of course bring into play certain political ideas here: that male sport helps construct male dominance through the idealisation of the super-strong male body.[46] But I also want to argue that male sport caters for that intense male desire to look at male bodies. Sport permits a considerable displacement of this desire: the spectator need not be aware that this is what he wants at all.

Thus Mulvey's claim that 'Man is reluctant to gaze at his exhibitionist like' seems spectactularly (!) incorrect both within and outside cinema. What is interesting is to locate those contexts where men want to look at women, and those where they want to look at men. Without doubt the latter activity is more hedged about with taboo, and has to be mystified and camouflaged.

The notions of 'having' and 'being' can be applied again, for on the surface men look at women in order to 'have' them; and look at men in order to 'be' them, that is, identify with them. But one can suggest that unconsciously the relations are also reversed: at times, the male wants to 'be' a woman and 'have' a man.

5 Westerns

The western is something of a test case for a book such as this, for it is a masculine genre par excellence. The western novel and film are 'phallic discourses' taken to an endpoint – men gaze at each other, pump bullets into each other's bodies, and lust after women as bar-room 'whores'. Is the western therefore simply a celebration of patriarchal values? Does it represent a male extirpation of the female, a homoerotic expression of hatred and envy of women?

I don't think the western is as coherent as that. One can point to other aspects – for example, its presentation of the male body as spectacle, its view of the male as a suffering person, the sheer stoicism involved in being a western hero, the solitary, cut-off quality of some protagonists.

If one of the core *overt* meanings of the western concerns 'law and order', that is, patriarchal and colonial law imposed by a white male hero figure, I shall argue that there are other *covert* subtexts of the western, for example male love, male suffering and a defiance of bourgeois values. The western explores some of the contradictions of American masculinity: it is required to be 'tough', but not too tough or it becomes outlawed; it must excise the need for love and tenderness, yet it helps to construct a world in which these can flourish; ultimately, as 'the desert turns into a garden', it makes itself redundant. Thus there is a tragic tinge to the western, as men find that they are cast out from the towns they helped to build, or watch others marry and raise children, while they are condemned, in the haunting words used in *The Searchers*, to 'wander forever between the winds'.

ANTECEDENTS

The western is a long-lived and tenacious genre. Its literary antecedents can be traced back at least to James Fenimore Cooper's Leatherstocking stories, for example, *The Last of the Mohicans*, and also arguably to Mark Twain's *Huckleberry Finn*. In both these classic American novels we find a world of males, who in different ways reject the world of women, the domestic world. Huck lights out for the territory, feeling persecuted by his do-gooding aunts and other women. There he finds Jim, black slave, who becomes his bosom friend. In *The Last of the Mohicans*, Hawkeye is a mythical figure, austere, almost impersonal, who lives in the forest with Chingachgook and Uncas, and similarly avoids the world of marriage and women.

56

At this point, it seems imperative to cite a comment by Leslie Fiedler who, in his startling critical work *Love and Death in the American Novel*, makes the claim that American literature rejected the 'European' theme of love between men and women, and rebelled against the 'gentle tyranny of home and woman':

> There is a relationship which symbolically joins the white man to nature and his own unconscious, without a sacrifice of his 'gifts'; and binds him in life-long loyalty to a help-meet, without the sacrifice of his freedom. This is the pure marriage of males – sexless and holy, a kind of counter-matrimony, in which the white refugee from society and the dark-skinned primitive are joined till death do them part.
>
> The very end of the pure love of male for male is to outwit woman, that is, to keep her from trapping the male through marriage into civilization and Christianity. The wilderness Eros is, in short, not merely an anti-cultural, but an anti-Christian and Satanic Eros.[1]

This is a controversial analysis of American literature, and in relation to western novels and films it is only half right. There are plenty of westerns that in fact take the hero through various struggles and obstacles towards the goal of heterosexual marriage – for example, *The Big Country*. And there are some fascinating westerns which contain both types of men: the uxorious and those who shun marriage. For example, in *Shane* the married farmer solicits the help of the romantic but unknowable gunfighter. There is an immediate sexual attraction between Shane and the farmer's wife, but Shane must move on, once he has carried out his ceremonial execution of the bad man, leaving the family safe in their valley.

The same divide is found in *The Man Who Shot Liberty Valance*: the lawyer, played by James Stewart, brings constitutional law to the west and marries John Wayne's girl. John Wayne, the rancher, represents a western value that is now seen as regretfully out of date. And in *The Searchers* Wayne plays another character – the embittered Indian-hating Ethan Edwards – who is shut out from home and family at the end of the film. Perhaps more than any other director, John Ford explored the tension within western masculinity, which is required both to be ruthless in the taming of the desert and the 'savage' Indian, and then to be 'civilized' within the tranquillity of the social order.

Thus Fiedler's argument works for westerns in this respect: that marriage is never the central theme of the western, although it may be the formal culmination of the narrative. It is the tensions between male love and heterosexual love, between the wilderness and civilization, between outlawry and legality, that lie at the heart of the western, and give it such a rich texture and a seemingly inexhaustible energy.

One can also tie in here Jane Tompkins' book *West of Everything*, which argues that westerns represent a revolt against the sentimental literature of the nineteenth century, dominated by women.[2] In this sense women are perceived in the western as dangerous scouts for the bourgeois order, and the western mounts a rearguard action against being taken over by this overwhelming force. To an extent, woman is perceived as the symbol of romance, marriage, commitment – which spell bourgeois emasculation. But ironically, men are caught in a trap of their own making: they exuberantly set out to construct a civilization, only to find that their future role in it spells constriction, loss of vitality and often death.

Tompkins also examines less prestigious literature than Mark Twain or Fenimore Cooper – for example Zane Grey and Louis L'Amour. This is vital to an understanding of westerns, since so much of the early western literature consisted of dime novels, with few literary pretensions, yet none the less hugely popular. The dime novel also provided much of the material that went into the B-western film, which existed almost as a separate genre from the more prestigious A-western such as *High Noon* or *Stagecoach*.

Thus the western became a very flexible and wide-ranging genre, able to encompass the unpretentious dime novel, whose descendant is surely the TV western series – *Bonanza*, *Rawhide*, *Gunsmoke* and so on – as well as the complex and poetic works of John Ford. In addition, if we look at the genre historically, we see a shift in the postwar era towards darker themes, which gave the western a new psychological depth.

Both Fiedler and Tompkins ignore a political analysis of the western, which could point to the construction of a masculinity in tune with American imperialism in the twentieth century.[3] In this sense the conflict with the native American is used as a parallel with later conflicts, as America began its mission of economic colonialism. But post-war westerns begin to show a darkening of tone, a more critical view of the notion of 'manifest destiny' which had seen the westwards expansion as wholly good. And masculinity itself – posited as the essential requirement for the construction of civilization – is seen as paradoxical. The toughness that is required for the drive westwards is seen as dangerous once social stability has been established, and more feminine values are needed. The hero turns into an outlaw, and one common western plot has two old friends turn enemies, as one cleaves to the path of constitutional law, while the other keeps to his old wicked ways (for example, *Pat Garrett and Billy the Kid*).

It is this paradox that gives the western much of its energy: 'the conflict between male toughness and social order has embedded unresolvable tensions in the western's representations of masculinity'.[4]

CINEMA

The western was for decades the staple genre of Hollywood. Up to 1960, between a quarter and a fifth of all films produced there were westerns.[5] This is a massive proportion of the market, and for some studios the western was their bread and butter, particularly the 'independent' studios such as Republic. The decline began in the 1960s, accelerated in the 1970s, and the western seemed to die in the 80s. But the 90s seem to be seeing something of a resurrection – more westerns are being made, following the success of *Dances with Wolves*, *Unforgiven* and the TV film *Lonesome Dove*. The 90s are also seeing a diversification of the western: black westerns and women's westerns are being made.[6]

But raw statistics conceal important distinctions among different types of westerns. The great bulk that were produced in the 30s, 40s and 50s were series westerns, mass-produced in blocks of six or eight films at a time, and B-westerns, produced to fill the bottom half of the double bill, and therefore not considered prestigious films.[7] In fact, the series western and B-western have their own fervent aficionados, since they have their own qualities of charm, timelessness, and at times a quite surreal quality.[8] In addition, there are a surprising number of gold nuggets amongst B-films, films of genuine power and vision, for example, the magnificent *Day of the Outlaw* by André de Toth, and the series of films directed by Budd Boetticher. In addition, certain individual performances stand out in the B-western – for example, John Cassevetes in *Saddle the Wind*.

The A-western only began to develop momentum in the 40s and 50s, partly inspired by the success of John Ford's *Stagecoach* (1939) and Henry King's *Jesse James* (1939). And it is the A-western that saw a new kind of 'revisionism': the 'psychological' western, the film noir western, the western with sexual themes. Such films took the western a long way from Roy Rogers and Hopalong Cassidy into more adult territory. In particular the ethical simplicity of many B-films (the hero and villain clearly demarcated in dress and behaviour) gave way to a new ethical uncertainty and relativity.

The B-western began to die in the fifties, but for a period television took over. Series such as *Bonanza*, *Gunsmoke* and *Rawhide*, dominated the television ratings until the early 60s.[9] Then it seemed as if both streams of western film – low- and big-budget – would die out. New genres appealed to young audiences – horror and sci fi in particular – and the western iconography began to seem old-fashioned in the space age. But the end of the western has been prophesied many times – for example in the thirties with the coming of sound. It is quite likely that as a mythical creation, the western contains complex and rich meanings that are not ephemeral.

WESTERN MYTHS

The western is a true mythical system. It has been constantly elaborated over time, until it has achieved the complexity and richness of more ancient mythologies. It provides a set of symbols which are instantly recognizable – for example, the shoot-out in the street, the card-game in the saloon, the horse-chase, the ambush, the Indian attack. Of course such symbols become too stereotyped if used in an unthinking manner, but they can also be used creatively.

The patriarchal framing of the western is not in doubt: men have come to the untamed west to create homes and build empires. Women are their helpers, and have a subordinate role. A certain number of westerns deal explicitly with the theme of the 'patriarch', although interestingly he is often portrayed as an evil figure, who is trying to block the lives of ordinary people. Indeed the evil patriarch became a stereotype, and the conflict between cattle baron and homesteaders a standard plot.[10]

Thus the western acquires a populist current to it, supporting the ordinary people against the rich. Nonetheless it is still a patriarchal populism: it is the ordinary *man* who is supported against the rich *man*, for example in *The Big Country*, *Shane*, *Pale Rider* and *Once Upon a Time in the West*.

There is also a utopian strain in the western: the land to the west is a kind of Eden, a land full of milk and honey. At times this paradisal vision is tinged with bitterness, as in *Across the Wide Missouri*, which shows that Eden is inevitably ruined by the relentless march of white civilization. At the beginning of this film the director shows us French and Scottish trappers and Indians coexisting in harmony: Clark Gable marries a Blackfoot woman. But Gable's own desire to push on to new territory carries the seed of destruction within it.

But the western is not usually as critical of white colonialism – that is, not until the 1970s cycle of westerns, such as *Little Big Man*, began to make parallels between the destruction of native Americans and the war in Vietnam. Most westerns uncritically accept the 'manifest destiny' of the white man, which is to advance westwards, driving the 'savages' before him.

However, the most complex westerns explore the contradictions within this colonial drive: that while much is gained, much is lost. And the 'pro-Indian' westerns, common in the 1920s and the 1950s, and perhaps re-emerging in the 90s, look with regret at the ancient values destroyed by the rush westwards. And there is a dislike of urban values in the western which is hopelessly romantic: the western hero helps to set up towns, but hates them for their constrictiveness and small-mindedness. His only solution is to ride out to the 'far country', and the process starts all over again. One of the implicit themes of westerns is 'Paradise Lost': it was fun taming the wilderness, but what have we lost in the process?

The western is so complex that I can only look briefly at several key themes concerning masculinity. There are a whole range of ideas – to do with nature and civilization, the individual and society, agriculture and industry, the nature of constitutional law, youth and age – that are of great interest, but must be omitted here.

I have focused on two main areas concerning men: first, men in relationships – with women, with other men, and as solitary figures; and secondly, the way men relate to three themes – nature, language and violence.

MEN WITH WOMEN

As I have said, in relation to the western, one can make too much of Fiedler's idea of the male fleeing society (and women) into the wilderness. Many westerns concern themselves with male exploits which lead toward heterosexual relationship. The 1940 film *Dark Command* is typical of its period: in a rather tortuous plot, John Wayne plays the drifting cowboy who arrives in Lawrence, Kansas, becomes sheriff, helps to tame the local guerillas who are using the Civil War as an excuse to loot and pillage, and eventually shoots the leader of the guerillas. Then Wayne woos the wife of the dead guerilla leader. Thus the woman, significantly, is exchanged between two men, and is, as it were, 'won' as the spoils of battle. Woman is the prize.

This can be related both to notions of the patriarchal treatment of women as 'exchange commodity', and also to an archetypal mythic structure, whereby the male hero goes through many obstacles to find a woman. He is tested through ordeal and the risk of death, before he is considered acceptable to the heroine. Of course this means that generally the function of the woman in the narrative is to stand and wait while the hero is tested.

As many critics have commented, women are essential to the formal structure of the western, but are not given any psychological depth, except in
off-beat westerns such as *Johnny Guitar*.[11]

Another important function that the woman plays is as an obstacle
herself. Frequently she opposes her man's determination to fight. She is
for peace and against war. The traditional plot then has the man resist the
woman's arguments: he goes off and has his fight, and is welcomed back
by her as a hero.

Jane Tompkins makes the perceptive comment that this conflict is set up
in the western precisely in order that the man can resist the woman:

> The man's reasoning is always that honor demands he meet the chal-
> lenge, with honor presented as an exigency only he understands. But
> what honor is is the need to do exactly that which the woman most hates
> and fears in order to prove that you are not under her control.[12]

In other words the western illustrates a rite of passage for the male: his
cutting the umbilical cord. In this sense it is similar to those rituals found
throughout the world in tribal societies, whereby young males are cut off
from their mothers, often in ceremonies of great violence and harshness.

But in the western this is also seen as a powerful tension for older men.
In *Unforgiven*, Clint Eastwood, an ageing and ineffective pig farmer, starts
the film very much a reformed character, and keeps telling his friends that
his dead wife helped him stop drinking, killing and so on. Significantly,
near the end of the film, when he has mown down the sheriff and his
henchmen, he downs a glass of whiskey. He has cast off the woman's
influence again, and can kill with efficiency and vigour.

One might argue that this is a childish demonstration of freedom –
'Look Mummy, I can drink whiskey, and kill people, just like you told me
not to', or alternatively a reimposition of patriarchal values and authority.[13] However one can also point to the oedipal tensions present in such
narratives, tensions that are internalized in the viewer. In other words the
struggle between honour and safety-first, or between one's own wishes
and mother's counsel, goes on inside all of us all the time. In that sense,
although the western is saturated in masculine ideas and values, it does
appeal to some women, since they too have had the problem of separating
from their mothers. Thus the woman in the western is shown very much as
a *maternal* figure: it is maternal authority that constantly has to be resisted.
Women are rarely shown as sexually energetic, except in their role as
whores: the 'good' woman wears those long dresses that shroud the body
in respectability. Only the bad woman (or the Indian woman) shows her
flesh.

The wife or wife-to-be in the western is therefore a wife-mother, who wants safety, domesticity, gradual progress. The man often revolts against this and craves violence, danger, abrupt changes in fortune. In this sense woman in the western often represents bourgeois values, which are resisted by the drifters, cowboys and gunfighters, who romantically hold out for another way of life, an impossible one, a purely mythic world that rejects family and property values.

MALE FAMILIES AND CORPORATIONS

Westerns are full of competing male gangs. The gang of outlaws is opposed by a trio or quartet of drifting cowboys, who clean them up before going on their merry way. Whole series of westerns were built around the exploits of such groups: the 'Three Musquiteers', the Bar 20 ranchhands in Hopalong Cassidy films, the Texas Rangers. The 1985 film *Silverado* celebrates such B-films in its amiable tale of a quartet of heroes who spike the plans of the villainous sheriff.

But the theme of the male group was also developed in more depth in the A-western. For example, John Ford portrayed the US cavalry as a kind of male Eden, a male family, in which men have all their needs met. The heroes of his famous trilogy – *She Wore A Yellow Ribbon*, *Rio Grande*, *Fort Apache* – are all men without women, who are devoted to their men.

In the 1960s, westerns focused on groups of men who had work to do. They were 'professionals', hired to do a job – in films such as *The Magnificent Seven*, *The Professionals*, *The Wild Bunch*. The notion of 'corporate work' had filtered into westerns from the business world.[14]

An early example of this theme is *Rio Bravo* (1959). This is a magisterial film, showing Howard Hawks working at the height of his power. This is shown in the first five minutes, which are entirely silent, and which lay bare the basic premises of character and plot. Dean Martin creeps into a bar, visibly panting for a drink. One of the professional gunfighters spots him, and contemptuously throws a dollar in a spittoon for him. Martin starts to grovel for it, but John Wayne intercedes and stops him. Then there is a shooting, and the killer is hauled off to jail by Wayne and Martin.

This is a brilliant mime-show, rapidly executed yet utterly solid. Simultaneously it lays down the basic plot – for the rest of the film, Wayne and company have to defend the jail against the killer's accomplices – and shows a prime set of male images: the broken man, the professional killer, the professional lawman.

Rio Bravo has often been described as a right-wing film, made in response to *High Noon*. Yet *High Noon* is curiously hostile to ordinary people, and *Rio Bravo* is hostile to big money.[15] Although Wayne himself attacked *High Noon* for its suggestion that the professional should seek help from amateurs, *Rio Bravo* is not an isolationist tract. Indeed, quite the reverse: Wayne's isolationism is criticized in various ways. He attacks Angie Dickinson for card-sharping, completely erroneously, and eventually she brings a kind of humanity to him.

And crucially, Wayne eventually finds himself head of a male family, consisting of the reformed drunk, the old-timer and the Colorado Kid. These are western stereotypes, yet in this film, Hawks fleshes them out, and uses them to amplify the theme of redemption. Dude, the drunk (Dean Martin), is redeemed by being given a job to do, but the sheriff himself (Wayne) is redeemed by being brought back from his initial cut-off state. It is interesting to note how often Wayne does not play the semi-fascist patriot with which he is associated.

There are complex threads running through this film concerning gender. For example, there is a famous scene when Angie Dickinson (playing a gambler) stops at the door of a hotel room, to find Wayne holding up a pair of women's red bloomers. 'They have possibilities, but not for you', she says to him. The red garment is a sign of female sexuality, with which Wayne obviously feels uncomfortable, yet which he is waving in the air – as a distress signal? And later Dickinson taunts Wayne when he accuses her of hiding playing cards. She asks him to search her – 'are they in my stockings, my garters?'. Wayne just looks dumb-founded. He cannot deal with the power of female sexuality.

Dickinson is therefore played as a rebellious female presence, both sexually alive and, as a professional gambler, transgressive within standard western iconography. It could be argued that Wayne brings her under the patriarchal heel, but in addition, he finds in her something he lacks.

But the core of the film is the male family, which gradually is assembled out of unpromising material. Hawks stresses the need for professional work as a means of male bonding: the four men have a job to do. But they also have fun, especially in the famous sing-song in the jail, in which Wayne, significantly, refuses to join.

But why the male family? Is it simply about professionalism and work? If we follow Fielder's thesis about 'male marriage', this would suggest that there is also a resistance here to domesticity and heterosexuality itself. Men construct their own world, free from the demands of marriage, children, and so on. This can be seen both as a central plank of patriarchal rule – following Eve Sedgwick's idea that the 'homosocial' bonds between men form the backbone of patriarchy – and also as a partial rejection of it, since in the male family, men reject some of the demands put on men by patriarchy – that is, to produce children and provide for families.

THE MALE COUPLE

Fiedler's remark about the 'holy marriage of males' has particular resonance to the cowboy and his sidekick, or the two friends who have become enemies and fight to the death, or the white man and his Indian helpmeet (The Lone Ranger and Tonto) or his Indian doppelganger (as in *The Searchers*) – these are staple elements in westerns. As we might expect, in the pre-war western these male couples are simply presented without examination; if we want to find a closer inspection, we have to turn to the post-war era again.

One of the outstanding films on this theme is *Gunfight at the OK Corral*, which is a long, rather tortuous work, dealing with the relationship between Wyatt Earp and 'Doc' Holliday. The action shifts from town to town, the relationship between Holliday and Earp goes through many changes until the final denouement at the OK Corral. Some critics have seen this as an overwrought film.[16]

But the overwrought quality is a result of tensions that are concealed, tensions about the love between Doc and Earp. This love cannot be openly explored in the western, or indeed in any mainstream Hollywood film, and so has to be hinted at. And there are many hints in *OK Corral*. For example, Doc's woman colludes with the planned murder of Earp, so that Doc will be free to be with her. Doc and Earp engage in earnest discussions as to who needs who. The emotional climax arrives as Doc lies dying in bed from TB, and Earp bends over him in anguish: 'I need you, Doc', while Doc's woman watches balefully from the corner.

Lawrence Kasdan's 1994 version of the Earp saga – *Wyatt Earp* – makes the rejection of heterosexuality quite explicit: Wyatt Earp finds dependence on women, and the possibility of loss, unbearable. 'Wives come and go; they leave you; they die', he retorts to a sister-in-law during a quarrel between the Earp brothers and their wives. And the relationship between Earp (Kevin Costner) and Holliday (Denis Quaid) is again the emotional fulcrum of this film, linked with a dark obsession with death and revenge.

Space does not permit a lengthy analysis of other films, but I must mention two that enshrine the male couple. First, the elegaic *Monte Walsh*, which portrays the cowboy as a dying breed, filmed with beautiful autumnal hues. In this film, Jack Palance and Lee Marvin form a couple who are destroyed, first by the ravages of capitalism, which is taking away the cowboys' livelihood, and secondly, by heterosexuality. Palance marries, and becomes a storekeeper: he is then killed by an unemployed cowboy. The film ends with Marvin talking to his horse, the only companion left to him.

Another remarkable 'couple' film is *Butch Cassidy and the Sundance Kid*. In this film, as well as spoofing many western cliches, Robert Redford and Paul Newman present a slow motion mutual seduction, full of glamorous good looks and derring-do.

The western presents us with a 'homoerotic' male couple, who are not a 'homosexual' couple. This seems to confirm Eve Sedgwick's ingenious claim that male bonding is so intense in patriarchy that it must contain a built-in guarantee against homosexual desire (see Chapter 2). But in addition, I see the western constructing a space that simultaneously rejects heterosexuality and homosexuality. This is a space that exists between categories, and therefore, if only in fantasy, enables men to float for a while, unencumbered by the ferocious demands of patriarchy and the either/or rigidities of gender and sexuality.

LONESOME

The novel *Lonesome Dove* has some very full descriptions of relationships between men and women, but significantly both main male characters in *Lonesome Dove* – Gus McCrae and Woodrow Call – have walked away from important relationships with women. In the end they are devoted to each other, and to the exploration of unconquered territory. When Gus's old love, Clara, argues with him to stay near her and settle down, he replies: 'We've heard Montana's the last place that ain't settled ... I'd like to see one more place that ain't settled before I get decrepit and have to take up the rocking chair'.[17]

In the end, this gives the western an awful bleakness. Although there is considerable glamour and heroism in the hero's quest for new land – 'before the bankers and lawyers get it' in Gus's words[18] – it also leads to a desolate existence. And *Lonesome Dove* is for me a desolate story, and Gus is a desolate man. He has a Zen-like wisdom, and an ability to get through life's difficulties. He is a great survivor, but at some fundamental level he cannot connect with people. His relationship with Woodrow Call – which is the emotional heart of the novel – can never be talked about. Both men are locked in a kind of autistic dumbness. Their mutual love can only be hinted at, or expressed in action. Thus Call takes Gus's dead body back from Montana to Texas as a last despairing gesture of love for him. *Lonesome Dove* is one of the greatest of western novels, and part of its greatness is that it doesn't shrink from a delineation of the stunted nature of the male-only world.

The word 'lonesome' is almost a western patent, along with 'lone' and 'lonely'. The lone hero is caught in a dilemma: he is needed by settlers, homesteaders and small towns to control outlaws and other lawbreakers, yet he is never really at home with them. He is reminiscent of those animal slaughterers employed by Hindus, whose task is both necessary yet disdained.

Both the cowboy, and his descendant the gunfighter, are 'lonesome'. Society needs them for various tasks, yet also wishes to expel them beyond the pale.

If we stand back from the western for a moment, it is interesting to speculate whether this image of loneliness says something about masculinity as a whole. It is a powerful image of male alienation. Men are needed to carry out many onerous tasks: they do heavy work, they fight in wars, they provide for families, propagate children, yet they also feel useless, unwanted. Somehow they remain 'uncivilized'.

Another way of putting it is that there is a basic clash between bourgeois civilization and men. Men fear that their basic identity will be destroyed if they become too absorbed into the warp and woof of society. Castration looms, not as a punishment from father or mother, but as a concomitant of being a 'citizen' at all. The bourgeois order – represented in the western by the woman in an apron standing at the door of the cabin – is overwhelming in the long run, but can be resisted temporarily.

The western is also deeply anti-technology. Cars are often portrayed with heavy irony, as in *The Ballad of Cable Hogue*, in which Jason Robards, in a scene of great farce and pathos, is killed by one at the end of the film. The railroad – seen positively in early westerns such as *The Iron Horse* (1924) and *Union Pacific* (1939) – becomes in later westerns the symbol of a destructive capitalism. This is shown most intensely in Leone's *Once Upon a Time in the West* in the toad-like figure of the magnate, Ferzetti.

In the western, the movement away from civilization and technology is portrayed quite graphically: the cowboy gets on his horse and rides out, or the gunfighter, having accomplished his unwelcome but necessary task, takes his money and goes to the next town. This exodus also connects with the theme of nature: the western hero is always longing for the hills or the plains, or to be alone with his horse. He feels uncomfortable in drawing-rooms, in fact in any room except a saloon or a bleak hotel-room. When he has a bath, it becomes an embarrassing and painful ordeal, and he tries to temporize with it by keeping his hat on, or smoking a cigar.

The lonesome hero doesn't feel comfortable with women, except saloon bar whores. In *Lonesome Dove*, Gus's ease with women is rather atypical. The other cowboys are more characteristic of the western: they are basically terrified of women, yet also worshipful of them.

At times this fear of women attains quite extreme expression: in *Jeremiah Johnson*, the mountain men shun towns and women, and the old timer that Robert Redford befriends makes this bitter pronouncement: 'a woman's breast is the hardest rock that the Almighty ever made on this earth, and I can find no sign on it'.

Similarly in some westerns, marriage, and anything connected with marriage, is disastrous. In *Shane*, Starrett's wife wears her wedding dress to a dance, and while this is partly a symbol of the values of community and relationship, it also signals trouble. In *Monte Walsh*, Palance's marriage is the prelude to his death.

Do these themes indicate a male supremacist tone? On the contrary, for me, they express a male sense of hurt and solitariness. Nobody wants *him*. He is required for certain functions in society, but his deeper self can only be found in solitude, with his male companion, or in communion with nature.

SHANE

Shane is one of those westerns which appear as instantly classical formulations. The theme of the loner is given a self-consciously mythic aura, which has irritated some critics, and delighted others.[19]

Beneath the surface story of *Shane* – gunfighter helps farmers resist cattle baron – there is a covert story conveyed primarily in the visual images. In this subtext, Shane is a wounded stricken man, who can offer the farmers a kind of male potency, but who is himself cut off from other men and women, cut off from the land, forced to ride on alone. There is a symmetry here: Shane is able to contest the will of the cattle baron, but he is asocial; the farmers have their community, but cannot fight – if they do they are gunned down. Thus male potency and sociability are inversely related.

The casting of Alan Ladd has often been criticized, and it is true that he is very static, wooden even. Yet whether conscious or not, the choice of Ladd as the gunfighter actually brings out this theme of male autism. In one brilliant John Ford-like tableau in the cemetery, the farmers and their wives mourn the death of Elisha Cook, killed by the gunfighter (Jack Palance). But Alan Ladd stands alone in the cemetery, separate from them.

He falls in love with the wife of the farmer he befriends (Jean Arthur), but this is an impossible love, as both of them tacitly recognize – another reason he has to leave at the end. He has also been a kind of masculine mentor to the farmer's son Joey, who laments his departure at the end of the film: 'Come back, Shane'.

I find something poignant about Ladd – his face often carries a haunted wounded look quite different from the farmers' faces, who are purposeful, utilitarian. Even Ladd's pretty fringed clothes add to this impression – they are useless for work. Ladd himself is useless, except for carrying out the primitive task of justice that is required. But such men then become outcasts, scapegoats. They carry too much blood on them, and must be cast out from the community.

In the male psyche there is a terrible wound here, a split between action and community, power and the ability to relate. One can be potent or one can be social – but not both.

Shane also has a rather ambiguous eroticism about him. Everyone stares at him: in the beginning, the boy Joey, but then the wife and the farmer begin to look at him intently. In the saloon the gunmen stare at him, trying to castrate him with their macho contempt. The farmer's wife seems to long for him in a veiled sexual manner; the boy longs for him as a super-father; and possibly the farmer himself longs for him as a male lover.

This aspect of *Shane* gives it a rather strained feel: somehow the director is trying to put something across that he is either not fully aware of, or which cannot be fully shown. Shane is a male pin-up, a kind of vamp, seducing everyone in sight with his buckskin fringes and his fluttering eye-lashes. There is something both beguiling and irritating about this portrayal, increased by Alan Ladd's rather inert presence. But then Ladd's deadness gives another quality to the role: Shane is shut off from his erotic relations with others.

There is also a doomed feel about Shane. When he argues with the cattle baron, who is attempting to drive the farmers off their land, Shane tells him, 'You've lived too long', and the rancher says the same is true of gunfighters such as Shane. Shane makes the interesting reply: 'The difference is, I know it'. Thus the coming of civilization will wipe out such men as Shane: their romantic existence cannot exist in ordinary society.

How much yearning is conveyed in such a film! Shane is a kind of Arthurian knight transplanted to the west. He has seemingly forsworn sexuality, even companionship. At the end of the film, he heads for the hills, while the blood drips from an untended wound. Thus beneath such beguiling film surfaces lurk quite subtle messages about men. They are not simply all conquering heroes: a terrible price is paid for their assumption of certain duties. In the end Shane has made a kind of living sacrifice of himself.

MEN IN NATURE

It is no accident that Shane rides off into the mountains: for while many of the narrative structures of the western can be found in other genres – the male couple is found in gangster films, thrillers and the 'buddy' genre; the male 'corporation' is found in films such as the Godfather trilogy and *The Untouchables* (1990); the shrinking from domesticity and the emphasis on violence and death is found throughout American culture, 'high' and 'low' – one important aspect of the western marks it out: the background of nature. Thus, while it may be correct in one sense to argue that space adventures such as *Star Wars*, or TV police series such as *Starsky and Hutch* or *Miami Vice*, are really westerns in disguise, they do lack the element of wild nature. In this sense, they are not westerns.

In fact to call nature a 'background' to the western is a misnomer: it is the central 'character'. The western film is utterly sensuous. It is anti-language and anti-metaphysics. It presents and presents, and does not describe or reflect. It is full of physical beauty – the immense prairies, the mountains covered in snow, the green valley, the 'far country' that calls to men.

Yet this is not without meaning at all – indeed its deepest meaning is its sensuousness. It seems to say – 'Here is life; seize it, live it, for tomorrow (or maybe today) we die'. Life is a spectacle, at which one marvels and catches the breath.

At times the western can become so self-consciously beautiful – as in *Shane* perhaps – that the sensuousness over-reaches itself. Shane's fringed buckskins, against the backdrop of the snow-covered Grand Teton mountains, are perhaps a tiny bit too aesthetic.

The western gives us sounds, sights, colours and action. Cowboys bivouac by a fire at night, hats tilted over faces, the coffee-pot next to the fire. A man on horse-back crosses a stream, looks over his shoulder – is he being pursued or is he the pursuer? Cattle mill about like a river of brown flesh, or thunder past like a torrent. The snow lies on the mountain peaks, and the men on horseback swallow whiskey to keep warm. The rain beats hard on the dusty street and turns it to mud. A rider races into town and is off his horse in one fluid movement. The buttes rise up in the desert, stark, unmoved by human suffering, ancient, indestructible. An Indian scout leans into the wind, listening.

Anyone who knows the paintings of Frederic Remington and Charles Russell will appreciate the extraordinary beauty of the west, and some directors of westerns have had the same painterly ability. Indeed, John Ford claimed that he tried to copy the Remington style.[20] Certainly, a central 'character' in Ford's westerns is the awesome backdrop of Monument Valley, filmed magnificently in colour in *She Wore A Yellow Ribbon*. Men are dwarfed by this gargantuan landscape; their activities seem to shrink to those of tiny ants, ephemeral beneath the eternal rocks. The land is also austere, hard, sculptural: one might say, a homoerotic landscape!

Even in the rather hackneyed western novels there is the same grasp of the essential sensuousness of the western myth. Here is Louis L'Amour:

> Barren crags loomed above the way I chose to go, and there were no more oaks, but here and there ancient cedars and patches of cholla cactus. We were nearing the desert now, the harsh Mohave that lay off to the south, mile upon mile of the Mohave, until it merged with the Colorado desert.
>
> Now the coolness of early morning was gone and the heat was coming. Turning sharply to the right, I went down a steep slope among the cacti, crossed a wash, following it through a natural gate in the rocks, and then found what I sought, a place among the rocks and a gnarled old cedar.
>
> There was more than expected, for in a shallow pool scarcely an inch deep and a foot across was water left from a recent rain. I wet my lips, then sucked some up as I waited.[21]

Not a particularly resplendent passage, but characteristic of L'Amour's style: action taking place in a landscape that is sharply delineated, focused like a pair of binoculars on the relevant objects – trees, cacti, rocks, a pool. These are the landmarks that are crucial to this man, who is being pursued – his ability to steer by them and survive among them will determine whether he will be captured and killed or will escape.

Here is something better – the beginning of that magnificent novel, *The Ox-Bow Incident*:

> Gil and I crossed the eastern divide about two by the sun. We pulled up for a look at the little town in the big valley and the mountains on the other side with the crest of the Sierra showing faintly beyond like the rim

of a day moon. We didn't look as long as we do sometimes; after winter
range, we were excited about getting back to town. When the horses had
stopped trembling from the last climb, Gil took off his sombrero, pushed
his sweaty hair back with the same hand, and returned the sombrero, the
way he did when something was going to happen. We reined to the right
and went slowly down the steep stage road. It was a switch-back road,
gutted by the run-off of the winter storms, and with brush beginning to
grow up in it again since the stage had stopped running. In the pockets
under the red earth bank, where the wind was cut off, the spring sun was
hot as summer, and the air was full of a hot, melting pine smell. Rivulets
of water trickled down shining on the sides of the cuts. The jays
screeched in the trees and flashed through the sunlight in the clearing in
swift, long dips. Squirrels and chipmunks chittered in the brush, and
along the tops of the snow-laden logs. On the outside turns though, the
wind got us and dried the sweat under our shirts and brought up, instead
of the hot resin, the smell of the marshy green valley.[22]

Here is a western Eden, full of animals, plants, fertile growth, the smell
of hot resin and the marshy valley. But within the landscape there is
action: the two riders have reached the divide, and begin their run down
into the valley to the town. The divide is both physical – separating two
valleys – and later a moral one – the divide between justice and unjust
revenge, which is depicted at great length in the lynchings that take place,
and which the two cowboys collude with. The man and the landscape are
sometimes in unison, sometimes at odds with each other, the man dwarfed
by the huge land.

The end of the same novel gives us a neat vignette of the relation of
man and nature:

Downstairs we could hear Rose talking and then laughing and all the
men laughed after her, the way they had in the afternoon. She was on
show all right.

'If I started a fight with that guy, it would come to shooting,' Gil said.

'We've had enough of that,' I told him.

'I know it,' he said, 'but I don't know how to start a decent fight with
that kind of guy.'

And then, like he was giving it a lot of attention, 'He's a funny guy. I
don't know how you'd start a decent fight with him.'

Tink-tink-a-link went the meadow lark. And then another, even
farther off, teenk-teenk-aleenk.

Then Gil said, 'I'll be glad to get out of here,' as if he'd let it all go.

'Yeh,' I said.[23]

After all the traumatic events of the novel, and even while Gil is still caught up in thinking about fighting another man, the meadow lark calls the two men back to nature, back to simplicity, and Gil can let go of everything. The bird's song tells them something profound if indescribable. Isn't such a passage akin to a Zen teaching? 'What is Buddha?' 'The log in the log-room; the frog jumps in the pond.'

But what is the meaning of nature in the western? One could relate it to the ongoing current of Romanticism prevalent in much twentieth-century art: we yearn for an Eden without industry and pollution. But what is the significance of nature for men?

Of course the white man is obsessed with the conquest of the land, and in westerns there is much sentimental talk of farming, wives and children, building a school and a church. In such scenes, small-town America constructs an image of itself and smiles approvingly.

But I think that the western also symbolically restores to men something they have lost – not simply being able to live in nature and its beauty, but *their own nature*, their own beauty. The snow-covered hills, the immense plains, the 'pretty country' that men gaze at in wonderment – surely these are symbols of something internal to men, that has been cut out of them. Let me call it simply enough their own sensuousness. There is a utopian vision here, a recovery of lost harmony with nature.

But nature is also shown as something which defeats men: an implacable enemy. In that icy film *Day of the Outlaw*, the reformed bad man (Robert Ryan) deliberately leads a gang of outlaws into the mountains, knowing that no one will survive. The outlaws begin to fight each other, but some of them freeze to death in the snowy wastes. In this film, the black and white photography attains a starkness and purity that is akin to Greek tragedy.

TOWNS

Westerns are not fond of cities. They denote eastern corruption, corporate sleaze, the break-down of community. The western tolerates the 'town', which usually consists of the basic rudiments of town life: blacksmith, church, saloon, livery stables, bank, railroad station. But there is a paradoxical feeling about the taming of the wilderness and the establishment of towns and law and order – many films are based on that very process, but there is something regretful about it. When Dodge City has been cleaned up by Errol Flynn and company in the film *Dodge City*, it becomes rather boring. Solution? Why, go off to the next town that needs cleaning up – Virginia City! There is a wonderful ironic tension here – the film is entertaining precisely because the town is so lawless. How would you make a western film about the tamed Dodge City? Very difficult.

There is a splendid scene in *Gunfight at the OK Corral*, which bears this out – the cowboys hot off the trail break into the Church Bazaar dance, ride horses across the dance-floor, swing from the chandeliers, fire guns, grab the women and try and make them dance. Of course Wyatt Earp and Doc eventually control the cowboys – but what fun the audience has had in the meantime! This scene summarizes a fundamental tension in the western: too much law is dull, but an absence of law is anarchy.

Towns have to be tamed, but once they're tamed, the western isn't interested in them. This is of course quite a natural dramaturgical principle, that can be observed in gangster films and the thriller in general. The thriller is thrilling because there are plenty of bad men around.

But there is more to it than this in the western. The tamed town is also abhorrent because it puts roots down, it settles people, ties them down. This infringes the Romantic vision of the western – the vision of the drifter, the man wandering from place to place. There is a splendid line in *Dakota Incident* when someone asks a minstrel travelling on a stagecoach where he is from, and he replies 'I'm the frommest man you ever did see'. He isn't a cowboy, but he is a drifter, and this is the Romantic fantasy – a man who wanders free as the wind, lives off the land. As Shane says, in reply to Joey's question ('Where do you want to go?'): 'Somewhere I've never been'.

'YOU TALK TOO MUCH'

The above remark is made by John Wayne to James Stewart in *The Man Who Shot Liberty Valance*, and it illustrates an important aspect of western men: they tend to be impassive and silent. Stewart with his lawbooks and his loquacity is seen as contradicting the western ethos, both by the outright villain Valance (Lee Marvin) – 'I'll show you law – western law!' – and the more moderate rancher Doniphon (Wayne). This film therefore articulates more consciously than most westerns the contrast between the traditional western male image and the new post-western one.

The western hero has a poker face; he isn't fazed by disaster or triumph; he doesn't shed tears; if he smiles it is tight-lipped.

Since the 1960s the western has been dominated by Clint Eastwood, both as actor and director, and it is worth spending a moment considering the persona he projects in most of his westerns. In the Sergio Leone trilogy, Eastwood adopts an extreme impassivity that became an essential part of the Man with No Name identity. One might even call it a placidity in the face of life. This is conveyed by Eastwood's lack of facial animation and by his voice – low, rather toneless, at times sounding uncomfortably throaty. The effect is also enhanced by the extreme fetishism that is given to his body, that is extreme close-ups of body-parts.[24]

Eastwood has been haunted by this persona. In both *High Plains Drifter* and *Pale Rider* he plays supernatural figures, returned from the dead. He is literally non-human. In *Drifter* he gazes impassively at the horrific events around him: after raping a girl, he simply says 'That'll teach you some manners'. Indeed, this film shows the 'gothic western' taken to its limits, to the point of horror.

Eastwood also developed a kind of dead-pan humour, one-liners that seem to be treasured by Eastwood aficionados. The idea seems to be here that in the face of catastrophe, while other men and women are freaking out, the hero spits, gazes at life untroubled, and finally makes a gnomic comment. Thus in *Hang 'Em High*, the sheriff quarrels with him, and tells him to go to hell. Eastwood replies: 'I've already been there'. In *High Plains Drifter*, amidst the plans to kill three bandits riding towards the town, the dwarf Mercado anxiously asks Eastwood: 'What do we do after?', that is after killing them, and Eastwood replies tersely: 'Live with it'. In *The Outlaw Josey Wales*, Eastwood's dislike of language is made explicit: the film is full of characters who talk a lot, and Eastwood falls asleep, tells them to shut up, or simply looks at them with a face like iron. The western hero cultivates a massive stoicism in the face of death and other misfortunes, but at times the stoicism is akin to autism.

Of course this impassivity is not unique to Eastwood. Westerns are full of terse one-liners that actually refute language. Some of them are very enjoyable: one of my favourites is in *Four Faces West* – Joel McCrea goes into the town bank to carry out a robbery. He pretends to be asking for a loan, and the manager asks him: 'What's your collateral for the loan?' McCrea pulls out his gun and says 'This!' A rather similar line is found in *Arizona Raiders* – during a poker game, one man exclaims 'I've got a full house', and another responds, 'I've got a better one', and pins the man's hand to the table with a knife!

Such gnomic utterances carry very strong ideological overtones: for example, in *Man with the Gun*, a town is suffering from the attacks of gunfighters, hired by the local rancher. The townspeople debate what to do, and one farmer in exasperation finally says to his fiancée: 'You can't keep turning the other cheek with a cemetery as big as the one we've got'. This is an irrefutable argument! And there is a powerful vein of anti-

Christian feeling in the western: enough of all this blather about forgiveness and repentance. Life is short and then you die!

But at times the one-liner is despairing. Thus in *Hud*, when Hud (Paul Newman) and the young boy Brandon de Wilde go out one evening, de Wilde comments: 'Lonesome old night' and Hud replies laconically: 'Ain't they all'.

Thus the gnomic style of the western hero resists language. He's not going to foam at the mouth, he's not going to get hysterical. He doesn't trust language. In *Dakota Incident*, a loquacious senator assures everyone: 'Never underestimate the power of words'. Anyone familiar with the symbolism of westerns knows instantly that he is doomed. And sure enough, when a stagecoach full of travellers is waylaid by Indians, the senator goes out to reason with them, and is shot. The woman on the coach has the correct western response: 'What do we do now? Turn the other cheek?'

The question is rhetorical. The whole rationale of the western is not to turn the other cheek, but to act. Thus in these terse statements there is hidden a massive movement against intellectuality, against Christianity, against Western verbalization. It is a complex stance, in one sense stunted, refusing to be emotional, to mourn or celebrate; yet in another sense, it is Zen-like, it refutes the *hypocrisy* of liberal Christianity. Thus in *Ulzana's Raid*, the wise old Indian scout (Burt Lancaster) opposes the liberal lieutenant, who is horrified by the savagery of the Apaches: Lancaster says he has no hatred for the Apache – 'it's like hating the desert because there ain't no water'. And when the lieutenant is equally horrified as white soldiers mutilate a dead Indian, Lancaster is phlegmatic: 'Kinda confuses the issue, doesn't it?'

At times this terse acceptance of life is attractive, for it seems to cut through the complications of Western intellectuality; but at other times it falls into portentousness. Having just watched most of Eastwood's westerns, I can vouch for it becoming extremely irritating! But Eastwood took the dead-pan persona to an extreme – by comparison, John Wayne was a positively vivacious actor.

The dominance of Eastwood in the western over the last thirty years is clear-cut, but difficult to explain. Why should 1960s audiences have enjoyed the bizarre spectacle of No Name? Why has this persona – half-dead, cut off from feeling, cut off from women – become so dominant in popular cinema? From the political point of view, one could argue that Eastwood has presented a masculinity that fits American imperialism like a glove: get things done, and don't fuss about liberal morality. Eastwood's non-western films are relevant here: above all, *Dirty Harry*'s vigilantism.[25]

However, one can also point out the mutilation that is revealed in the Eastwood western. These men are not alive; in two films they are literally dead (*High Plains Drifter* and *Pale Rider*); they relate to other people with great difficulty.[26] In other words, it strikes me that Eastwood has, wittingly or not, held up a mirror to modern men. This is the demand made by patriarchy to men: deaden yourself, show no feelings, do not speak, carry out your duties and don't complain, and then die. The western makes a virtue of necessity: the hero is obliged to suffer in silence, to show no tears, ask for no compassion. Ultimately western masculinity is *suicidal*.

The Indian male is often put forward as a supreme exponent of suicidal stoicism: *Ulzana's Raid* has one chilling scene when Ulzana – the ferocious Apache chief – about to be killed by the Indian army scout, Ke-Ni-Tay, sings his death song. This movement towards death is echoed when the white scout (Burt Lancaster), fatally wounded, asks to be left alone to die. 'It's not Christian' the liberal lieutenant remonstrates, while Lancaster gets on with rolling a cigarette – one can sense the director Robert Aldrich rubbing liberal noses in the dirt. The masculinity being presented is not simply destructive, it is self-destructive, half in love with death. This also makes the western very attractive as a fantasy: stop worrying, just keep the ammunition dry!

VIOLENCE

Violence is at the heart of the western, its raison d'être. The traditional western posited an ethical violence, that was necessary in building civilization, along the lines of the 'just war' argument. Clearly this means that the spectator gets to have his cake and eat it. The violence is justified ethically, salving our guilty feelings, but then we can settle down and enjoy it for its own sake!

But this ethical violence can also be seen as justifying American imperialism, which has frequently used violence against other peoples, usually cloaked in a veneer of righteousness, just as the British Empire did in its heyday. This criticism has particular cogency since the main mythical events in the western are historically grounded, particularly in relation to the annihilation of the native Americans.

The pre-war western does not question the use of violence as an ethical force. Thus many B-films posit a simple enough Manichean world: there are heroes and villains, and the job of the heroes is to shoot down the villains. Or the 'town-taming' type of western requires the violence of the hero to purge the town of evil. There is a *regeneration through violence*. This point is clearly controversial. Many critics have condemned this stance, for it can seem almost fascist in its political implications.[27]

However, I think there are other reasons for the presentation of violence. By this, I mean that in westerns (and of course other genres such as the thriller, the detective film, the horror film) we get to satisfy our sadistic desires in safety. The safety is guaranteed by several things: the violence is 'justified' in the text by social need; the targets of the violence are usually suitably demonic or unpleasant; the hero is left with no other option; and of course the film is a fantasy, permitting us a safe catharsis.

This argument brings up the relation of fantasy to external reality. We are all violent, if not in deed, then in thought and feeling. Which of us does not sometimes harbour thoughts of revenge? Which of us does not subtly or not so subtly punish those around us? This is the violence within us. In fact, Jane Tompkins makes this point about the murderousness found in academic life![28]

It can be seen clearly in young children. Their hatred can be ferocious. When Mummy is expecting a new baby, little Jimmy or Sally partly wants to kill it – there is no doubt about that, and we set out to civilize their hatred and murderousness, and make them hide it. But at the same time, all societies require rituals, or cultural forms, which permit a journey, in fantasy, through violence and homicide. Indeed, Western theatre and cinema could be said to be obsessed with violence and cruelty.

'If looks could kill,' we say. But in the western, looks do kill. One man looks at another, holds him in his gaze, and turns him into a corpse. Let me be frank – I find this both enjoyable and satisfying to watch. It is more satisfying than the techno-killing we get in modern films such as *Predator* or *Terminator*, because it is more personal and more honourable.

The western can of course present killing like a cartoon – the gun pops, the villain or the Indian slews off the horse. End of story. When I was a kid in the Saturday morning cinema, we'd cheer at that. Another bastard bit the dust.

But there is much more intense killing than this in the western – a contest of one man against another in the dusty street, the climax of the film, a kind of righteous murdering, that includes a homoerotic fascination between the two men. This is taken to extreme lengths by directors such as Sergio Leone and Sam Peckinpah, who dwell on the death-scene, film it in slow motion, with an ornate music sound track. Surely here, we are being shown a panegyric to the male orgasm?

Is this potential fascism? This is one of the fears about the heroic avenger and his eroticised violence – he is a prototype storm-trooper. Of course, fascism is a collective movement, not an individualistic act – nonetheless I remember the chilling cry of Spanish Fascism: 'Down with intelligence, long live death!' At times the western gets close to this.

Some of these issues are explored in Lawrence Kasdan's *Wyatt Earp* (1994), which shows brilliantly how 'law and order' is itself historically constructed as a legitimized form of violence. Indeed in this film, Wyatt Earp, played by a grim-faced Kevin Costner, enters into a private world of dark savagery and blood-lust, captured superbly in the last hour of the film. Kasdan films one scene of revenge against a nightmarish background of dark shadows and steam in a railroad station: Earp shoots one of the Clancy gang, and pumps bullet after bullet into his body, lost in his own private rapture.

This film shows nicely the ambivalence of the western in relation to violence: on the one hand, one can see a clear political point, whether intentional or not – patriarchal law and order is just another form of savagery, no better or worse (just more hypocritical) than the savagery of the outlaw. But on the other hand, Kasdan films these scenes with a superb sense of choreography, so that the violence in itself becomes intoxicating, transcendent. Earp becomes a god-like figure, untouched by any bullet, a dark American Macbeth. 'I'm a dead men,' Holliday says to him, and he is therefore a fitting friend for Earp, who is more than half in love with death. This is a film about necrophilia, and reminds me very much of the *Godfather* trilogy, which also peels away the veneer of civilization, revealing to us a culture steeped in blood and death.

The same ambivalence can be found in Eastwood's *Unforgiven*: Eastwood has a stab at showing the nastiness of western violence. The two cowboys who are shot in revenge for mutilating a prostitute die in the most horrible manner: one of them shot in the belly and gasping for water, the other one shot in the shit-house with no warning. But then in the final sequence of the film, violence reaches a thrilling climax, as Eastwood shoots down the sadistic sheriff, who had tortured his friend Ned. Of course this violence is justified by revenge, but it is also transformed into a luxuriant and cathartic eroticism. The depiction of violence is simply pleasurable.

But there is another aspect of violence in the western: there is a strong vein of masochism, which in certain films becomes a quasi-erotic frenzy, for example *One Eyed Jacks*, *High Plains Drifter*.

There has been much theoretical exegesis on the nature of male masochism,[29] but I think one straightforward interpretation is often missed: that the image of the tortured male represents the damage done to men by patriarchy. In other words, a genuine male suffering is represented. Furthermore, this portrayal is fraught with tension in Hollywood westerns, since it infringes the orthodoxy, that women are suffering (and erotic) victims, men are supreme (non-erotic) heroes.

Clint Eastwood's westerns form a fascinating blend of sadism and masochism – in *The Beguiled* he suffers a kind of castration by women; in *High Plains Drifter* he is flogged to death, and returns from the dead to take a terrible revenge; in *Unforgiven*, his best friend is tortured to death.

My interpretation of this masochism is quite prosaic: pain is represented as a symbol of real pain. Male masochism speaks of a real pain in men, a real destruction and dereliction.

THE DANCE OF DEATH

There are westerns with no violent deaths (for example, *Four Faces West*) but they are rare. Death often provides both the initial dramatic tension that sets the story going, and the denouement. In fact, the deaths in *Lonesome Dove* become wearisome: in the novel there are at least thirty, most of them violent.

We could leave this as a straightforward matter – revenge stories are exciting, full of action, satisfying morally, and so on. But is there something else going on in this fascination with death?

In the first place, death transforms life. The western reminds me of those Zen stories which show the sweetness of life by reminding us it could end tomorrow. For example, the man hanging off a cliff has time to taste a wild strawberry before he plunges to his death.[30] In that sense I find the western has a salutary tale to tell about death: that it exists, is common, and will come what may.

Death is also connected with male love. Men who love each other cannot demonstrate it very easily in our culture. They do not exchange tender embraces, they do not exchange orgasms, in fact they do not refer to love at all. In the western the only thing that one man can give another – apart from water, tobacco, a horse maybe – is death.

And what is this death? The end of separation, the dissolution back into the universe, the merging with everything. Death is the end of our alien stay on earth. Thus in the western, death is given a most solemn and ritualized choreography, and in the Italian western becomes operatic, balletic and farcical. There is this wondrous, comical, majestic thing, Death. The individual man who seeks death or dispenses death becomes mythic: he is the Man with No Name. He has gone beyond individuality, beyond humanness, and has become divine or demonic. He *is* Death.

Death brings about a strange intimacy in the western. One of the most interesting shots in *Shane* is the moment when the two gunmen – Shane, and the hired gun Wilson (Jack Palance) – meet. Both men speak quietly, and there is a strange smile on their faces. What does this odd scene mean? The two men recognize each other in a way that no other people in the film do. They are both angels of death: a white and a black angel, but none the less both of a kind. When Shane rides into town to face down Wilson, he dons his ceremonial robes: buckskins, fancy guns, and so on. He is going to a religious rite, a communion, a meeting place beyond earth and sky. It is interesting that despite his paucity of lines, Palance was nominated for an Oscar, such is the power of his presence, the shiver that we feel when he arrives. He *is* death in his black robes. He is Lucifer, and while we root for the white angel, Shane, somehow the black angel has a magnificence that chills the blood.

But why are these strange myths needed by men and not women? There is something quite disturbing and sinister about this. It suggests that men yearn for death. And they yearn for death in each others' arms, finally babbling of their forbidden love for each other.

I am not sure where this yearning for death comes from. Some feminists have suggested that it is inherent in men, just as a love of life is inherent in women.[31] This strikes me as implausible. I feel that the male yearning for death is partly indicative of a failure to live. I am reminded here of D. H. Lawrence who wrote about this yearning copiously, and one can guess, had it himself.

Death also has a spiritual or religious quality in the western. Westerns by and large kick Christian values out of the window, and instead we find a worship of death, an eroticism around death, that is both disturbing and exciting.

CONCLUSION

I have only skimmed the surface of the western in this chapter. There are other very important themes that I have to ignore. For example, the western hero is a kind of anti-Christ, who solves problems with human endeavour, not divine help ('There's no time for praying,' Ethan shouts out in *The Searchers*). And I have not devoted any attention to the great directors who used the western as a basic metaphor within which different ideas could be explored: for example, Ford, the great Shakespeare of the western; Fuller, the raw primitive; the complex career of John Wayne as actor and director. And then the western actors, both major and minor.

In a sense, I want to reclaim the western from those, such as Ronald Reagan, who want to reduce it to a simplistic conservative formula:

American white might is right. Unfortunately, some radical film critics and cultural studies scholars have tended to support Reagan's reductionism. For example, Paul Smith, in his book *Clint Eastwood*, often accepts that the right-wing view of westerns is a correct one: 'there are many possible points of articulation between the public discourses of Reaganism and the habitual ideological profferings of the western'.[32] I have argued that westerns are much more complex than this. They contain much else: a desolation and a yearning that speak of another side of masculinity.

Perhaps I can make a personal point here. I grew up in a very dour culture: north of England working class. In such a culture the values of westerns seemed perfectly at home, especially the stoicism of men, their inability to speak, their recourse to violence. As I grew older I became both fascinated and horrified by westerns, because I saw in them too much of the stoicism that I had painfully learned to wean myself from. The western presents a stunted world for men, and for women, a world that is utterly one-dimensional. Yet there is also much beauty and visual poetry in it, and a great yearning for an impossible paradise.

6 Horror Films

Horror films are often believed to have audiences which are primarily young and male. Thus in her book *Men, Women and Chainsaws*, Carol Clover summarizes what available evidence there is about horror audiences, and concludes that pride of place goes to adolescent males.[1] This is also confirmed by James Twitchell in his book *Dreadful Pleasures*.[2]

However, there are significant exceptions. First, certain horror films are not low-budget cult films, nor aimed at the video-rental market, but are designed as mainstream big-budget films. Obvious examples are *The Exorcist*, *Alien* and *Silence of the Lambs*. In such cases, one might assume that audiences would be more mixed in age and gender.

The second exception can be found in horror fiction, where a burgeoning women's horror movement has developed, particularly in America. In Britain, horror seems to be so narrowly defined that women horror writers are either lifted up to the category of highbrow fiction – the clearest example being Angela Carter – or in fact find it very difficult to get published.[3]

In this chapter, I am primarily interested in the dominant young male audience for horror, and the possible meanings they may extract from it. What are they horrified by? and why?

Horror is in many ways a conservative genre, because it exploits the tensions between the safety of repression, indeed the requirement for repression in society, and the fascination, terror and disgust we feel at letting go of repression, and seeing what lies underneath it. Thus Dracula is tamed by the crucifix because Christianity is the repressive force required to check his unbridled lust. In the horror movie we get to have our cake and eat it: the vampire is permitted his oral excesses, to our enjoyment, but he is also vanquished, to our relief.

The sub-genre of 'body horror' reveals to us those things that secretly fascinate us about the human body – for example, in *The Exorcist*, the little girl Regan gets to do those things that are normally forbidden in film and in public life: she urinates on the carpet, she vomits green bile, she masturbates (with a crucifix!), she asks her mother to lick her genitals, she grabs the genitals of the psychiatrist, and so on. Secretly we are fascinated by her letting go of normal restraints, although also disgusted and shocked by the green bile and so on. But the end of the film sees a closure to these kinds of activities: Regan's demonic possession is lifted. Thus traditional horror narrative introduces some kind of disruption to normal life, then removes it. Order is subverted by disorder, which is then returned to order.

However, there is also a species of 'radical' or 'paranoid' horror which refuses us this kind of closure, and this kind of horror became more common in the 1970s and 1980s, for example in George Romero's zombie films. Romero's *Night of the Living Dead* provides a famous example of non-closure: at the end, the man who has held out throughout the whole film against the relentless tide of zombies is finally shot dead by the posse who have come to 'save' the survivors. The cure is worse than the illness. Throughout this film Romero shows a ruthless ability to take every cliché of classical narrative heroism and subvert it.

It seems plausible to read into this paranoid horror scenario a bleak political vision: the world is decaying with no hope in sight. The demons and zombies and psychos have been let loose on the world, and there seems to be no exorcism available.[4]

Sexuality itself is treated conservatively in the horror movie, but this is something predictable in a Puritan society. Western cinema finds it almost impossible to construct genuine eroticism, not because of official censorship, but because of our inner censorship – we find it too embarrassing and frightening. Horror therefore appropriates eroticism and blends it with sado-masochism and evil. Hence horror doesn't offer a celebratory liberation about sexual matters – that isn't its function. It presents to us both our disgust and fascination with sex. In a sense, sexuality *is part of the horror*.

Therefore horror genres tend to flourish in Puritan cultures – it's interesting in this light to consider the importance of the gothic in American literature, from Hawthorne's *The Scarlet Letter* to Faulkner's novels. *The Scarlet Letter* achieves its great intensity partly because of the perceived horror of adultery, but also because of the power of sexuality that unconsciously grips society.[5]

Under order lies disorder: the disorder terrifies and fascinates us, while the order irritates us.

This also produces a paradox about the enjoyment of horror movies or novels: the enjoyment is tinged with shame. At the moment when we catch ourselves fascinated by some sado-masochistic scene, or a display of visceral excess, we realize instantly that we 'shouldn't' be enjoying this. This issue seems to polarize along class and gender lines, at least in Britain. Audiences for horror movies tend to be young, male and working class – quite possibly they too are ashamed about enjoying horror, but they can go to the horror movie as a kind of bourgeois bashing exercise in defiance. If the horror movie fan is caught in a kind of double bind, because he is setting out to enjoy the reprehensible, for the young male this may be precisely his aim, since he is in a mood to kick against the traces temporarily. Watching horror may therefore provide some rudimentary rite of passage for adolescents.

There is another paradox about horror, pointed out by Barbara Creed in her book *The Monstrous-Feminine* – we go to look at horror, but when the horrific climax occurs, sometimes we have to 'not look' – people actually look away from the screen, cover their eyes, and so on. Speaking of the famous chest-bursting scene in *Alien* she says: 'Such scenes satisfy a morbid desire to see as much as possible of the unimaginable'.[6] I am not sure about the word 'unimaginable' – I think frequently we have already imagined something terrible, and we can't bear to see it realized. The horror novelist Stephen King points this out in his book *Danse Macabre*: revealing the nature of the horror is a risk for writer or director, since the reader/viewer has imagined something much worse![7]

But certainly Creed's notion of not-looking is very important: to see the terrible thing threatens our equanimity considerably. It may even threaten our sense of identity, since it represents the eruption of the unconscious into conscious life. By not looking, we refute the terrible spectacle, thereby refuting the unconscious, although the next instant probably finds us looking again in fascination. So there is a kind of rhythm between withdrawal from, and return to, the film and its awful disclosures.

I find when I watch certain films on video that the fast forward has the same function! I can have a sneak preview of the terrible scene I know is coming, and then go back and watch it at the correct speed, because by then I have managed to readjust to it. It has become manageable because it has been realized on the screen, and I have the comfort of knowing it is nothing worse.

This notion of not-looking points to the deep masochism that is inherent in watching horror. The viewer is assaulted by the film (and director); the viewer is hurt, wounded by the fearful sights on offer. Why then do people go to see horror movies? I don't think we need a tremendously complex theory of masochism here: simply, we all have deep dark feelings which we have to compulsively rehearse, like probing a sore tooth, in the hope of understanding them, getting rid of them, enjoying them. Horror therefore provides a useful vehicle for our private shadows: sado-masochistic pleasures can be rehearsed in fantasy but not acted out in reality.

MALE ORDER/FEMALE DISORDER

The issue of order versus disorder is particularly relevant to the role of masculinity and men in horror. From the 1950s through to the 1980s we see a gradual dissolution of male order and expertise. In the sci-fi horror film of the 50s, male order is temporarily disrupted, then restored. Thus in *The Beast from 20,000 Fathoms* (1953) there is never any doubt that the beast – a dinosaur thawed out by an atomic explosion from a deep frozen state – will eventually be conquered by the assembled scientific and military experts, led by Professor Nesbitt, the atomic scientist. Thus patriarchal order is briefly disrupted but rapidly restored. But this also represents a partial critique: for the disaster has usually arisen through male arrogance or over-reaching, or excessive rationality.

The same structure is followed in many 1950s films: for example, *Them!* (1954) has gigantic ants, who have mutated following atomic explosions, and who invade the sewers of Los Angeles, but are eventually conquered by the same military–scientific alliance, led by an ageing professor, expert on ant behaviour.

A most interesting character in both *Them!* and *The Beast from 20,000 Fathoms* is the young woman scientist, daughter of the professor, who takes quite a prominent role. Thus in *Them!*, the professor's daughter insists on going down into the underground nest-chamber of the ants, and rejects the 'This is no place for a woman' kind of remark. Is this a nascent feminist voice speaking?

The central thematic tension in horror is the clash between reason, which is repressive, and unreason, which is repressed and therefore eruptive. But male rationality is treated very ambivalently, for although it provides a means of reimposing order, frequently it is itself seen as the source of chaos. Unreason is often seen as female, as in films such as *Carrie*, which shows a teenage 'witch' possessed with strange telekinetic powers.

In her book *The Monstrous-Feminine* Creed describes the various categories of the female monster which have permeated horror: the terrible mother, the vampire, the witch, and so on. All of these female roles stem from the ultimate horror: the female reproductive body, shown very graphically in the *Alien* trilogy.[8] Thus part of the horror of *Invasion of the Body Snatchers* lies in the archaic reproductive ability of the giant 'pods' which produce carbon copies of human beings. The real threat in *Them!* is posed by the queen ants, who threaten to fly off to found new nests. Then there are the many films associated with menstruation: Carrie's superhuman ability is associated with its onset. *The Exorcist* began a cycle of films about adolescent girls possessed by the devil, and the 1970s also saw a number of female vampire films.

But female intuition also provides a critique of male reason: this can be seen very clearly in *Audrey Rose* (1977), which is a spin-off from *The Exorcist*. In this film, a little girl (Ivy) is possessed by the tormented soul of a dead girl (Audrey Rose), who desperately needs to be healed. There are two important men: the father of the dead girl, who understands these psychic mysteries and knows how to calm the unquiet soul of his dead daughter, and the father of Ivy, who refuses to believe in such supernatural goings-on, agrees to Ivy being hypnotized to find out the truth, and watches as she dies during the traumatic reliving of the other girl's death.

Audrey Rose is almost schematic in its arrangement of characters: the child's mother is sympathetic to the 'irrational' notion of reincarnation; the dead child's father is convinced of it; and Ivy's father is sceptical. This kind of horror therefore critiques male rationality and 'objectivity', and suggests that there are deeper worlds, which reason cannot fathom. The male viewpoint is shown as split between a rational and non-rational one.

The ultimate end-point of male rationality is the mad scientist, exemplified by Frankenstein, who will stop at nothing in the pursuit of his inflated scientific dreams, and whose experiments often lead to disastrous consequences in the natural world, and whose rationality creates its counterpart in the monster.

It would be incorrect, therefore, to see horror simply as a 'patriarchal' set of texts, which denigrate feminine 'irrationality' and long for the imposition of male reason and control. Stephen King – probably the most important figure in contemporary literary horror – makes this point about his heroine Carrie: 'She's also Woman, feeling her powers for the first time, and like Samson, pulling down the temple on everyone in sight at the end of the book'.[9] And surely this is right: in both book and film Carrie is a sympathetic character – we enjoy her ability to bring destruction upon her tormentors.

In the 1970s and 80s, the male himself becomes problematized in films such as *The Driller Killer*, *Halloween*, and *A Nightmare on Elm St*. In such films, male order is subverted and annihilated, and disorder found to have its source *in the psychotic male*. Then the closure found in the 1973 *The Exorcist* (the male priests exorcise the demon, although at considerable cost) is missing, and we are confronted with an even more terrible vision: the horror is endless and will return. Freddy's back! In addition, in a number of contemporary horror films, women provide the closure, and bring to an end a reign of male terror, for example, *Silence of the Lambs*. Thus the hero becomes female. *Alien* is an extraordinary film in this sense, since both the horror and the hero are female, and men are sidelined.

One can therefore offer these interesting if very simplified trajectories for horror in the post-war period: the male role shifts from heroic rationality to a homicidal psychosis; the female role shifts from sexual/reproductive horror to heroism and power. There are of course many films which do not fit into this schema, and many which fit only partly, or which blend the traditional and revisionist patterns, but none the less it can be seen as a thread running from the 1950s to the 80s. In a sense, horror has deconstructed both genders: the rationality of the male has been peeled away, revealing a core of psychotic destructiveness; the archaic sexual threat posed by woman has been partially replaced by a sense of female power.

In a parallel development, the role of victim – historically nearly always filled by women – has been taken up more and more by men. Thus although the famous poster for the film *Jaws* shows a woman swimming above a massive shark, the chief victims in the film are in fact men. And there is the interesting sub-genre of films which show women terrorizing men: for example, *Play Misty For Me*, *Misery*, *Fatal Attraction*.

Out of the very complex set of themes found in horror, I would like briefly to examine five. They are the male vampire (Dracula); the mad scientist (Frankenstein); the zombie; the male psycho-killer (or slasher), and the female monster.

DRACULA

The vampire is clearly a sexual symbol. As he sucks blood from the victim's neck there are all kinds of associations with oral sex, breast-feeding, intercourse, menstruation.

But the vampire is sexually indeterminate: his mouth is always shown as soft and red with sharp white teeth, often with blood trickling from it. This reminds us of the *vagina dentata*. Thus Dracula is a femininized man, partly phallic, partly vaginal – this gives him his fascination and his horror. In Coppola's *Bram Stoker's Dracula* there is an extraordinary scene, taken directly from the novel, where Dracula presses a woman's mouth to his own breast, and makes her suck the blood. He breast-feeds her with his blood. Thus in Dracula we see a hybrid male/female parental figure, who may well correspond to infantile perceptions about sexuality and gender.

The vampire is usually portrayed as a most primitive creature: for example, he casts no reflection in mirrors. This can be related to Lacan's notion of the mirror-stage, that is, the stage when the human infant can identify with its own image in the mirror.[10] Why does the vampire cast no image? Surely because its identity is non-human, we might say pre-human.

And vampiric sex ultimately kills the victim, who becomes one of the undead, and also a vampire. Thus there is a transmission of vampirism from unhealthy bodies to healthy bodies, as if vampirism was a sexually transmitted disease. One wonders in the age of AIDS if the vampire film, with its rich associations of blood, is used as an indirect comment on AIDS. There is also a transmission from male to female: Count Dracula usually vampirizes a group of young women, who then become sexually voracious. Thus Dracula is seen as highly dangerous to the bourgeois order in releasing the full threat of female sexuality.

In terms of boundaries, the vampire transgresses at least three: that between life and death (since he lives for ever); gender boundaries (since he is both masculine and feminine); and between Christian order and pagan disorder.

Dracula also represents the incestuous parent who has to be killed off to release us for adult sexual life, and for full creativity. The stake through the heart symbolizes our need to kill the parents who hold on to us, and us on to them, and involve us in a perverse sexuality. I have found that a number of clients in therapy see their parents as vampiric figures who are draining them of life and blood, and who have to be symbolically killed off. In the original *Dracula* novel, this is demonstrated by Lucy's submission to Dracula, thereby turning away from her fiancé. Vampiric sexuality destroys heterosexuality and family life.

One of the greatest non-horror films to describe family relationships of this kind is Orson Welles' *The Magnificent Ambersons*, in which a decaying family is poisoned by its incestuous relations: son and mother cling to each other in one family, as do daughter and father in the other. The movement outwards towards exogamy is blocked, and the family dies. This is a kind of vampire film without vampires.

The vampire is frequently used in literature as an image for parasitic forces. There is a memorable example in Dickens' *Bleak House*, in the lawyer Vholes, who battens on the heir Richard Carstone and destroys him:

> He stood behind me, with his long black figure nearly reaching to the ceiling of those low rooms; feeling the pimples on his face as if they were ornaments, and speaking inwardly and evenly as though there were not a human passion or emotion in his nature.
>
> So slow, so so eager, so bloodless and gaunt, I felt as if Richard were wasting away beneath the eyes of this advisor, and there was something of the Vampire in him.[11]

George Eliot also uses the image of the vampire in *Middlemarch* to describe Bulstrode, the banker who feeds on other people's weaknesses:

> There were many crass minds in Middlemarch whose reflective scales could only weigh things in the lump; and they had a strong suspicion

that since Mr Bulstrode could not enjoy life in their fashion, eating and drinking so little as he did, and worreting himself about everything, he must have a sort of vampire's feast in the sense of mastery.[12]

These examples show how vampirism has passed into the common cultural stock, particularly as a symbol of financial exploitation: the bourgeoisie sucks the blood from the poor.

But the cinematic Dracula is often shown as the symbol of *aristocratic* degeneration against which the bourgeoisie struggles. The fact that this aristocracy is associated with a perverse sexuality indicates the need of the bourgeois order to maintain rationality and sexual repression.

In the Hammer production, *Twins of Evil*, the Puritan elder (Peter Cushing) exclaims bitterly at one point: 'The aristocracy is evil' – but the elders in his village are too afraid to take on the decadent vampire Count, and instead take revenge on innocent peasant girls. Thus gender war acts as a screen that obscures class war, but by the end of the film the people of the village gather in traditional fashion to destroy the vampiric Count: class war explodes into the open, and the war against women fades into the background.

This film is also notable for its schematic structure: there is a Puritan male, who punishes young females simply for being sexually alive (Cushing); in contrast there is the degenerate Count who makes blood sacrifices to the devil and draws women into his sexual frenzy. Cushing has twin nieces who are also divided: one of them wants to be vampirized by the Count and is shown as sexually energetic; the other one is the traditional demure female. But people have difficulty telling them apart, which is not surprising since the female twins represent the traditional splitting of the image of woman in patriarchal society: whore and madonna.

Thus, in this film, both males and females are shown as divided between repression and indulgence, Puritanism and vampirism. This is a kind of trap set up by the film, from which there is no escape. In the end the licentious pair (Count and girl) are killed. Then the Puritan male is killed, and the virginal girl is left to find her heterosexual mate. Thus bourgeois order is maintained both through the destruction of the aristocracy and of sexual energy, a rather mordant comment on British social history! The bourgeois order is shown as unable to tolerate sexual vitality.

For British audiences, the Dracula myth therefore provides a continual reenactment of the Civil War and its aftermath, perhaps because that War resulted in a kind of paralysis – the monarchy restored, the aristocracy maintained in positions of power right down to the twentieth century, and the Puritan clampdown on instinctual energy forcing men into the world of manufacturing and Empire, and women into the domestic world. The vampire therefore provides a brilliant image for the way in which sexuality and orgiastic energy have been repressed in modern society.

Dracula is perverse in gender, sexuality and social class, but in a sense the Dracula myth is a conservative one, since in its classical form the bourgeois male expert is called for: Van Helsing, who is able to drive the stake through Dracula's heart. Thus patriarchy is reinforced, as in exorcism films, which also require the help of male experts. The original Dracula novel provides such a closure; but many directors subvert this, and suggest that 'He will return'. In Werner Herzog's vampire film, for example, although Dracula is destroyed, he has vampirized Jonathan, who will continue his work. Incidentally, this film (*Nosferatu*) contains the most haunting contemporary image of Dracula, played by Klaus Kinksi, who conveys both an enormous decadence and a deep sadness. The moment when he finally fastens his teeth on the neck of Lucy is one of great delicacy, chilling perversity and deep melancholy.

Thus the overt conservatism of the Dracula myth (Dracula is defeated) may be contradicted by the sensual imagery with which his sexuality has been presented, suggesting that it might well be a close-run thing between vampiric sexual excess and the rigours of the bourgeois order. There is a further paradox, which Phil Hardy describes succinctly with reference to Terence Fisher's *Dracula*:

> The most disturbing aspect of it all, vociferously objected to by some critics, is that the sadistically brutal actions are performed by the representatives of Christian morality: they are the ones who brutally drive the stakes into the flesh of sexually aroused women.[13]

There is a nice paradox here: the vampire is shown as perverse, but the representatives of secular and clerical rule are seen as sadistic in the extreme. But these comments demonstrate admirably how the horror film (and novel) has been able to debate quite profound historical and political themes by means of its lurid iconography.

FRANKENSTEIN

If we compare Dracula with Frankenstein, we can see that while Dracula is over-feminized and over-sexualised, Frankenstein is under-feminized, too reliant on an inexorable and inhuman logic that makes him transplant brains, graft sculptor's hands onto criminals' bodies, and so on. Frankenstein is a mirror image of Dracula: bourgeois rationalism (which seeks to annihilate Dracula) has itself become excessive and monstrous. Mark Jancovitch describes this hyper-masculinity as a kind of splitting:

> Frankenstein's 'sin' is not hubris, but his refusal to define knowledge in terms of human interest and 'domestic affection'. He accepts the separation of spheres which isolates scientific activities from the domestic sphere, and which associates masculinity with the former rather than the latter.[14]

The contrast between the feminized male and the over-rational male is found throughout horror films and novels: for example, in *Silence of the Lambs*, Hannibal Lecter is the remorseless intellectual who (literally) penetrates and devours people, whereas the serial killer Buffalo Bill is obsessed with his mother, endlessly watches movies of her, and kills women to make a suit of their skin.

Thus, horror for the male lies in two directions – either too much or not enough femininity. The prototype of excess femininity is Norman Bates in *Psycho*, who is overly identified with his mother and her ferocious jealousy – thus he is condemned to kill the woman he desires, because he is not sufficiently differentiated from her. Lack of femininity is demonstrated in the legions of mad scientists found in horror movies – a gruesome example is seen in Romero's *Day of the Dead*, in the scientist who exults in his operations on zombies, removing their brains, hearts and so on, and who appals the main female character. The mad scientist is also affectionately spoofed in *Ghostbusters* and the *Back to the Future* series.

But behind Frankenstein there is a shadow: the monster he creates. Karloff's monster in the 1931 film (*Frankenstein*) is a magnificent creation, because he conveys the sadness of being trapped in such a body, yet from the sadness he moves to the savagery of revenge at being so hated and feared. This sadness is an extra dimension of horror, difficult to achieve, and usually not found in the bloody films of the 1970s and 80s. Its greatest exponents have been Karloff, and Barbara Steele in the Italian horror films such as *Black Sunday* and *The Terrible Secret of Dr Hichcock*. Steele had the ability to convey immense melancholy, terror and desire in one look, and she is undoubtedly the chief female icon of horror.

The Frankenstein myth, which seemed to disappear in the cinema after the mid-thirties, was reinvigorated in the 50s by Terence Fisher's *Curse of Frankenstein* (1957), which revolutionized horror films and brought a much-needed energy to British films.

There is a welter of themes in this film – the mad scientist, whose cold rationality is conveyed very well in Cushing's elegant performance, also has an undercurrent of black humour. He casually wipes blood on his frock coat as he decapitates his dead criminal, stolen from a gibbet, and examines charnel house eye-balls with a feline delicacy. Fisher also brings sexual and class themes into the myth: Frankenstein is cynically having an affair with a maid while getting ready for marriage to his cousin. When the maid, in a fit of lower-class revenge, threatens to expose his experiments, Frankenstein shuts her in with the monster. There is a superb transition at this point: the next shot has Frankenstein and his cousin at breakfast: 'Pass the marmalade' he intones exquisitely.

This film therefore shows that beneath the ornate surface of conventional bourgeois mores, and beneath Frankenstein's detached rationality, there is a savagery that is projected into the monster. Thus the monster, played with great pathos by Christopher Lee, is the obverse and twin of Frankenstein's cold rationality. In later Frankenstein films, Frankenstein is more openly monstrous, for example in *Frankenstein Must Be Destroyed.*

Curse of Frankenstein orchestrates these elements in long flowing sequences. The end of the film is particularly symphonic: the monster escapes, clutching Frankenstein's fiancée. Frankenstein shoots her by mistake, sets fire to the monster, who falls into a vat of acid. Then Frankenstein sits in his cell waiting for the guillotine, and attempts to strangle an old friend, bringing out his kinship with his own monster. But all of this is constructed as a long rhythmic sequence: psychological imagery is blended with socio-political symbolism in an effortless manner.[15]

Whereas Dracula represents a perverse sexuality that threatens the bourgeois order and conventional gender and sexual structures, Frankenstein represents the great Western striving for reason and omnipotence, which is forced in the end to recognize its own product: something abhorred by nature. Thus the mad scientist theme critiques conventional masculinity, with its rationality, its autism, and its disdain of 'female intuition'.

But Frankenstein also embodies a kind of repressed male motherhood: the male scientist tries to emulate women and produce his own offspring by means of his own rationality and experimentation. Here the theme of male envy of women is explored, and the sublimation of that envy into male creativity. This provides another example of the way in which horror is able to explore quite deep unconscious psycho-social themes.

THE DEAD WALK!

The zombie film had been a minor sub-genre in horror until Romero's *Night of the Living Dead* (1968) spawned numerous copies right across

Europe and America, some of them achieving truly horrible effects through the benefit of modern make-up techniques and special effects. Romero's zombies are both male and female, but the significant zombies are male. Thus in *Day of the Dead*, the mad scientist has a pet male zombie, whom he keeps on a chain, and tries to train, in a rather nice parody of behaviourist psychologists.

The zombie transgresses one of the basic boundaries of human existence: that between life and death. They are the 'living dead', and the manner in which they have been woken from the grave usually has a contemporary ecological reference. Thus in *Night of the Living Dead*, radiation from an abortive rocket launch has stirred them to life; in *Pesticide* and *Bloodeaters*, pesticides have had the same effect. The zombie is therefore a product of patriarchal ecological disaster.

The zombie breaks another boundary: he eats human flesh. The dead come back to prey on the living, to tear their bodies apart and devour them. This can be interpreted both psychologically – our present experience is often vitiated by some trauma from the past – and politically – the zombies are a huge underclass, utterly deprived and decaying, whose only function is to attack those still living. In *Zombi 2*, the earth itself is shown rising up to disgorge long-dead victims and conquerors from the Spanish Conquest.

The cannibal theme also works as a bitter comment on the need of capitalism to 'devour' people: for example, in *Motel Hell*, in which people are turned into food, solving the world's overpopulation and hunger problems at one stroke.

One of the most innovative films based on cannibalism is the British production *Death Line* (1972). Unusually this combines visceral horror – rows of rotting corpses line the hide-out of the cannibal who haunts the London Underground – with a sympathy and compassion towards the plague victim, who kills and devours passengers. He is shown mourning the death of his pregnant partner, and howls out his grief in the subterranean passage-ways. There is also a powerful contrast between these Dantean scenes underground and the facile life shown above ground.

The zombie film also acts as a comment on contemporary urban life: Romero's shuffling figures, walking autistically along the road, ignoring everyone else, are reminiscent of the crowds in any big city.

Romero's *Day of the Dead* is a nightmarish political and physical presentation. The male body is shown as corrupted, decaying, yet unable to die, often shown with parts missing or hanging out; and the body politic is likewise in ruins. There is also a very interesting use made of the female gaze. The main female character – who will prove to be one of the few survivors of the zombie attack – keeps seeing men whose bodies are in terrible shape. Half is missing, or part of it falls out, and she is appalled. But consider this 'look' against the conventional male look at the female sexual object. Here the male is in a degraded state, he is disintegrating, and he is watched by the woman.

THE SLASHER

If the zombie film shows men in tatters, degraded and disintegrating, in the 'slasher' film masculinity itself is the source of chaos, personified in the mad killer who prowls through the suburbs of the American Mid-West, targeting young women.

One of the problems with the slasher film is that of identification: do we identify with the slasher in his crazed attacks on sexually active women, or does the film encourage us to distance ourselves from him? Argument has raged on this issue. Some feminists have argued that the psycho-killer film glamorizes a basic male drive, and that male adolescents in the audience cheer on the killer, just as football crowds in England chanted approbation of the Yorkshire Killer: 'Ripper 13, Police 0'. In this view the slasher film is an intense exercise in misogyny.[16]

However against that some critics, notably Carol Clover, have argued that the slasher film can work as a critique of this violence. Certainly in such films the male presence is no longer the calm dominant presence that is traditional in disaster films such as *Towering Inferno*. The male expert is feeble or simply absent. The emergence of the female hero who often single-handledly dispatches the killer completes the gender reversal. The male has been transformed: from being heroic saviour of heroines, he has become the horror![17]

Psycho is often reckoned to be the prototype of slasher or psycho-killer films, but perhaps no subsequent film has approached its rich texture. It provides one of the greatest disjunctions in identification in Western cinema: our identification with the main female lead is carefully prepared in the first part of the film and then torn apart. We watch Marion with her boy-friend, we appreciate her financial difficulties, we see the tedium of the office she works in. Thus, when she steals money from the office we identify with her, and we share the increasing paranoia of her journey, followed by the policeman in sun-glasses, regarded with suspicion by the second-hand car salesman. Her sudden murder is a massive blow to the audience. What are we to do? Hitchcock's solution: identify with the killer.

This can be seen partly as Hitchcock's black humour, but surely *Psycho* is more profound than that. The film demonstrates to us our moral relativism: we become engrossed with Norman Bates and the mystery of his 'mother' in the dark house, while our nerves are still jangling from Marion's murder.

We are suddenly immersed in a different world, far away from the gossip of Marion's office, or her arguments with her boy-friend. The conscious world seemed to be going on in its usual way, admittedly portrayed with Hitchcock's sense of the bizarre, but then a door opened and we descended into a world of madness and nightmare. Surely, in this sense, *Psycho* is saying something about the twentieth century, and its juxtaposition of the mundane and the horrific. Every night on TV we see this: interspersed between the glossy car ads and the deodorant ads are dreadful pictures of Bosnia, Africa, Northern Ireland. Is the same species involved in both activities? We know it is, and we know that in *Psycho* Norman is as human as Marion, and as much part of us. Hitchcock stretches our concept of the human to include both, and in a strange way, without condemnation. Norman almost exists as a force of nature. He chills us, fascinates us, thrills us. Yet there but for the grace of God ... . This is also a political vision: the capitalist world order, apparently so orderly and mundane at the beginning of the film, begins to collapse before our eyes, revealing the terrifying world of the repressed, where desire takes on nightmarish forms.

There are many other levels in this film: for example, there are many images to do with looking and eyes: Marion's dead eye, the policeman's sun-glasses, Norman's voyeurism, his dead birds staring down, his mother's eyeless sockets. There is also a constant play on the theme of penetration: Marion is sexually penetrated by her boy-friend and then by Norman's 'mother' in the shower scene. Norman himself has been psychically penetrated by his mother's image. The camera penetrates the lovers' hotel room at the beginning of the film – above all the spectator is penetrated by the film's assaultive images.

Norman is a gender monster: he has forsworn heterosexuality for a necrophiliac carnival and a devotion to taxidermy. Yet he is played with great delicacy by Anthony Perkins, and the audience warms to him, since in the end there is no-one else to warm to! Hitchcock brilliantly circumscribes our moral universe, until Norman is all we care about. Yet this provides a chilling commentary on the amoral history of the twentieth century: the universe of *Psycho* is a helpless one, in which human beings struggle against overpowering unconscious forces. In this sense, *Psycho* is one of the great filmic texts of our century, displaying in graphic form the conflict between conscious and unconscious forces.[18]

Is *Psycho* a misogynist attack on women? Certainly Norman has been castrated and psychically destroyed by his devouring mother. However, it is surely significant that the first victim of this maternal monster is a young, sexually active woman: in other words, women are as much in danger as men.

Halloween is a much less dense text than *Psycho*, but none the less it is a highly accomplished film. The director, John Carpenter, synthesizes different elements beautifully: the iconography of Halloween – masks, pumpkins, fancy dress, horror movies on TV – children's songs on the sound track, the lives of teenage girls, the suburban houses, the rather camp psychiatrist, played by Donald Pleasance.

There are three striking differences from *Psycho*: first, the killer is not given any motivation. He simply exists. In the opening shots of the film, the famous and much copied subjective camera kills a young girl, then is revealed to be the point of view of a six-year-old boy. But we have no idea why he has killed his sister. There is no 'psychology' in this film as there is in *Psycho*. Male psychosis and rapacity simply exist *sui generis*.

The second interesting difference is the portrayal of male experts. In *Psycho* they are not shown in a heroic light, but in *Halloween* they are positively useless. Both psychiatrist and sheriff wander round the streets, usually in entirely the wrong place, while Michael gets on with his killing.

The third important difference is the character of Laurie, who fights off the killer. This is the figure whom Carol Clover describes as the 'Final Girl'. I have watched *Halloween* with groups of friends, and when Laurie's friends have been killed and she is alone in the house with the killer, people start to shout: 'Come on girl', 'Wack him' and so on. Thus there is a strong incentive for the audience to identify with Laurie, and to stop this relentless male killing machine.

Halloween could be criticized as misogynous. There is a distinction between the sexually active girls, who are killed, and Laurie, not sexually active, who survives. However to argue from this that the film condemns female sexuality strikes me as rather simplistic. This is correct, if we identify with Michael as a kind of Moral Majority judge and executioner. But do we? Surely the teenage girls are presented as positive figures, and doing the things that young audiences do. Female sexuality is shown as deeply disturbing to the male killer, provoking hatred and destruction in him, but does the film simply identify with that point of view? This strikes me as a bizarre interpretation. The hero of the film is Laurie: men in the film are shown as either psychotic or useless. In fact one can argue that it's not Laurie who has a problem, but the men who can't deal with her: as she says plaintively, 'They think I'm too brainy'.

Halloween is a model film with which to demonstrate the fluidity of interpretation. James Twitchell argues in *Dreadful Pleasures* that sections of horror audiences do identify with the killer in such a film, but that other sections identify with the female victim-hero.[19] I would also suggest that multiple identification is quite likely: one can identify with both simultaneously.

THE FEMALE MONSTER

In an earlier chapter, I pointed out the great value of Barbara Creed's book *The Monstrous-Feminine*. Whereas most writers on horror seem to have glibly assumed that 'woman is victim; man is monstrous attacker', Creed argues convincingly that in contemporary horror there are a great number of active female monsters. She subdivides the 'monstrous-feminine' into various categories, such as the archaic mother, the possessed woman, the monstrous womb, the vampire and the witch. Indeed, some of these figures are clearly not new at all, and Creed demonstrates how classical mythology is full of female monsters, such as Medusa and the Sirens.[20]

Why then has there been such a blind spot towards the active female monster in critical writings on horror? One major reason has probably been the classical Freudian stance of many writers on film. For in Freudian thought, woman is monstrous for the male because she represents the possibility of castration. Or in Lacanian language, she is a 'disavowed lack'.[21]

In the same theory, man is monstrous because *he is the castrator*. We might argue in this vein that males are compelled to watch horror films in order to relive (and relieve) their infantile terror at the realization that their father threatened to castrate them, and their mother was living proof that castration was possible. This scenario presupposes a male active position, and a female passive position.

However, films such as *Carrie* do not fit this scenario at all. Carrie is one of a legion of young adolescent girls in horror who are disturbed by the onset of puberty, and particularly menstruation, and develop extraordinary powers. This film has its justly famous climax, when Carrie – who has been tormented by her school-fellows, by having pig's blood poured over her at the school prom – carries out an apocalyptic destruction of the school, and later kills her own mother.

Carrie is a relatively sympathetic character, since she is so badly treated by the other pupils. There are also more negative female monsters, who threaten men with castration. The black horror film, *Def – By Temptation*, is an extraordinary remaking of the female vampire story, with a black vampire who seduces men in bars, and during intercourse kills them. *The Hunger* stars Catherine Deneuve as a contemporary female vampire who with chilling elegance feasts on the blood of her victims.

The 'maternal monster' thesis permits us to take a fresh look at *Psycho*. This film has become so familiar that one forgets that on first viewing, for most of the film, the truly horrific figure is the mother, who makes the assault in the shower, kills the detective Arbogast on the stairs, and terrorizes her son. And at the end of the film, she speaks through Norman, now completely taken over by her.

Low budget 'female horror' is exemplified by *The Evil Dead*, which shows a young male subject to a horrifying attack by demented and demonic young women.

In fact, once one starts to look for it, the female monster is ubiquitous – might not one argue for example that in *Jaws* the shark represents the *vagina dentata*?

This aspect of horror explains quite neatly the predominance of male adolescents in the audience: young males, who are beginning to experience their own sexuality, need to exorcise their fears of the archaic (and most crucially, seductive) mother before they can become sexually active.

WHAT IS THE HORROR?

If we think of the mad scientists, zombies, psychotics, vampires, ghosts, witches, demons, satanists, werewolves, mummies, who people the horror movie – taking some of the major categories that Andrew Tudor uses in his book *Monsters and Mad Scientists* – it strikes me that the notion of 'boundary infringement' applies to all of them. Thus creatures such as the werewolf blur the boundary between human and animal; the mad scientist crosses the margin between rationality and insanity; the vampire crosses many boundaries: life/death, male/female; the zombie straddles the boundary between life and death. We find horror in the blurring or dissolving of those boundaries that normally define existence for us.

In relation to gender, we can identify two kinds of fears present in horror: those about the opposite sex, and those about one's own sex. Thus for young males there are fears about the castrating woman, the phallic woman, and the devouring nature of female sexuality. And there are also fears about his own sexuality, his sado-masochism, and the stability of his own gender identity. The male monster is he who starts to become a woman, or on the other hand, he who starts to annihilate women. Through the 1960s, 70s and 80s the male expert is gradually dismantled, and we are left with the male monster on the one hand, and the male victim on the other.

We can also perceive a shift from oedipal horror to pre-oedipal horror. The former relates to sexual difference, to desire, incest and castration fears: the classic example being *Psycho*. The latter relates to fantasies of bodily disintegration, an orgiastic visceral apocalypse, where the boundaries of the body itself are smashed, and its innards are revealed, as for example in *The Evil Dead*. But such primitive body fantasies also seem to indicate deep political fantasies of disintegration and collapse. The horror movie is an intensely political genre: it has described the paranoia of the Cold War and the paranoia of urban collapse, and also the dread of gender collapse as part of an overall social disintegration.

MALE HORROR?

Why should men be particularly worried about boundaries, assuming that horror is very much a male genre? One possible answer is that males have had to cross the momentous boundary between female and male: they have to separate from their mother and carve out a masculine identity. Many men are haunted by this journey, unconsciously longing to return to the maternal womb, or to death, which is its counterpart. For young males, the female is both the ultimate fascination and the ultimate horror, for she might drag him back to a regressive identification, that secretly he craves, but which spells psychic and social death for him.

The horror film also provides a kind of initiation for male adolescents: they go along with their friends to demonstrate that they can face the terror and horror and laugh at it. In many cultures they would face physical pain, isolation, and other stringent tests to prove their manhood. And yet the best horror directors (Hitchcock, Bava, Cronenberg) go beyond adolescent fears and reveal to us those political and psychological aspects of modern life we would rather not face, yet which reverberate in our unconscious.

Horror genres also probably reveal men's fear of female emancipation and feminism. I can refer back to Jane Tompkins' argument about the western being a response to women's self-assertion in the late nineteenth century in America. In this view, the attacks by killers such as Michael in *Halloween* could be seen as the unconscious reaction of men to an emancipated female sexuality: to destroy it. But it is surely more accurate to speak of an ambivalence towards female sexuality and liberation.

7 Pornography

Is pornography part of popular culture? The fact that this question can be posed is in itself significant, for porn stands on the threshold of acceptability and visibility. Its function is in some ways to scandalize, to present 'on-scene' what is considered obscene.[1] But porn has also been commercialized and industrialized in this century. Not simply found in the leather-bound volumes of the upper-class connoisseur, it is blazoned across mass selling magazines, which are found in every newsagent.

It also strikes me that images of the female body are one of the most important aspects of popular culture, and pornography stands at the apex – or is it the nadir? – of such representations.

I feel myself sliding down a slope of respectability: from the western, to horror, and now pornography. Porn is the pit of contemporary culture, a reservoir of shameful desires, hidden masturbatory fantasies, and great loneliness. Porn seems irrevocably associated with sleaze, perversity and even criminality.

From the psychological point of view, this spectrum of decreasing acceptability is of great interest, as it presumably reveals an increasingly taboo set of desires, feelings and representations. There is also an issue here about audiences: the western, the horror movie and pornography are all non-elite cultural forms, normally associated with working-class or juvenile audiences, and therefore frowned on by 'high' culture critics.

Pornography has of course occasioned great ferment within feminism, and for a period in the 1980s seemed to become its dominant issue. It brought into focus the nature of male desire – often seen as inherently perverse or rapacious – the objectification of women, and also the nature of representation itself under patriarchy.

However, my view is that in the feminist debate, porn has often been treated reductively and monolithically. It has been said by some feminists to represent the inherent depravity of male lust, or the central demeaning patriarchal view of women. Thus Andrea Dworkin, in her book *Pornography*, articulates a view of male sexuality that is absolute and categorical:

> Male sexual power is the substance of culture. It resonates everywhere. The celebration of rape in story, song and science is the paradigmatic articulation of male sexual power as a cultural absolute.

Pornography reveals that male pleasure is inextricably tied to victim-
izing, hurting, exploiting; that sexual fun and sexual passion in the
privacy of the male imagination are inseparable from the brutality of
male history.[2]

In my experience of working with men in therapy, this description of
male sexuality is very blinkered. For some of these men, sexuality is not a
parade of triumphant brutality at all: it is an area that fills them with terror
and shame. In addition, male impotence seems to be increasing massively,
and frequently crops up as an issue in the therapy consulting room. In this
sense Dworkin's comment about the way men see women – 'Male perceptions of women are askew, wild, inept'[3] – strikes me as applicable to
her own perceptions of men.

Dworkin also provides quite a narrow view of pornography – for
example, the growth of gay, lesbian and bisexual porn is practically
ignored in her book, as it is by many anti-porn activists. Indeed, the
development of porn *for women* becomes an important issue here, for the
Dworkin thesis seems to suggest that women who like porn are simply
being indoctrinated by 'male perversity'. But is this true? This seems to
freeze both men and women into essentialist positions: men have a pornographic imagination, women don't. Ironically, this view perpetuates a
neo-Victorian view of women – they simply don't have 'dirty thoughts',
unless they have been contaminated by men! It can also lead to the
project of suppressing the male pornographic imagination, in which feminists have found strange company, including New Right and Christian
groups.

However a number of feminists have opposed the anti-porn movement,
and have criticized its censorious and simplistic attitudes, and its apparent
hostility to all images of explicit sex.[4]

It is interesting in this light to consider how the female body is portrayed in women's magazines. Glossy magazines such as *Vogue* are full of
portraits of semi-naked women, and many of the poses are remarkably
similar to those found in soft porn, although less sexually explicit.[5] Thus
both men's magazines and women's magazines use the female body as
their chief icon. Is this simply a patriarchal appropriation of women? I find
this too conspiratorial a theory, and also demeaning to women readers of
women's magazines, who are made to appear passive victims, accepting
what they are given. In fact one could reverse this view: the prevalence of
the image of the female body suggests the power of female sexuality,
which is being derepressed today. The same arguments can be made about
romantic fiction, which has become increasingly sexualized, and has led to

the sub-genre of so-called 'bonkbusters' such as Shirley Conran's *Lace* or Jilly Cooper's series of novels – *Riders, Rivals, Polo*. If this is not 'porn for women' (by which I intend no slur), what is it?[6]

But Dworkin argues that porn is a representation of fundamental *male* attitudes of conquest and despoliation. This argument is found in the writings of many anti-porn activists, for example John Stoltenberg:

> Male-supremacist sexuality is important to pornography, and pornography is important to male supremacy. Pornography *institutionalizes* the sexuality that both embodies and enacts male supremacy. Pornography says about that sexuality, 'Here's how'. Here's how to act out male supremacy in sex. Here's how the action should go. Here are the acts that impose power over and against another body. [original emphasis][7]

I find myself in disagreement with some of these comments, particularly the notion of 'enactment'. Stoltenberg stresses the correlation between porn and men's actions: 'here's how the action should go'. My view is that porn is fantasy, and that fantasy does not necessarily show us how to do things at all. Do we find that the consumers of porn act like this against women? This is an empirical question which no-one seems to have explored. However, I can offer some evidence on the basis of working in therapy with a number of clients who use pornography.

In my experience the users of porn are not a homogeneous group. At one extreme there are very solitary men, whose only sexual experience consists of masturbation and pornography. At the other extreme are couples who use porn, particular rented videos, to enhance their sexual pleasure. But one cannot homogenize the uses to which porn is put, or the moods in which it is used.

But certainly I have not experienced porn-users as triumphant male warriors, gloating over their spread-eagled female victims. If porn fetishizes the female body, it also fetishizes male loneliness, inadequacy and impotence. For porn is a substitute. My experience of the heavy porn-user is that *porn does not lead to contact with women*, sexual or otherwise, but provides a hiding place for the man who is terrified of that contact. It does not actually lead to a 'consuming' of women, but rather brings to bleak fruition a male inability to be with women. If the man using porn feels triumphant, I would argue that he is in the grip of a triumphant failure, or rather failure turned into triumph.[8] His conquest is illusory, his lust has no object except himself, the female body that he scrutinizes is in fact replaced as an object of desire by his own penis. Relations with others fall into a despairing narcissism; women become phantoms, shadows, projections of his own unmet needs.

One can draw a parallel here with sexual perversions such as exhibitionism and voyeurism which, in the criminal sense, are overwhelmingly com-
mitted by men. Dworkin's and Stoltenberg's argument, that porn enshrines
male power and brutality, would presumably lead them to claim the same
for exhibitionism – by which I mean genital exhibitionism. I have only
worked in therapy with a small group of exhibitionist men, but they struck
me as very damaged men, whose ability to sustain intimate relations with
either men or women was severely limited. Their exhibitionism – which
superficially could be interpreted à la Dworkin as a display of genital
supremacy – was a compensation for desperate feelings of inadequacy.[9]

Indeed, one thing that is not explicitly portrayed in soft porn is male sexuality. The female body is the chief icon, and through it, male desire and
male pleasure are depicted. But is this simply a male appropriation of female
sexuality, or does it not also represent *a denial of male sexuality*? Certainly
in Britain it is striking that it is the penis that still remains largely taboo in
soft porn. Surely if porn really enshrined the 'male-supremacist sexuality'
referred to by Dworkin and Stoltenberg, the penis would have centre stage?

Pornography is a puzzling and complex phenomenon. To suggest that it
simply represents the hegemony of male lust over women strikes me as
bizarre, for in fact porn is shrouded in shame and obscurity. So-called
'sex-shops' are not triumphant palaces, but grubby back-street hideaways.
It is true that soft porn is now freely available in newsagents, but I cannot
see any sense of triumph surrounding its sale.

Why is porn so seedy? Why is it seen as shameful? Are men guilty
about their lustful dominance over women via porn? This strikes me as
unlikely. Surely one major reason is the Western Puritanical fear and distaste for sexuality in general. By contrast, in many Asian countries newly
weds used to be given books of erotica on their wedding day to aid them
in their sexual relationship.[10]

But the word 'erotica' brings up an interesting issue: the distinction
between 'art' and 'porn'. Many attempts have been made to distinguish
them, probably the most famous being Kenneth Clark's distinction between
art as 'contemplative' and 'non-art', including porn, as inciting to action:

> To my mind art exists in the realm of contemplation, and is bound by
> some sort of imaginative transposition. The moment art becomes an
> incentive to action, it loses its true character. This is my objection to
> painting with a communist programme, and it would also apply to
> pornography. In a picture like Correggio's *Danae* the sexual feelings have
> been transformed, and although we undoubtedly enjoy it all the more
> because of its sensuality, we are still in the realm of contemplation.[11]

Under this rubric, both communist propaganda and porn are disqualified from being art, since they incite revolutionary fervour and sexual desire respectively. This seems a rather dismissive gesture towards Communist poets, such as Mayakovsky, film-makers such as Eisenstein, the playwright Brecht, and others, who did not necessarily see a contradiction in a didactic art. Clark's analysis also seems to leave 'erotic art' floating in a void, since it too presumably excites desire. Does this mean an erotic art cannot exist?

A further hidden sub-text is present in Clark's deliberations – art is for the elite, non-art for the masses. Thus 'erotica' denotes the connoisseur with his collection of rare books – porn is found in the local newsagents! It is the mass production and consumption of sexually explicit material that seems to offend, not just Clark and other art critics, but many others concerned to censor porn. Indeed, Lynda Nead, in her book *The Female Nude*, suggests that obscenity can be defined as 'that which, at any given moment, a particular dominant group does not wish to see in the hands of another, less dominant, group'.[12] Or to put it more cynically, erotica is what I like; porn is what you like!

CLASSICAL NUDE AND PORN NUDE

The distinction between classical nude and porn nude could hardly be more striking: the porn nude has been marginalized, while the female nude has been central in bourgeois culture. For example, in University College London, at the entrance to the art library, there is a life-size classical statue of the female nude. One can imagine the uproar that would ensue if a life-size porn photo were placed there instead.

Why has porn been marginalized? In the first place, an obvious difference is that it is more working class, and high art is more upper and middle class. In other words porn is 'non-aesthetic' within the political parameters of the art world.

It is also more sexual in its intent, whereas the female art nude mystifies female sexuality and euphemizes male desire. This is suggested in Kenneth Clark's attitude towards sexuality in his classic study *The Nude*: he argues that the erotic is present in paintings of the nude, but minimally: 'no nude, however abstract, should fail to arouse in the spectator some *vestige* of erotic feeling, even although it may be only *the faintest shadow*' [my emphasis].[13] One can make a comparison with ballet, in which sexuality is rendered acceptable, or sublimated, by all manner of artistic embellishment and softening. I am not criticizing ballet, simply pointing out the mechanism of concealment that goes on.

Porn is also more *traumatic* – it reveals trauma, or converts trauma into triumph – the trauma of sexual difference, sexual desire, frustration, female sexuality – deeply painful areas for many men.

The porn nude is more self-conscious than the classical nude. Often she stares at the camera. She invites the viewer to inspect her, to examine her proffered breasts, her splayed thighs, her genitals. She has a curious look on her face, a mixture of coy salaciousness (the 'come on' look) and aggression.

This direct stare is rare in the art nude. This is one reason Manet's *Olympia* caused such a furore, since the model here also stares at the viewer, not salaciously, but very directly.[14] Normally the painted nude invites the male gaze, while she looks away. But the woman in the porn photo often gazes directly at the male viewer. She looks at the man looking: looking itself is eroticized. And being seen to be looking seems to increase the eroticism (his looking is looked at). This is a curious kind of voyeurism, when the woman being watched watches back. Yet of course the woman does not really look: she is a two-dimensional image. This gives the male viewer his safety: he can *imagine* being seen to be looking.

Overall, one can suggest that the nude in high art is a highly multivalent symbol, one of whose meanings is the provision of a safe and deniable experience of sexuality. The female body, and the male desire that it incites, are 'spiritualized' and placed within secure boundaries. One can almost forget one is looking at a naked woman. By contrast pornography, which in modern times is usually photographic, explicitly presents the *baseness* of the body. The lighting is often harsh, the woman's body is not prettified but shown in a direct way that many people find disgusting or obscene. Here sexuality is not mystified or made mysterious: instead the model splays her legs, opens her vagina for the camera. Part of the intent is to demystify the mystery of the female body, and to lay bare the nature of flesh itself as a carnal substance. Some porn magazines have photos of the anus, perhaps the most taboo zone of the body, associated with the 'dirt' of defecation.

Porn therefore implicitly attacks Western art for its euphemistic attitude to the female body. Feminists can object with good reason that the female body is an inappropriate arena for such a 'debate' to be carried on, but in a sense porn is merely hi-jacking an already existing text and subverting it. The female body, one of the key icons in Western culture, had been resolutely sealed over – 'laminated', to use Laura Kipnis's eloquent word.[15]

The art nude presents an image of perfection rather than an image of reality. This idealization is brought out clearly in the sub-title of Clark's book, *The Nude: A Study of Ideal Art.* 'Obscenity', by contrast, is non-ideal, imperfect, non-contemplative, disruptive.

A remarkable emblem of ideal virginity can be found in a number of renaissance paintings of women, who are shown holding a sieve miraculously full of water. This represents the sealed female body, virginal, intact. The orifices of the female body are stopped up, thereby rendering women safe, non-sexual, allegorical.[16]

But porn is resolutely orificial. It presents us with the 'black witch' and her imperfect but energetic body. To masturbate over her is a kind of black sabbath, turning upside down many images and beliefs in Western culture. Surely these are some of the reasons why porn is so vilified: it returns the 'dirt' to a bourgeois world which had tried to pretend that no such thing existed. Laura Kipnis describes the bodies found in the American porn magazine *Hustler*:

> The *Hustler* body is an unromanticized body – no vaselined lenses or soft focus: here is neither the airbrushed top-heavy fantasy body of *Playboy*, nor the ersatz opulence, the lingeried and sensitive crotch shots of *Penthouse*, transforming female genitals into *objets d'art*. It's a body, not a surface or a suntan: insistently material, defiantly vulgar, corporeal. In fact, the *Hustler* body is often a gaseous, fluid-emitting *embarrassing* body, one continually defying the structures of bourgeois manners and mores and instead governed by its lower intestinal tract – a body threatening to erupt at any moment. [original emphasis][17]

This distinction between a spiritualized or exalted image of sexuality and a debased or highly carnal one, can be related to the ancient split between mind and body in Western culture. Indeed this split amounts to a hatred of the body, expressed eloquently in the famous words of St Paul:

> But I say, walk by the Spirit, and do not gratify the desires of the flesh. For the desires of the flesh are against the Spirit:
> Now the works of the flesh are plain: fornication, impurity, licentiousness, idolatry, sorcery, enmity, strife, jealousy, anger, selfishness, dissension, carousing, and the like.
> Those who belong to Christ Jesus have crucified the flesh with its passions and desires.[18]

In the long history of the hatred of the body in Christian culture, we can also point to a key projective process. Carnal pleasure and desire were projected on to women, who were therefore punished as inciters of desire, while the male witchfinders could congratulate themselves on their zeal and moral purity. Similarly, in contemporary controversies over censorship, anti-porn zeal probably conceals a fascination with the very thing activists seek to banish: carnality. In a barely concealed manner, the anti-porn activist is *excited* by porn, and must keep displaying it for our disapproval.[19]

PRETTINESS VS UGLINESS

As Laura Kipnis points out, within porn itself there are considerable differences of style. Whereas magazines such as *Penthouse* and *Playboy* display a 'pretty' kind of porn – soft focus, discreet poses, soft lighting, and so on – other magazines such as *Knave*, *Club International* and *Blue Climax* use harsh lighting and open genital and anal shots, in a way that seems rather ugly. Observers often make the point that the harsh porn is 'gynaecological', or looks like 'a butcher's slab'.

This is a kind of anti-aesthetic of porn, which can be related to Linda Williams' term, the 'frenzy of the visible'.[20] Whereas *Penthouse* goes along with the discreet concealment/revelation of the female body, other magazines seem concerned to shatter this with an abrasive explicitness.

This distinction strikes me as relevant to the repression of the flesh in Christian cultures that I have already alluded to. The repressed returns with a vengeance, shown in an unromantic light, as 'flesh on a butcher's slab'. The same kind of phenomenon can be found in horror movies, especially those specializing in some kind of 'body horror' (see Chapter 6).

Porn does not present the 'horror' of flesh, but its baseness, its materiality and vulgarity. It also demystifies the mysterious: the display of female genitals and female anus shatters deep taboos against such revelation. In a sense, such porn is utterly profane: the Holy of Holies is thrown into the market place. Marina Warner describes the long history of these taboos within Christian culture:

> Woman was mother and matter, and matter was volatile, dangerous, passive, opposed to spirit, and often judged the inferior principle. Her kinship with matter was linked to her reproductive processes, and these were frequently described, in a strong Judaeo–Christian tradition, as effluents, liquids and fluids oozing from the improperly stopped container of the female body. In order to stand for virtue, the physical condition of this metaphorical body had to be turned upside down, and the soft, porous, effluent-producing entity made hard, impermeable and corked, so that its contents, dangerous on contact, could be kept hermetically sealed and safe.[21]

Why should porn reverse this sealing up? Why should porn seemingly delight in turning upside down the sentimentality and romanticism with which 'femininity' has often been presented in our culture? I find one answer in Jung, who stressed the inevitability of it. He used the rather cumbersome word *enantiodrama*, suggesting that 'the rational attitude of culture necessarily runs into its opposite, namely the irrational devastation of culture'.[22]

Thus the sentimental portrayal of femininity, or the allegorical use of the female body, has depended on a severe curtailment and obscuring of female sexuality, and what I have called the spiritualizing of the body. Such intense repression must lead in the end to a violent reaction, since the repressed images will erupt back into consciousness. Thus the image of woman in much porn is almost deliberately harsh and unsentimental. As feminists point out, she is reduced to a collection of sexual organs: breast, vagina, buttock, and so on. Whereas classical art presented an image of woman as a sealed container, porn presents a vessel full of holes, leaking, messy.

Is this necessarily a denigration of women? Surely it may also represent female power, female actuality and vitality. Some of the images in porn magazines strike me as images of powerful women, who are *yearned for by impotent men*. It has often been pointed out that prostitution frequently caters for men yearning, not to dominate, but to be submissive to a 'dominatrix'.[23] One could of course argue that this is simply an erotic reversal of the normal power relations, but it certainly contradicts the Dworkin view that pornography and the sex industry in general give a representation of male dominance.

The vulgarity of porn also points to an assertion of matter as matter; a defiant riposte to the spiritualization of matter which has been enforced by Christianity.

Class differences also seem important in discussing different kinds of porn: *Penthouse* caters for the business man, with its in-depth interviews and its articles on high-performance cars. The tone of a magazine like *Blue Climax* is plebeian. The language used in the copy is deliberately harsh: there is much talk of 'tits' and 'cunts'. There is a kind of class resentment built into this kind of porn. The bourgeoisie has used the 'demure woman' as an ideological symbol to indicate certain virtues which have been felt essential to an ordered society – hearth and home, chastity outside marriage, a tyrannical heterosexuality, a deep shame about bodily pleasure. Porn obviously does not mount a considered critique of this ideology: rather, it presents an inchoate and unconscious rebellion against it.

I should emphasize that I am not trying to set up porn as 'good', in reaction to its nomination as 'bad' by some feminists. When I say that porn is 'anti-bourgeois' this does not necessarily mean it is 'progressive' or liberating. After all, anti-bourgeois ideas are used by fascism! None the less the development of porn since the war does show a fascinating 'return of the repressed', and I would assume, does not stop there. Which other areas can porn find to derepress?

INTERPRETING PORN

The anti-pornography movement over the past twenty years has often taken a psychologically shallow view of the pornographic image. It has taken representation as reality – if a man looks at a photograph of a naked woman, he is intent on 'possessing' her, 'consuming' her, 'objectifying' her. He is active, she is passive. Male lust devours a female victim. Porn promotes male pleasure.

To a psychotherapist such as myself, this is very limited. It is like interpreting a dream literally. You dream of a naked woman – what does this mean? I have no idea, since the dream is yours, but we would surely not limit ourselves to the active/passive interpretation.

Indeed in dream analysis, one of the most common types of interpretation is an 'internal' one: the naked woman represents part of yourself. For a man, this would suggest part of his feminine side, which he is perhaps out of touch with. Similarly when women clients dream of penises, men with erections and so on, it is quite likely this is a dream about themselves, and their assertiveness, which may be emerging in their life. Thus in dreams and fantasies and other projections of the unconscious, the subject/object split breaks down: I am what I see. And this dissolution also occurs frequently in waking life: for example, we are attracted to partners who contain hidden aspects of ourselves. To put it rather poetically, our inner psyche is spread out before us in the theatre of life, with its many characters, its plots, its happenings. Inner and outer interpenetrate.

Thus it is quite common for men to dream of young girls – I often see this as indicative of the immaturity of their feminine side – yet it is often a hopeful dream. One of my clients had a very vivid dream of a young Tibetan girl who had been embalmed for thousands of years, but gradually began to come back to life when explorers discovered her body. There seemed little doubt that the dream was about part of himself, that had been long dormant, but was beginning to awaken.

Another client dreamt of a couple in bed: the man wanted to make love, but the woman didn't. The client told me that he felt the dream concerned two sides of himself: the woman represented that part of him that sometimes didn't want sex, but felt ashamed to admit that, for it wasn't 'manly'.

Dream interpretation is empirical – we cannot publish tables of dream symbolism. And in principle I see no difference between dream-imagery and the imagery of pornography. Feminism tends to ascribe fixed meanings to pornographic texts, as if somehow these meanings were frozen in amber within the text, and there was no possibility of an alternative meaning. In particular this monolithic approach ignores the *uses* to which porn is put. How do men actually use porn? What emotional process leads to a man looking at porn, or masturbating, and how does he feel during and after using porn? As far as I can see, very few studies of pornography have considered such questions, and many of them have conducted very artificial tests on the results of exposure to porn in laboratory conditions. In particular, very little discussion has taken place on the meaning of masturbation in relation to pornography, which surely has a great deal to do with loneliness and feelings of inadequacy.

Space does not permit me to conduct any elaborate investigation here, but I have chosen to focus on a brief examination of a number of pornographic texts, both photographic and written, from which I have extracted a number of themes that strike me as important.[24]

1 Infantile sexuality

In the first place, porn strikes me as primitive and infantile. I do not mean this in any derogatory sense. I simply mean that the images in porn remind me of a male child's fantasies. This is his sight of the forbidden zones, these are the things he has been trained both to look at and not to look at.

The psychoanalyst Robert Stoller argues that the male child is given very complex messages about looking. First, that he may not look at female bodies. Secondly, that if he could look and see, 'the vision would be astonishing'. Thirdly, that if he is a 'red-blooded male', he will try to look.[25]

In fact the whole construction of 'sexual looking' is immensely complex, and also involves various aspects of female fashion, and aspects of female behaviour – for example, pulling down of skirts, leg-crossing, partial display of the breasts and so on. Thus girls are trained not to reveal their bodies, and also to reveal them.

Both sexes are thereby drafted into a complex and contradictory culture of looking. One must look, but one must not look (boys). One must hide the body, but one must display the body (girls). These rituals give considerable value to sexuality, and render it potent and magical.

Indeed Stoller concludes that pornography is inevitable in a culture which puts so much emphasis on sexual looking, and he relates the whole mechanism to the mystery and hostility which surrounds sexuality in our culture.[26] He does not offer a political explanation for this, but one might argue that it is part of the 'commodification', both of sexuality and of human beings, which has developed under capitalism. 'Value' is enhanced by rarity; therefore the female body – as prime exchange commodity in sexual, marital, reproductive and property transactions – must be rendered rare, concealed and hard to get to. Thus female genitals have often been referred to in pornography as 'jewels'.[27]

In addition, for boys the whole mixture is given extra excitement by the gradual withdrawal of his mother's body from him. He becomes aware that while her body was available to him as an infant, he must renounce it as he gets older. This reminds us of the idea of the 'male wound': men are permanently looking back to a golden age when the breast belonged to them.

The breast is certainly an 'overdetermined' symbol, for it recapitulates both childhood experiences and adult sexuality. The breast is maternal and sexual. Indeed it is sexual partly *because* it is maternal – men are permitted to covertly rediscover the lost breast in adult sexual behaviour.

In some kinds of porn, woman is *reduced* to a pair of breasts. This is shown clearly in some of the written copy found in porn magazines:

> With her mature and titillating attractions, Sharon makes an instant cleavagy Park Lane classic: Enjoy a mere trio of pages *udderly* devoted to this Birmingham-bred bra-bender.
>
> Mind you, she's small time compared with some of the cleavage queens eager to bare their ins and outs (and not just their devastating united dairies) to *Park Lane*. [original emphasis][28]

This is rather typical of the copy found in porn magazines, a rather strange mixture of puns and coy humour. The terms *udderly* and *united dairies* refer to breasts as providing milk. Thus Mummy is both 'titillating' and nourishing. Her breast stimulates the sexual appetite, but also feeds the mouth with milk. This is a very oral fantasy.

This extract also shows a typical fascination with large breasts. Many magazines have at least one photo spread of a model with large breasts, and there are specialist magazines devoted to them. The sense that the large breast is full of milk is often highlighted, as above. One can refer again to prostitution, and the practise of so-called 'baybism', that is, literally treating men as babies, dressing them in nappies, giving them feeding bottles, and so on.[29]

Such imagery suggests to me a feeling of deprivation, an infantile hunger that demands feeding. It is significant that portraits of the Virgin Mary used to show her with one breast exposed, but later portraits covered her up. This can be related not only to sexual prudery by the Catholic Church, but also to the symbolism of hunger and food.[30]

2 Eroticization of feelings and needs

Many men eroticize their feelings and needs. This is partly because sexual feelings are more acceptable to men than emotional ones. Thus, to want to have sex with a woman seems 'masculine'; to need her to listen to something, or to need a hug from her, or to show one's sadness to her – these seem less masculine. Thus there is a displacement amongst some men, from emotion to sex. The penis becomes the organ which articulates need, loneliness, grief, love, hatred, fear, anxiety, and so on.

At this point it is relevant to mention one of my clients who used both heterosexual and gay porn, and had both heterosexual and homosexual fantasies. Jim had massively eroticized his own psyche, so that many of his feelings and needs were encoded into sexual imagery. Breast, vagina and penis all had important meanings for him, which were not sexual, but had been sexualised. Eventually he was able to decode this symbolism, much of it tied up with his own creativity – he was a wonderfully talented musician – and he described to me how some days he felt 'breasty' and other days 'like a cunt', and yet others 'like a prick'. In fact, I am indebted to him: he taught me a huge amount about sexual symbolism and its non-sexual meanings. He was also unashamed about his own sexual fantasies, and his use of different kinds of porn, and saw it as a kind of map, wherein he could orientate himself, or as a kind of mirror in which to identify himself.

Thus sexuality has become an important symbolic system for some men, used to encode hopes, fears, yearnings, in fact all kinds of feelings.

This argument brings up an interesting if provocative question: is pornography about sex? Obviously at one level it is. But so many non-sexual issues seem to be articulated through porn, just as many non-religious issues are articulated through religion. However, one can extend this argument to sex itself, and the rather surreal question arises: is sex about sex? I am sure that frequently it is not: many people use sex to conceal yet half-express non-sexual feelings – need, anxiety, anger and so on. In fact, in Robert Stoller's book *Perversion*, perversion itself is defined as 'the erotic form of hatred'.[31]

3 Envy

Pornography is amazingly repetitive. Looking through a number of porn magazines, one gets used to a limited number of sub-genres: the 'lesbian' scene; the phallic woman (e.g., a woman with a hosepipe between her legs); outsize breasts; the 'spread-eagled' genital display; the woman licking her own breasts or touching her clitoris; and in harder porn: oral sex; a woman playing with two penises; domination by one sex of the other; the 'meat shot', that is, penis-vagina penetration. In her review of hard-core films, Linda Williams sees the 'money shot', that is, the shot of the penis ejaculating, as central during the 1970s.[32]

Why this repetitiveness? A classical Freudian explanation might be that the trauma of castration and sexual difference has to be constantly gone over again and again, because it is never quite believed: 'do women really not have a penis? Let me have another look'.

But I have noticed another feeling in men towards female sexuality and female sexual organs: a profound envy. Both the breast and the vagina must be compulsively examined, because they are 'treasures' not possessed by the man. Pornography enables him symbolically to possess them, masturbate over them, curse them, or do what he will. But this protest is futile: the naked woman remains invincibly different from him, and *superior to him*.

Thus I suggest that the pornographic urge to possess often stems from a sense of not having, a sense of failure, incompleteness, and a ferocious envy and hatred towards women for possessing these organs of fertility, sexuality and reproduction.

Sometimes porn seems to me to be about reproduction itself. In the 'spread-eagled' shot, the camera seems to be trying to gain access into the womb itself. The emphasis on breasts has a dual function: the men who stare at them want to suck them, and also own them for themselves. Here the intense 'mother complex' found in some men seems relevant.

Feminists have often appropriated the Freudian/Lacanian theory of castration to demonstrate how women are portrayed in popular culture: as symbols of 'lack'. But I feel that the male viewer of porn is consumed by his own lack, and the fullness of the woman he gazes at. She has it all, and he wants it.

4 Maximum visibility

In the depiction of female genitals in porn, the woman frequently opens her vagina with her hands, so that the camera peers into her. There is also the sub-genre of female masturbation shots – the woman strokes her clitoris, and often simulates sexual ecstasy.

The open vagina shot might be interpreted as an invitation to the penis – penetrate me. But there is something else here: Linda Williams describes it as making the invisible visible.[33] That is, the mystery of female sexuality is exposed to the camera and the viewer. What is the inside of a woman like? What is the nature of female sexual pleasure?

The written material found in soft porn magazines often raises such questions – for example, *Mayfair* has a regular feature entitled 'Quest: The Laboratory of Human Response', which purports to ask searching questions about sexuality. Of course its purpose is sexual arousal for the reader, but its questioning often suggests a puzzlement about female sexuality: 'Did you enjoy what happened next?', 'What were you wearing?', 'What happened next?', 'You didn't climax?'

But what are the driving forces in this hunger for visibility? This is surely very complex. Part of it can be ascribed to the tension between concealment and revelation that I referred to earlier: one might argue that we are still recoiling from the Victorian obsession with 'covering up', and are intent on 'stripping bare'.

There is also *a drive for knowledge*. This can be related to the phallic drive which underlies scientific and technological developments: men seem compelled to 'penetrate' nature's secrets. One can also refer to Foucault's thesis that sexuality represents a huge epistemological semiotic: that is, it represents a means of acquiring knowledge and power.

I am also reminded of a section in one of Paul Theroux's travel books, where he describes Japanese tourists in strip-tease bars, their heads shoved between the dancer's thighs, gazing into the ineffable mystery of her genitals:

There was something undeniably strange and solemn and even somewhat religious in the fervor of the men who sat like intense votaries waiting for a woman to come near. The man's patience, the woman's movements, edging nearer and nearer on the altar-like table, squatting, opening her legs very wide, her thighs enclosing the man's head, and the man staring hard in a frenzy of concentration as though a mystery were being revealed to him that he must memorize. It was public, and yet highly personal – only the chosen man could see clearly. There was as much veneration in this man's goggling at a woman's everted private parts as you would find in most church services. The man slipped a dollar or more into the woman's garter, and she lingered, and the man stared straight on, serious and unsmiling in his own private vision. From this sort of ardent behavior, it was a very short step to the Hindu worship of lingams and yonis, or to the cultism of the Komari, the vulvas carved in stone all over Rapa Nui.[34]

I find Theroux's description interesting in the way it relates the sex industry to ancient methods of sexual ritual and worship. In the worship of the goddess, the genitals are both taboo and sacred as source of fertility and sexuality. Porn strikes me as one of the few places in the industrial world where such primitive *religious* fantasies can be pursued.

5 Utopia

Theroux's prose also brings out quite a strange aspect of pornography and the 'sex industry' in general: it provides a utopian vision. This sounds odd when one thinks of the sleaziness associated with 'sex-shops', porn cinemas, prostitution and so on. But porn provides this message: you will be all right; your needs will be completely satisfied; your penis is not simply adequate, it is wonderful; the world is full of beautiful women who are panting for your sexual advances; orgasm is guaranteed; and orgasm will be an earth-shattering experience, which will make life worth while.

There is something pathetic about this message, but the pathos stems from the compensatory flavour of the vision. Utopia is offered to people who find life almost the opposite. They feel inadequate; women do not desire them; life doesn't seem worthwhile; orgasm is a whimper not a bang.

The issue of maximum visibility seems to be connected with the utopian vision: for whereas normal society covers up bodies, hides sexual passion behind bedroom doors, in fact leaves sexuality as an arcane mystery, porn turns all of this upside down. Whereas actual life is a constant compromise between desire and repression, porn offers a fantasy world where repression is dissolved and desire is magically enacted.

If porn as a mass industry has increased during the twentieth century, it is possible that one reason is the utopian cravings that beset people. In this sense, it is arguable that sexuality has replaced religion and politics as the 'opium of the people'. It has become a key symbolic system, through which we articulate our hopes and fears, but also our understanding of the universe. In this sense, porn is messianic or eschatological.

6 Female sexuality

In her book *Hard Core*, Linda Williams argues that hard core films have shown a shift from depicting male pleasure to female pleasure. Thus, speaking of the famous film *Deep Throat*, which in America revolutionized the public perception of porn, she says: 'its narrative is constantly soliciting and trying to find a visual equivalent for the invisible moments of clitoral orgasm'.[35]

Of course historically, women's sexual pleasure has been denied and destroyed throughout patriarchal societies: this is manifest in many ways, from the construction of the demure Victorian maiden to the practise of clitoridectomy carried out in some cultures. The phrase 'lie back and think of England' presupposes that you cannot lie back and enjoy it, if you are a woman. Nor can you demand greater sexual enjoyment, or visit a prostitute, as Victorian men did.

It is arguable therefore that contemporary pornography is witness to a kind of bizarre rehabilitation of women's sexual pleasure. As Linda Williams says: 'pornography is one of the few areas of narrative where women are not punished or found guilty for acting on their sexual desires'.[36] Of course traditional porn has framed female sexual desire within male looking; but that too is changing. Women seem to be using porn more frequently; perhaps even more significantly they have also started to make porn – for other women, for couples, even for men. Williams spends some time in her book describing how one woman pornographer, Candida Royalle, sets about creating such a 'revisionist' porn.[37]

7 Porn for women?

The issue of female sexuality brings me to a fascinating question: why is pornography for men much commoner than pornography for women? One could simply argue that this reflects its patriarchal context: male porn is commoner because it reflects the dominant position of men and their 'consumption' of women as sex objects. Another point is that men are perhaps more 'perverse' than women, because they are more traumatized by sexual difference. One might also predict that women's porn will increase as post-Victorian derepression continues.

However, the question itself needs to be examined, for it depends on a prior definition of pornography as 'sexually explicit photographs or film'. But it is quite reasonable to widen our definition of porn – for example, to include romantic fiction, whose readers are mainly women, and which has

become much more erotic in the last two decades. Thus one can argue that
there *is* a women's porn, which is very different from men's porn, so that
in some senses the two pornographies do not 'recognize' each other. Let
me cite a brief passage from a Mills and Boon novel:

> He tossed the towel aside, then climbed slowly into the warm bed, and
> his strong arms gathered her against him and his mouth descended to
> hers. It was a kiss of unbelievable sweetness, not soft, not hesitant.
> Skilful, warm and hard, and Toby's body curved helplessly to his. Her
> legs entangled with hard, sinewed calves, and as he fitted himself to her
> the kiss deepened, joining her soul to his for all time. Her body seemed
> made for his, despite the difference in their heights. There were no
> bones digging awkwardly into each other, no uncomfortable wriggling
> to get it just right, it was as though her body waited for just this man,
> just this hard body, and opened warmly to receive it. His mouth stayed
> with hers, not passive, not still, moving, demanding, giving, drawing
> the very core of her to the surface to be examined, welcomed, joined
> with his.[38]

This prose operates differently from prose in a porn magazine: it is
much less explicit, and relies on a kind of hazy sexual innuendo – for
example, the repetition of 'hard', and the use of phrases such as 'curved
helplessly', 'fitted himself to her', 'uncomfortable wriggling', 'opened
warmly', 'drawing the very core of her'. This is a skilful kind of code,
enabling the writer to refer to genital contact without the explicitness of
male porn. We cannot imagine the words 'penis' or 'vagina', or their
equivalents, in such prose, yet the reader is able to bathe in a warm erotic
luxuriance. In a sense the non-explicitness increases the eroticism.

Such texts surely cause many problems for those who wish to censor
porn, for why should romantic fiction be exempt? One obvious answer is
that it is not sexually explicit (although this is changing). But this seems to
take us back to a Victorian puritanism: sexual explicitness is the enemy.
On the other hand, if you want to ban male porn for its objectification of
women, romantic fiction is as guilty.

In fact this argument brings out a key problem for the anti-porn movement: how do you define porn, and who will define it?

8 Power

To argue that porn reveals the exercise of phallic power presupposes that
the male viewer of the female body 'consumes' or 'owns' or 'devours'
the female as object. But suppose I reverse this: he is in thrall to this

female body; porn symbolizes his impotence, for he can only relate to a 'paper woman'; his masturbatory fantasy covers up the trauma of his autism. This strikes me as an equally valid view.

This debate confronts us with the fascinating and complex problem of detecting power relations in texts: for the interpretation is partly affected by the felt power or powerlessness of the interpreter, that is, you or I.

What power relations do you see in a photograph of a man and woman making love? Or a photo of an erect penis? Or of a woman's breast? We cannot answer these questions in abstract. Your interpretation depends on your political views, your personal history, your attitude to the opposite sex, and so on. For example, the photo of a penis can excite envy, disgust, admiration, laughter, fear, excitement, and many other feelings, depending on the context.

The point I am making is that images in themselves are inert: it's our relationship with them that produces interpretations. Of course in patriarchal society one might suppose that images of women are phallic put-downs. But they can also be manifestations of female power.

Is there any evidence for this? In written porn it is striking how frequently women are described as being in charge:

> Without warning the brunette yanked my jeans and pants down together, making me start as my prick sprang up: "Mmm," she grinned, peering down below my waist. "Nice."[39]

There is also a wider issue here. Why is porn a scandal? If it simply helped construct a male supremacy over women, it would not be as scandalous as it is. Surely it is plausible that the scandal partly arises from the revelation of female sexuality and male impotence, both long concealed in patriarchal societies.

This, I suggest, is the source of the shame men feel when buying porn or visiting porn cinemas, peep-shows, and so on. They are 'caught in the act', not the act of oppressing women, but the act of admitting to their own needs, and their own lack of fulfilment. They are 'wankers'. That word is one of the great put-downs of men in our culture, hurled by car drivers at each other, and by politicians and academics at each other in private. But porn is the literature of wanking; it presents wanking as a theatrical spectacle, which makes it more glamorous and exciting, and temporarily dispels its loneliness and the sense of inadequacy it frequently covers up.

Thus porn may in fact betray one of the dark secrets of patriarchy: the powerlessness of men before women.

9   Identification

The issue of multiple identification is important in the analysis of pornography. Who does the male viewer identify with? This is particularly interesting in relation to the sub-genre of 'lesbian' scenes, where two or more women look at each other's bodies, touch each other, induce each other to orgasm. Such scenes are very common, found in nearly all magazines, and in hard core films.

One could argue that these scenes show a truly patriarchal rapacity: women are organized as groups for male amusement. But I wonder if the male viewer has another investment in the all-female cast: he can surreptitiously take part – as a woman! He can take a respite from phallic sexuality.

I am reminded again of Carol Clover's thesis that the mutilated female body in horror films is identified with by men.[40] I cannot see why the same interpretation does not apply to porn images at times. The naked woman represents the viewer, or rather a hidden part of himself, which yearns to be revealed, naked, brazen even.

The question of identification becomes even more puzzling when we consider images of the penis. The penis is rarely shown visually in soft porn magazines, but there are interesting descriptions of it in the copy. In certain written texts – particularly the letters (presumably concocted by the magazine staff) – we find ourselves looking through a woman's eyes at a man's penis, which may be described in great detail.

In one letter, there is a bizarre scenario: a man and his wife are spying on a male friend in the toilet. He finds some photos of the woman and begins to masturbate over them. This excites the couple, who eventually make love as he ejaculates. But what is interesting here is that the focus of erotic interest is the solitary man masturbating and the suggestion that his masturbation excites women:

> I couldn't speak. Something like a sob came from below. Gary arched his back, eyes half closed; his right hand closed round his shaft, just below his neat round knob. He began to pump the stretched foreskin, slowly, rhythmically, jerking from his hips, fucking the tight circle of his thumb and forefinger as if it was my cunt.[41]

Perhaps the female viewer in the scene is a convenient fiction: what really excites the male reader is the male penis. The reader who might masturbate over this text is in fact being excited by a couple watching a man masturbate over photos of a woman. This is both complex and indirect, but in the end penis connects with penis, masturbator connects with masturbator. The man who is actually masturbating is excited – by the image of male masturbation!

Another story has an equally complicated setting: a woman hires a man to come to her house and make love, while her neighbour watches them from an adjacent house. But again the focus is on the male body, through the woman's eyes. His penis is described in great detail:

> It was long (extending up to beyond his navel), thick and seemed to be dragging his balls up tight to his body. A prominent blue vein twisted its way up the shaft, and Marian traced its winding course with her tongue, abandoning it when her lips closed over the shiny, plum-like head.
>
> She gulped it in, tightening her cheeks round it, sucking hard. It felt tender and soft, but meaty – but like a piece of fruit does, she thought, when you pop it into your mouth, just before you bite it. She took it lightly between her teeth for a moment and pressed gently, feeling the tender flesh yield. But she resisted the temptation to bite harder and returned to her slow, sensuous sucking action.[42]

Again if we consider that most readers of this are male, we are presented with an odd series of 'gazes', that in the end produces a kind of telescope, at one end of which is the male reader, and at the other end is another man's penis. The woman in the story is the intermediary who connects one man with another. This allows men to be turned on by other men's penises, since they can rationalize that they are really turned on by the woman's excitement over the penis.

These are quite complex, indeed labyrinthine connections, and presumably one reason for this is that the focus of erotic interest is the penis. Is this one reason for the barring of photographs of erect penises? Not because women might find them exciting, but men might?

In hard core porn, a common shot has a woman holding two penises in each hand, or sucking one and holding the other – again, there is the suggestion that the woman acts as a conduit for the two penises to meet each other.

One can make a similar point in relation to the 'money' shot in hard core films. Of course this demonstrates to the male viewer that everything is OK in relation to male prowess. But might it not be also that the ejaculating penis is a turn-on? Of course this has to be concealed: a woman is present in the film as well. But is the woman camouflage?

10 Soft/hard/gay

One of the crucial distinctions between soft and hard core porn is the presence of the (hard) penis. This can be seen as a kind of Lacanian 'lack': soft porn lacks the penis, which in hard core is one of the key images, and is shown ejaculating, penetrating, being sucked by women and so on. It is rarely shown in non-erect form.

But what is the meaning of the erect penis in porn? Simply enough, one could answer that it serves to reassure the male viewer that male performance, male conquest, male dominance have no inhibition placed on them, are triumphantly celebrated. In this view, the penis is identified with by men: it is the *subject* of the text. However, one could also argue that the penis is desired by men, is the *object* of desire.

But a third interpretation is possible: that both points of view are present. One can both want to be that rock hard inexhaustible penis, and have it. One can want to be the penetrator, and the penetrated. In other words, there is no need to decide in an either/or way as to the hetero- or homosexual tone of such images.

This blurring of meanings can actually be seen at work in certain texts. In one text, pictures of a man inflating his penis with a mechanical device give way to pictures of women inflating his penis, which give way to pictures of men on their own, displaying their penis. The text moves from autoerotic to hetero to gay images, showing perhaps the lack of clearly defined boundaries between such categories. The model in question is in fact Jeff Stryker, formerly a gay model, who shifted to heterosexual porn.[43]

Linda Williams has argued that 'bi' porn also shows a blurring of boundaries, genders, sexualities.[44] A further example can be found in Constance Penley's account of women's Star Trek fanzines, involving sexual fantasies by women around Spock and Captain Kirk.[45]

Pornography therefore seems to have certain radical capabilities for melting the hard boundaries of gender and sexuality. This flexibility seems particularly present in bisexual and gay porn, but surely exists also in 'heterosexual' porn. In fact, the provocative question arises: *is porn heterosexual*? Does it simply represent a rapacious male desire consuming an inert and fetishised female body? Rather I see porn as dream-like, a world where such clear terms and concepts melt like Dali's watches, where the desirer merges with the desired, where the female body is 'put on' by the watcher, where the masturbator pays homage, not to the other, but to himself, reflected in the hallucinatory image of the sex/gender that he is not.

Gay and lesbian porn seem very important in the debate over images of sexuality, for they have challenged the view that porn is necessarily masculinist and devouring of the female body. However, some feminists have still argued that porn is porn and that, for example, lesbian porn is still demeaning to women.[46] And gay porn has been criticized for being overwhelmingly phallic: 'In pornography, the homosexual male, like the heterosexual male, is encouraged to experience and enjoy his sexual superiority over women'.[47] Indeed one could argue that gay porn, by completely getting rid of women, and focusing on the penis, heightens the sense of male power.

However, gay porn does seem to be relaxing its phallic obsession, and the theme of 'anality' – much more dangerous for men, for here there is a switch in gender as well as sexuality – is being presented more.[48]

The growth of gay and lesbian porn demonstrates the flexibility of pornography: it need not reflect a male propriety over women's bodies. In a sense, one can construct a pornography for any sexual taste.

CONCLUSION

Porn is a deeply complex and contradictory cultural form. In one sense, it attacks Western notions of art and decency, and could therefore be described as 'counter-hegemonic', that is as a resistance to the bourgeois world order.[49] At the same time, for some men who use it, it seems to betoken their great loneliness and inability to relate with people. At another level, I see it as an expression of the 'Great Goddess' theme, which has been so repressed in Western Christianity, yet which periodically resurfaces. Here is a sexual goddess, whom men worship in solitude, who fills them with yearning and hatred.

In psychodynamic terms, one can see it both as an expression of Oedipal trauma: the naked woman must be gazed at repeatedly to discover whether castration is a fact or not; and of preoedipal trauma: she is also the hallucinatory image of one's long-lost mother, with her endlessly available body, her capacious breasts, her womb which men yearn to re-enter. She also represents men's frustrated yearnings to be mothers and bearers of life.

If ever a cultural form was 'over-determined' it is porn. One of the wisest things I have read about it is by Harriet Gilbert, in her essay on Dworkin's novel *Mercy*:

> Because we have laughably little idea about what anyone, male or female, is actually doing when writing or reading about sexuality and violence, we are in no position, either moral or practical, even to attempt to stop them.[50]

I am also struck by the non-discreteness of porn images. By this, I mean that one cannot wall off pornography as a separate category of representation. Porn has an intimate connection with high art, since it turns upside down many of the conventions used in the representation of women. As we have seen, porn unveils and unblocks the orifices of the female body, which had been stopped up and hidden by centuries of Christian ideology. Of course this deeply offends many women and men, but this can be seen in part as testimony to the radicalism of porn's representation.

Secondly, one cannot separate porn from other images of women that are found in our culture – on TV, in women's magazines, in film, and so on. Women are shown in an increasingly sexual manner, so that many of these images could have appeared in porn magazines twenty years ago. And as I have mentioned, romantic fiction seems to be being considerably eroticized, and overlaps with pornography – and interestingly, excites a parallel disapproval from 'high' culture critics.

Do all these images simply signify a patriarchal appropriation of the female form? This is partly true, but I also see massive contradictions here. The female body is envied, hated, adored, feared, enjoyed, perhaps simultaneously! The woman in porn is mother, whore, goddess, trash, all at once.

Porn is scandalous. Its function is to scandalize. Porn can only be defined as the set of sexual images that currently stand on the frontier between the permissible and the impermissible, a frontier that is constantly moving, and that is policed by all manner of critics. Thus banning porn, or wanting to ban it, actually creates it *as porn*, since it cannot have its scandalous reputation unless someone wants to ban it. When porn excites, it does so because one knows that one's excitement is taboo. This takes us back to Stoller's young boy, who simultaneously knows he is forbidden to look up women's skirts or down the front of their dresses, and also that if he does, he will be rewarded by a fabulous vision.

I suggest that part of porn's scandal is not so much that it eroticizes and theatricalizes the dominance of men over women, but rather that it reveals how deep men's needs are of women. Men are prostrate before these images; their masturbation is a cry of loneliness; the body that is most fetishized is their own. I echo Mary McIntosh's claim that 'far from being the socially approved blueprint for sexual behaviour, pornography is the repository of all the unacceptable and repressed desires of men'.[51]

It may well be that the explosion of sexuality in the present century is not in fact to do with the need for pleasure, or the need to desire, but shows the construction of a complex semiotic code. In this light, porn is part of an enormous epistemological upheaval: using sexuality to understand ourselves and understand the universe, and to rediscover the power of matter itself. To an extent, sexuality has replaced religion, politics and science as a means of acquiring knowledge and power, establishing one's identity, and seeking salvation. One might, of course, retort that pornography is an extremely degraded and degrading system of knowledge, but that may indicate the depths of repression from which it is being dragged today, and also that this search for knowledge has been largely the preserve of working class, non-academic men, rather than middle class academic ones.

8 Male Images in Rock and Pop Music

Being part of patriarchal society, popular music has been dominated by men at all levels: composing and playing music, arranging and engineering it, and making the business deals about it. But in certain areas of popular music, quite complex divisions of labour have operated between men and women. For example, although in jazz the greatest instrumentalists have been men – Louis Armstrong, Sidney Bechet, Charlie Parker and so on – the greatest jazz/blues singers have been women – Ella Fitzgerald, Bessie Smith, Billie Holiday, Sarah Vaughan.

In other areas of popular music, women are very prominent: for example, in gospel music, Mahalia Jackson and Sister Rosetta Tharpe; in soul, the towering figures of Aretha Franklin and Gladys Knight. And in the 1950s, alongside the emerging rock 'n' roll singers, there were many popular hits by women: the McGuire Sisters, Winifred Atwell, Kitty Kallen, Kay Starr, Jo Stafford, Doris Day, Vera Lynn.

Furthermore, although the initial outburst of rock 'n' roll was dominated by men (Elvis Presley, Little Richard, Buddy Holly, Chuck Berry), as was the development of rock groups in the 1960s (the Beatles, Rolling Stones, the Who), other developments in rock/pop show a strong female influence.[1] There is the whole phenomenon of 'girl groups' in the 1960s – for example, the Supremes, the Shangri-Las and the Crystals – and then the emergence of many solo women singers (Diana Ross, Annie Lennox, Kate Bush), culminating in the domination of Madonna in the 80s.[2]

What is striking in all these areas is how women are almost always seen as singers, while men are instrumentalists, composers, sound engineers and producers. A similar division can be found today in contemporary dance music, where many records have a male rap section and a female melodic sung section – for example, in the dance records by the 'Euro-pop' groups, Snap, 2 Unlimited and The Real McCoy. Men speak; women sing. This has interesting connections with gender assignments, since singing is more emotional and expressive; speaking is more declarative.[3]

Women therefore find it very difficult to make their way into areas of technical expertise such as guitar playing. The growing number of female heavy metal groups often find it difficult to find acceptance (or record deals!), since record companies and music audiences refuse to accept that women can play with the virtuosity demanded in metal music.[4] Guitar playing is therefore seen unconsciously as a 'phallic' activity, restricted to men, as is sound arrangement and song-writing. However, during the 1980s this began to change slowly, as female metal bands such as Girlschool, Heart, and L7 showed that they could 'rock it up' as wildly as men. Female rappers also found it difficult at first, partly because the media has tended to demonize rap as the wild expression of criminal black men. But again female rap artists such as Salt-N-Pepa and Queen Latifah have broken down the gender wall.[5]

ETHNICITY

As with gender, ethnic distinctions have had a complicated impact on popular music. American popular music – which via jazz, the blues, rock 'n' roll, rock music and pop music, has been the major force in the creation of contemporary Western popular music – has shown a fascinating interaction between white and black musics, sometimes described as an 'appropriation' of black music by whites. However, the reality is probably more complex than that. The relation between white and black music has involved mutual borrowings, unconscious assimilations and so on.

One can to an extent turn the argument round. Rather than saying simply that white music borrowed shamelessly from black music, it can be said that black music has come to dominate popular music in the twentieth century. The music critic Peter Gammond puts this quite graphically:

> In the whole of musical history, let alone popular musical history, there has never been quite such a revolutionary and drastic change of emphasis as that brought about by the implantation of the emerging Afro-American idiom on the existing white American strains …
>
> The revolution that occurred might well have appeared to be a sudden one; but in fact it was simmering for centuries. The emergence of black music was of a volcanic nature. The pressures had been building up for some 300 years before the eruption came.[6]

This revolution happened through ragtime, jazz, the blues and rhythm and blues, the rise of rock 'n' roll, and the subsequent spread of pop music. The 'implantation' of black music was seen most dramatically in the sudden appearance of Elvis Presley, who was the prototypical 'white man with a black voice'.

But there is no simple formula available to explain the relation between white and black musics. While white rock stars have shamelessly ripped off black song writers and singers, black music itself has been deeply influenced by white music, often to the dismay of purist critics. But then black music has often felt itself under threat from a massive white commercial establishment, which is quite prepared to move in and make a financial killing from black music, and in the process often bowdlerize it.[7]

It is easy to think of white musicians profoundly influenced by black music – the Rolling Stones above all – but black musicians such as Michael Jackson and Prince have been influenced by white pop. The 'cross-over' operates both ways: reggae had a huge impact on punk rock; but Tamla Motown soul shows a smoothness partly derivable from pop. One of the outstanding musicians of the 60s – Sly Stone – blended soul, psychedelic rock and jazz in a fusion that revolutionized both pop and rock.[8]

Many powerful myths have operated, and continue to do so, in relation to 'black' and 'white' music. Let me repeat that by using the term 'myth', I am not suggesting that these beliefs are false, merely that they act as collective organizers of people's perceptions and experience.

One of the most important myths about black music is that it is especially 'authentic' or 'natural'. The musicologist Allan Moore relates this idea to the 'assumption that blacks in the southern USA lived in a state of mindless primitivisim, in which they expressed themselves through music, without the intervening of musical "theory"'.[9] White musicians often see 'going back to the roots' as meaning a return to the blues or rhythm 'n' blues. Today, this also connects with the interest in 'world music', often based on a belief that non-European music is 'primitive' or 'immediate'.

Black music has also been seen as the music of enslaved people, and therefore white fans and musicians seem to identify with it in that light. For example, the attraction of white working-class youth for black music in Britain has been a sustained phenomenon since the 60s, and while some of this identification can be seen as connected with notions of 'cool' style and sexuality, it is likely that white youth, unconsciously or not, empathize with black music as the expression of rebellion by the powerless against the powerful.

A striking example has been the Northern Soul phenomenon: working-class youth in the North of England dancing in clubs to the most obscure soul records on small US labels. This movement began in the 60s, as psychedelic and progressive rock became popular in the South of England, but it persists into the 90s. Other important areas of black music popular among British white youth have included Jamaican ska in the 60s, rock-steady in the late 60s, reggae during the punk era, and hip-hop in the 80s and 90s.[10]

Corresponding myths about 'white music' have tended to exaggerate its emptiness and commercialism. Thus Nelson George, in his fierce diatribe against the corruption of black music, *The Death of Rhythm & Blues*, sees assimilation, in all its guises, as the great danger: 'the two greatest black stars of the decade, Michael Jackson and Prince, ran far and fast ... from blackness'.[11]

Thus musical purism has tended to form demarcations between 'white pop' and 'black rhythm 'n' blues', whereas in reality the two are constantly intermingling with each other. There are of course many other purisms – for example, white country music has also been seen as tainted by the commercial success of singers such as Dolly Parton: 'by the 1950s there was a clear divide between the authentic school, with its often scholarly adherents, and, as in the wider folk-music field, the country music which became part of the commercial world of pop/country fusion'.[12]

There are many other aspects of black music which have had a powerful impact on popular music. For example, distinctions between the anonymity of the blues, the ensemble playing of jazz, and the individual virtuosity also found in jazz and in rhythm 'n' blues, seem to be important metaphors for the changing social structures of African-American communities.[13] But these metaphors have also become leit-motifs in the history of pop. For example, one of the distinctive qualities of contemporary house and techno music is that individual achievement is abolished: in the dance club, the audience is the collective performer.[14] On the other hand, heavy metal turns the individualism of the rock performer into a melodramatic and exaggerated performance, emphasized by the long hair, bared torsos, spectacular stage-sets and, in some bands, use of make-up and jewellery.

ROCK 'N' ROLL

Rock 'n' roll has been one of the great artistic explosions of the twentieth century, and it was at first an explosion of male aggression, sexuality and delinquency, fused into a kind of raucous urban blues. Frequently tamed, lobotomized, castrated by commercialism, it manages periodically to go back to its roots again and find new reserves of energy.

The *Cambridge Music Guide* describes 'the rock explosion' as 'an attempt to recreate music as orgiastic magic', and their comments on the Rolling Stones emphasize an affinity with African tribalism:

The Rolling Stones ... still represent the closest approach pop has made to an orgiastic music comparable with that created in tribal societies. This is seen in the group's singer Mick Jagger's Africanized yelling and bodily gyrations ... Amplification intensifies primitivism ... Percussion is more violent than real tribal drumming.[15]

Thus post-war youth in a blind manner found their way back to some very ancient roots of ritual. And rock music has an intimate relation with dance – the first rock 'n' roll films saw people dancing in the aisles, not to mention ripping up the seats.

The best rock is raw, elemental, for that connects it with the streets, and the ordinary kids on the block, and their grievances and dreams and fantasies. Of course the rawness quickly gets smoothed out, and then the shift into pop begins. This is one of the fascinating processes that seems to go on endlessly in contemporary music: thus the rise of the 'Seattle sound' in the 80s (groups such as Nirvana, Soundgarden and Pearl Jam) was seen partly as a return to 'rock authenticity'.

Above all, rock 'n' roll brought the body into music in a very sensuous and aggressive manner. This is described by Paul Willis in his account of 'motorbike boys':

This music allows the return of the body in music, and encourages the development of a culture based on movement and confidence in movement. The European classical tradition has steadily forced the body and dancing out of music ... The absolute ascendancy of the beat in rock 'n' roll firmly established the ascendancy of the body over the mind.[16]

Thus in rock 'n' roll the white working class asserted itself musically, and tore itself free from the schmaltz and sweetness associated with much popular music. And men in particular reached out for a music that wasn't smoothed over. It is arguable also that men looked for a refuge from the domestic world, seen as feminine: 'women – this is obvious in many rock lyrics – were a threat, a threat to male independence, a threat to male art'.[17] One of the contradictions found in rock music is that some young male musicians have used women as targets in their war on their own sense of imprisonment and suffocation: 'how unambiguously degrading to women is the language of aggressive masculinity through which the lads kick against the oppressive structures they inhabit'.[18]

We can draw a parallel with the western: in rock music young men express their rage, rebelliousness, and their refusal to be coerced into bourgeois society and into domesticity. This rebellion often didn't last very long – it's amazing what difference a £100 000 recording contract can make, but there has been an inexhaustible supply of angry young men.

One of the fascinating aspects of pop and rock is the opportunity it gives young white men to display themselves, physically, sexually and emotionally. The white singer who really turned emotion into musical display was Johnny Ray, whose stage gimmick was to end a song by collapsing into sobs. This provoked riots at concerts, airports, hotels. Nik Cohn gives an impression of Ray's act:

> He'd hunch up tight into himself, choke on his words, gasp, stagger, beat his fist against his breast, squirm, fall forward onto his knees, and finally, burst into tears. He'd gag, tremble, half strangle himself. He'd pull out every last outrageous ham trick in the book and he would be comic, embarrassing, painful, but still he worked because, under the crap, he was in real agony, he was burning, and it was traumatic to watch him. He'd spew himself up in front of you and you'd freeze, you'd sweat, you'd be hurt yourself. You'd want to look away and you couldn't.[19]

The interesting aspect of this is that Ray was showing the taboo side of white male identity: the pain, the tears, the self-doubts. Ray was much more popular in Britain than in America, and had many more hit records in Britain. But then in America, Ray was part of a huge R & B movement, whereas in Britain he was an absolute novelty. But it is also possible that his self-laceration connected more deeply with British audiences, perhaps more concerned with male self-doubts at that time than in America.

BLACK ROCK 'N' ROLL

In the beginning of rock 'n' roll there were great black singers – Fats Domino, Little Richard, Chuck Berry – but subsequent rock bands were nearly always white. At times this has provoked feelings of bitterness among black singers, that their music was being stolen by white musicians. For example, Chuck Berry seems to have been embittered by the fame of Elvis Presley as the 'father' of rock 'n' roll, when he felt he had a greater claim to the title.[20]

Certainly Berry has been one of the greatest of rock lyricists, combining a genuine poetic perception of adolescence with great wit, in such songs as 'Maybellene', 'Roll Over Beethoven', 'School Day', 'Sweet Little Sixteen', 'Johnny B. Goode' and 'Memphis Tennessee'. Berry also played the guitar with a ringing quality that is quite distinctive, and helped to make rock music a guitar-based music.

Berry had an enormous influence on the spread of rhythm 'n' blues amongst white bands – the Rolling Stones, the Beatles and Bob Dylan were hugely affected by his music, and for a period in the 60s any British rock band worth its salt would always include some Berry numbers as part of its act. Charlie Gillett describes his influence as follows:

> If importance in popular music were measured in terms of imaginativeness, creativeness, wit, the ability to translate a variety of experiences and feelings into music form, and long term influence and reputation, Chuck Berry would be described as the major figure of rock 'n' roll.[21]

Is it simply then that Presley was white and therefore more acceptable than Chuck Berry to the music industry, TV and cinema? There is some truth in this, but I think Presley did have qualities that Berry lacked. In particular, Presley oozed an outrageous sexuality and aggression that youth hooked into, whereas Chuck Berry has always had a rather distant and sardonic persona.

Among the other black singers, Little Richard provided an outrageous extroversion, hammering the piano and screaming out the often rather meaningless words of his songs, of which the famous 'Awopbopalooobopalambamboom' is a splendid example. But Richard made a kind of wild poetic frenzy out of these nonsense lyrics, and this anti-linguistic drift has been found periodically in rock music, and indicates the sensuousness of rock and pop. This has been difficult to swallow for literary-biased critics, who have tended to praise Bob Dylan for his poetic lyrics, while ignoring dance music, which often reduces language to a chanted mantra.

Chuck Berry and Little Richard therefore represent two important strains in rock and pop: the narrative and the anti-narrative. Berry's lyrics are full of fine detail – for example in the song 'You Never Can Tell', there is the 'coolerator crammed with TV dinner and ginger ale', there is a cherry-red '53 Jidney car, there are 700 records in somebody's collection. This is part of the great hedonism of rock, the celebration of life – the blue suede shoes, the Thunderbird, listening to the radio. Berry brings such elements together in wonderfully compressed stories, but Little Richard fragments them into splinters, disconnected from any narrative. One tendency uses language in a poetic fashion, celebrating urban life; the other dismembers language, so that it is desemanticized, and becomes simply music.

ELVIS

Perhaps the key 'creation myth' about rock 'n' roll is that it began when white country music blended with black blues, R & B and gospel, Tin Pan Alley and other influences. This musical miscegenation produced a sound that was electric, raw, sexual, and that acted on young people like a magnet. Elvis Presley's first recording actually had on one side a blues song, 'That's Alright Mama', and on the other side, a country song, 'Blue Moon of Kentucky'. These early Sun recordings by Elvis can be compared to a seismic earthquake in popular music: furthermore, Elvis also looked great – rough, sneering, lascivious. He was nothing if not male. Sexuality oozed out of him, poured out of his body.

If pop is mythology, then Elvis is prime hero and villain. His early appeal was precisely as villain to the moral majority in America, and a hero to the youth. He looked angry and was disdainful of conventional manners and, so it seemed in those days, conventional music. There is an interesting description of him in Alan Clayson's biography of Roy Orbison:

> Presley, sneering, didn't seem to care how badly he behaved up there – breaking guitar strings, spitting out his chewing gum, swivelling his hips in a rude way, doing the splits, knee-dropping and crawling to the very edge of the stage ... Even those who barracked still felt sick of the corny monotony they still had to endure at graduation balls, village hops and other occasions arranged and supervised by grown-ups to keep teenagers off the streets.[22]

But as well as presenting this charismatic and disruptive persona, Presley was a more complex musician than he is often given credit for. After all, he had the ability to fuse disparate elements into a very heady brew. Here is one description of an early recording, 'Heartbreak Hotel':

> He sings it lyrically, with a ripe romanticism almost comparable with that of a concert artist; he thus invites us to take the love experience straight. At the same time he rebelliously undermines it by rhythmic displacements derived from the triple drag-style of piano boogie and by conscious pitch distortions suggested by gospel singing. Presley uses both black barrelhouse and Pentecostal styles as part of his performing expertise. Straight romantic lyricism is held in tension. The performance stimulates because it is precarious.[23]

In fact, this ability of Presley's to play off different musical styles against each other became almost parodic later in his life. Some of his Las

Vegas concerts show him display such a dazzling ability to switch mood,
tempo and style, that one can only mourn his inability to sustain such
work. And frequently one catches him laughing at himself and at us; there
is a kind of contempt in him that spells self-destruction.

But Elvis was also a great symbol of white working-class exuberance.
He let out a shout of defiance, confidence and joy. He offended conserva-
tives because he seemed to embody carnality; he offended some radicals
because he sang about 'Blue Suede Shoes' and other trivia in a way that
turned them into joyful symbols. He embodied the contradictions in rock
music: it is both rebellious and hedonistic; as Simon Frith says, 'disturbing
and relaxing'. It casts a snook at bourgeois forms of music (hence Chuck
Berry's classic song, 'Roll Over Beethoven'), but it is not a worked-out
political statement. In fact attempts to produce 'political rock' are usually
doomed to failure, since they are usually not much fun!

Elvis helped release a great dam of energy which was lying dormant in
post-war youth. But Elvis Presley became not only an icon of rock 'n' roll,
but an icon of Americana itself, or even an icon of the twentieth century:

> The version of the American dream that is Elvis's performance is blown
> up again and again, to contain more history, more people, more music,
> more hopes; the air gets thin but the bubble does not burst, nor will it
> ever. This is America when it has outstripped itself, in all of its extrava-
> gance, and its emptiness is Elvis's ultimate throwaway.[24]

At times his fame is surprising. I had a glimpse of this when my son's
school put on a year-end concert, and to my amazement, my son volun-
teered to do an Elvis impersonation. I dug out some old film of Elvis from
the 50s, and eventually, after plenty of practice, his impersonation was a
very good one.

But what connection was there between these ten-year-old children and
this musician who died before they were born? I think partly that the
image of Elvis provides a lurid outsize masquerade of masculinity, that
can be put on self-consciously, half-ironically, like a huge suit of clothes.

Also, Presley fascinates because he did combine many different images.
He was the poor white trash who made it; he was the man with the golden
voice who could sing anything – and did! He projected a startling image of
sexuality; he was insolent and rebellious, and still appeals to delinquent
youth; but he also became a god for the middle-aged swingers in Las
Vegas. In other words he blended within himself – or within his image – a
huge number of twentieth-century myths. The King in gold lamé suits; the
brash kid with sideburns and swivelling hips; the syrupy singer of country
music; the sincere gospel and hymn singer; the overweight male stud,

leering at middle-aged women; the polite Southern boy, who collected teddy bears and loved peanut butter and jelly sandwiches (and adored his mother). There are many Elvises. This kind of multiple projection is very dangerous for the receiver of it, as other figures such as Marilyn Monroe found out, for the real person is ignored in the process.

Elvis was King, but perhaps he didn't realize that in some ancient religions kings were eventually executed to make way for a new king. In other words, Presley got sucked into the maw of publicity and fame and got chewed up like meat in a mincer. Furthermore, there are signs that he was a massively depressed person, and his mother's death seems to have devastated him.

There is something awesome in Presley's career: both in its genuine achievement, and its degeneration. In many ways his career is a paradigm of the contradictions in rock music. Here was this raw talent, with one of the great male voices of rock, and within a few years he was singing sub-Italian ballads, wearing tuxedos, and churning out an endless series of shoddy films.

It is tempting therefore to see Presley as a 'noble savage' corrupted by the record producers and the entertainment industry in general. Greil Marcus – finest of contemporary rock writers – pinpoints the romanticism that underlies this idea: 'There is a deep need to believe that Elvis (or any exemplar of America one cares about) began in a context of purity, unsullied by greed or ambition or vulgarity, somehow outside of and in opposition to American life as most of us know it'. Marcus calls this the 'Faustian scenario'.[25]

This romantic approach to Elvis – pure country/blues singer corrupted by record companies and Hollywood – is wide of the mark, for it ignores his own musical tastes. One of his favourite singers was Dean Martin; he liked Mario Lanza, lachrymose country music, hymns. He liked lashings of kitsch on everything – music, clothes, cars, houses.

We should also note the ferocity of purism that operates in rock music, and in other areas of popular music. For example Muddy Waters was booed when he first played electric guitar and sang blues, as was Bob Dylan when he played electric guitar at the Newport Folk Festival.

There has been a persistent attempt to freeze musical forms in some kind of pure state, which is of course a fantasy. So the rock 'n' roll purists have hated Elvis for singing romantic ballads and for becoming popular with a very wide audience – 'It's Now or Never', adapted from the Italian song 'O Sole Mio', was his biggest seller. In a sense, this attitude expresses contempt for Elvis's non-rock fans, the audiences who bought the ballads and the hymns and so on.

In an article entitled 'Sexing Elvis', the feminist Sue Wise describes her own experiences as a fan of Elvis, whom she did not perceive as a macho sex machine at all. She describes her reaction to his death: 'the memories that were evoked were nothing to do with sex ... the overwhelming feelings and memories were of warmth and affection for a very dear friend'.[26]

Sue Wise's tribute to Presley touches me, for I too remember being an Elvis fan, not out of some kind of macho bravado, but in a mood of tenderness, sentiment, and loneliness. I remember friends at school who collected every record put out by him, and they were not 'hard nuts' at all. The country music origins of Elvis are important here, for country music has been described as a music of defeat, self-pity and stoicism, all of which Elvis possessed in abundance.[27]

THE 1960s: BEATLES, STONES, BEACH BOYS

In the 1950s, British musicians could only watch and imitate. But in the 60s a genuine home-grown musical explosion happened, and significantly in one of Britain's most aggressive, poverty-stricken and witty of cities – Liverpool. The Beatles were heavily influenced by black music, but they brought something new to rock, a fresh urban poetry that blasted the cobwebs out of the music business, a very English eccentricity and surrealism reminiscent of Lewis Carroll, and perhaps an echo of the music-hall and pantomime.

And in Lennon and McCartney they had popular song-writers of genius, beautifully balanced: Lennon, despairing, romantic, but with an outer persona as the hard sneering cynic, McCartney, the soft doe-eyed choirboy. Lennon was a kind of English Elvis – full of hate and pain, and later in his life Lennon learned to scream his pain out, and made some devastating recordings ('Working Class Hero'). George Harrison was remote and mystical; Ringo Starr, a kind of English plebeian Harpo Marx. Thus the Beatles became a balanced quartet of males: a kind of family, with something to please everyone. There was the thug, the choir-boy, the mystic and the nerd.

They were witty, iconoclastic, aggressive, and working class. They enabled adolescents to create their own world, entirely separate from adults. The Beatles, in their interviews and press conferences, would suggest that the adult journalists were fools really, and that they, the Beatles, were taking them for a huge ride. Young people loved this, and drank it up, and asked for more. This was particularly true of John Lennon, the most aggressive, the best singer, with a genuine hard blues voice, and with a really acerbic wit.

The Beatles also provided a kind of do-it-yourself quality in music that was refreshing and encouraged identification and imitation. They wrote their own music, played the instruments, sang, sometimes in a rough and ready way in the early days – this was a far cry from the smooth products of Tin Pan Alley.

The success of the Beatles in America provided a kind of historic irony: for the music of Chuck Berry, Little Richard, Fats Domino, and other black singers and composers, which had been exported to Europe, was now being reimported in a different form. Some black music critics have seen this as a typical white appropriation,[28] but this is surely an historical and musical misjudgment: the Beatles were not simply paraphrasing Berry and Richard, but blending with them other musics and other cultural influences.

But something else happened to the Beatles, that has been alternately praised and damned: they discovered ART and MEANING. These two concepts have always been dangerous for rock, since rock is in some senses anti-language or anti-semantic. Nik Cohn correctly points out that the whole essence of rock is contained in Little Richard's 'Awopbopaloobopalambamboom!'[29]

The Beatles' album *Sgt. Pepper's Lonely Heart Club Band* is a crisis point for rock. For some it represents a moment of genius, a blend of poetry, melody and surrealism that is a landmark. At the same time it was possibly disastrous. Along with Bob Dylan, it has disoriented rock more than anything else.[30]

The Beatles were always compared with the Rolling Stones, and the comparison is still interesting. Whereas the Beatles quickly assumed an acceptable image ('lovable moptops'), culminating in their acceptance of the OBE from Harold Wilson, the Stones didn't get smoothed over, stayed loyal to the musical roots, and of course musically outlived the Beatles. Gradually they emerged as the iconic rock band – quite simply, the Stones have been the best white rhythm 'n' blues band. A track such as 'Gimme Shelter' shows a ferocious and intense R & B, awesome in its sheer attack, menace and poignancy. The Stones had realized, and never forgot, that rock music must seem *dangerous*, or it dies.

But the Stones also had important non-musical qualities. They evoked an eerie sense of corruptness and demonism that was spell-binding to youth in the 1960s. There is a wonderful description by Nik Cohn, of seeing the Stones quite early on in their career:

The limousine came up the street towards me and stopped directly outside the Odeon stage door. The police formed cordons. Then the car

door opened and the Rolling Stones got out, all five of them and
Andrew Loog Oldham, and they weren't real. They had hair down past
their shoulders and they wore clothes of every colour imaginable and
they looked mean, they just looked impossibly evil.

In this grey street, they shone like sun gods. They didn't seem
human, they were like creatures off another planet, impossible to reach
or understand but most exotic, most beautiful in their ugliness.

They crossed towards the stage door and this was what the girls had
been waiting for, this was their chance, so they began to surge and
scream and clutch. But then they stopped, they just froze. The Stones
stared straight ahead, didn't twitch once, and the girls only gaped.
Almost as if the Stones weren't touchable, as if they were protected by
some invisible metal ring. So they moved on and disappeared. And the
girls went limp behind them and were quiet. After a few seconds, some
of them began to cry.[31]

That is not only wonderful prose, it gives a haunting flavour of rock
music of the period, and the strange and surreal images that suffused it.
The sense of evil, the image of 'sun gods', the ugliness that people found
almost ecstatic, the cut-off quality – 'the Stones weren't touchable'. What
do these astonishing images represent?

I have already referred in Chapter 4 to the religious or transpersonal
images that are found in popular culture, with reference to the posthumous
cult around Elvis Presley. Here is another version of the yearning for the
non-human or super-human. In Cohn's description, the Stones are gods of
evil, pagan priests of a Dionysian cult of pleasure and amorality. This was
a part of the 1960s movement that was anti-Christian, anti-work ethic, and
pro-pleasure, pro-sexuality.

Of course it all went terribly wrong: the Stones concert at Altamont
descended into violence and murder; Brian Jones, the Stones' rhythm
guitarist, died in peculiar circumstances; many other musicians of the
1960s died from drugs – Jimi Hendrix, Janis Joplin. In a sense it was
bound to go wrong, for it was chaotic and reactive. The Stones represented
a kind of inchoate anti-bourgeois movement, espousing drugs, free sex,
wild music, yet the limits of such a movement were swiftly exposed.

MALE HARMONIES

In America a different kind of male pop was being developed. In the
Beach Boys, and to a lesser extent the Four Seasons, pop found artists of

the sensuous, creators of great rafts of sound, voices undulating, words turned into oceanic waves. This is a great concrete music. And there is something important here in terms of the male drive into music: the hunger for beauty.

Pop is the most sensuous of all art forms – the loudness, the beat, the use of language in an abstract manner, the repetition – one gets inside the music, or blends with it. Of course this is why some people hate it, for it is atavistic, primordial: 'pop music is a fusion of image and sound, a pastime, and there is nothing wrong with that, but *music lovers cannot take it seriously*' [my emphasis].[32] But young men have been driven into it to find things that were forbidden them under the iron aegis of masculinity: beauty, poetry, femininity, as well as rebellion, and delinquency.

A word that springs to mind about the Beach Boys' sound is *exquisite*. The blend of male voices, quite high-pitched, light, riding fast and loose over the instrumentation, gives a unique feeling of innocence and charm. There is nothing dark in their early songs. They talk about the beach, the Honda shop, the T-Bird that a girl's father took from her, long summer days, California girls. This could be judged as infantile, yet I prefer to see it as a dream-like world, a fantasy world, where there are no shadows.

But it is the vocal texture that transforms this apparently jejune world into high baroque pop art. Brian Wilson constructs vast arches of sound from voices that glide overhead, interweave, in an infinite golden male choir. The 1963 B-side hit 'In My Room', unusually slow, shows this to perfection – play it quite loudly, and the room is full of voices sliding, mingling, caressing each other and the listener. This is sensuousness taken to a height of luxury, voluptuousness. Yet this song shows Wilson working at a fairly simple level. Move on to 'Good Vibrations' from 1966, where Wilson uses his favourite structure of high tenor, followed by falsetto and the chorus, using three vocal lines at once. On 'Heroes and Villains' (1967) the choral effects are pushed out even more, to highly abstract vocal patterns, deliciously slowed down in the middle of the record, and then speeded up. Here Wilson is losing touch with song lyrics and semantics altogether, and one wonders also whether he was losing his audience along the way, as 'Heroes and Villains' did not sell all that well in the USA, although it was a Top Ten hit in the UK.

In a sense, Wilson had nowhere left to go. He had pushed the Beach Boys' sound out to unheard-of territory, involving highly abstract, multi-tracked, vocal instrumentation. In terms of popularity, 'Good Vibrations' was perhaps their apotheosis, although the delightful 'I Can Hear Music' followed in 1969. Anyway, the 70s approached, and the innocence and charm of the 60s could not be perpetuated. Interestingly, the Beatles – those other children of nature – disbanded right on the edge of the decade in 1970. The age of innocence was dead.[33]

I'M BLACK AND I'M PROUD

Black music in the 60s pursued quite separate tracks from Beatlemania. The great flowering took place in soul music, which blended gospel, rhythm 'n' blues and pop, and produced singers of great intensity, such as Otis Redding, Wilson Pickett, Ray Charles and Sam Cooke. Furthermore, soul had a massive 'cross-over' and dominated the pop charts in the mid-60s. This led to the inevitable commercialization and, some argue, dilution of the music, as white music companies tried to cash in. Two record companies highlight some of the contradictions in black music: Motown – black-owned, but dedicated to crossing over to the pop charts; and Stax – originally white-owned, but aiming primarily at black R & B fans.[34]

Other contradictions in the black music business can be seen in the figure of James Brown, famous for his physical and emotional intensity: 'Brown whined, begged, pleaded, reassured, declared, preached, exclaimed, cried and exultantly shouted'.[35] Brown is also famous for determining his own music direction, and travelling with his own band, the JBs. In a sense, Brown single-handedly created a musical genre, funk. He was also very much a black musician for black audiences, and did not permit the same degree of softening to his music, in order to cross-over to the white pop charts.

Brown became wealthy, and owned radio stations and real estate. This led him to espouse the notion of 'black capitalism', and eventually he came out with explicit support for Richard Nixon, who also favoured black capitalism – so long as welfare programmes could be cut. Brown also projected an intense machismo, which in the 60s did not arouse much attention, but which later began to antagonize black women.[36]

Brown is therefore a very confusing figure, the Soul Brother who backed the Republican Party, but this confusion, as with Muhammed Ali, reflects both the tensions in black American life, and the tensions present for black males, who have been in turn demonized, patronized and crushed. Brown was imprisoned in 1988 for drug offences, and this aroused great anger, since it seemed that yet again, a successful black man was to be pilloried.

IT DOESN'T MATTER IF YOU'RE BLACK OR WHITE

So sang Michael Jackson on his album *Dangerous*, illustrating his tendency to blur categories of gender, sexuality and ethnicity. His career
began in 1966, the year that the Beatles released the album *Revolver*, and
proclaimed that they were more popular than Jesus, and the year Elvis
Presley had a big hit with the single 'Love Letters'. An eight-year-old boy
climbed on to a stage in Gary, Illinois, and set in motion one of the most
extraordinary careers in pop music. It is a career that is still going on in the
mid-90s, although now surrounded by controversy.

For nearly thirty years Michael Jackson has been the boy wonder, Peter
Pan, a man who seemed to retain the sweet voice and the asexuality of a
choir boy. Purely as a music phenomenon, Jackson has had an extraordinary career – first with the Jackson 5, and then as a solo singer. But as a
male figure he is both bizarre and disturbing.[37]

His plastic surgery seems to have abolished blackness, but I wonder
also if its real function is to abolish masculinity, especially any resem-
blance to his hated abusive father. If one looks at successive photos of
him at different ages, he comes to look less and less like his father, and
more and more like his mother, his sister Janet, and Diana Ross. He is like
a Frankenstein's monster in reverse: everything that is pretty is combined
together to produce a perfect androgyne.

It is interesting to compare him with Prince, the other great black talent in
pop in the 80s. Prince has favoured a tacky kind of sexuality, so that his concerts are a blend of erotic extravangza, fashion show and pantomime. The
word often used about Prince is 'raunchy', he is so insistent on sexual overtones to much of his music. But his music energy and ability is prodigious,
producing in his best tracks a kind of jazz-funk-rock music that is tremendously exciting. If Prince therefore connects with the sexual roots of black
music, Jackson abolishes sexuality and produces instead a child's fairy land.

Michael Jackson is like a little boy, squeaking, screaming, groaning,
sounding in torment. But his voice expresses very well the agony of a little
boy growing up in an adult world, finding it confusing, indeed 'dangerous'. He is not so much asexual as presexual – the song 'Dangerous'
seems to describe female sexuality as a tremendous threat.

Nonetheless Jackson produced some great records in the 1980s – tracks
such as 'Billie Jean', 'Beat It', 'Thriller', 'Smooth Criminal', 'Liberian
Girl', which blend soul and pop into an exciting mix, and which also show
his great melodic talent.

How can a child produce such great music? I think because there is
something genuinely pained inside him, something anguished and lonely,

which keeps breaking out. The funky music is a kind of framework which he wraps around himself, like the mythology of being 'bad', being a 'smooth criminal', and so on. But his real voice is one of bewilderment and hurt.

To see him dance is itself a physical experience. His body is something pliable, something fantastic, almost non-human. He is able to do things with it that look impossible, as with the famous moon-walk. He doesn't walk, he glides, he flows like water, and the audience erupt at this piece of magical theatre, this *trompe d'oeil*. He becomes a machine, or a robot, but then suddenly melts again, and then is violent, crude. This is great mime.

There is the macabre as well, as in the 'Thriller' video. This is a hypnotic piece of movement and music – corpses dance with Jackson in a sinuous snake-like way. But still it's the little boy delighting in the grotesque and gruesome. Jackson brought the infantilism of pop to a pinnacle.

Part of Jackson's charisma rests on his ability to fuse many oppositions that exist in music and in American society. White and black, male and female, pop and soul, child and adult – Jackson seems to inhabit a place in between all of these categories. One can only speculate on the internal psychology that allows him to do this, but certainly it has permitted a very wide range of fans to identify with him. In a sense, he is not simply a gender-bender: he bends everything, dissolves the hard categories of the external adult world into soft melting shapes, more akin to a cartoon world or a dream world. It is easy to see why he loves Disney, for his music and his image provide a kind of one-man Disneyworld.

It is unclear whether his career is now in abeyance, following the allegations of child abuse made against him in 1993. Jackson has never been legally accused of any offence, but the tabloid press and TV have produced massive amounts of rumour and innuendo, and seem to have spent large sums of money trying to dig up dirt about him, so that possibly his image has been severely damaged. This episode demonstrates yet again how 'idols' are destroyed by the very forces that raised them up in the first place.

WHITE POWER CHORDS

Let me finally return briefly to some of the developments in white rock which, post-60s, became more inflated and portentous, as 'progressive' rock turned into 'pomp' and 'stadium' rock. Various fusions with other music fields also occurred – particularly country rock – and in the late 70s there was the violent revolt into punk rock, which punctured the pretentiousness that rock music had attracted.

One other important development in the late 60s was the growth of 'hard rock' bands like Cream, Led Zeppelin and Deep Purple, who in turn were heavily influenced by white blues bands, such as the Yardbirds, and also by Jimi Hendrix, who had inaugurated a new era in guitar virtuosity. Such music is now seen as the early beginnings of heavy metal.

As heavy metal became 'codified' in the 70s, it was vilified throughout the music press and beyond, and in a sense became a split-off and ostracized part of the music scene. It seemed as if heavy metal was fixed for all time, both musically – with its high volume, distortion, and spectacular performances – and in terms of its fans, who vehemently asserted their identity through heavy metal.

Heavy metal therefore appears on the surface to be a straightforward kind of male exhibitionism and, thus, part of the construction of patriarchal male dominance. As with football matches, certain very male pubs and so on, music such as heavy metal provides a kind of fervent male camaraderie. But does this represent the male domination of women?

In fact, heavy metal represents a clear case of a genre, or in fact a set of genres, where the iconography of power, heroic fantasy and intense romanticism can be seen as compensatory in the lives of the audience. Thus, Will Straw argues that heavy metal appealed to white suburban youth without college education, and Robert Walser sees the audiences as 'a group generally lacking in social, physical and economic power'.[38]

This also means that heavy metal music has had very low prestige, and has often been seen as devoid of musical interest, depending on loudness and the musical ignorance of the fans; in the words of *The Oxford Companion to Popular Music*: 'the bands tend to produce the basic rock and roll that appeals to the unsophisticated follower of the music'.[39] This comment is remarkably wide of the mark, since the Ur-metal bands, such as Cream and Led Zeppelin, in fact extended and *elaborated* the rock 'n' roll song: many famous metal tracks have never been released as singles, as they are too long and dense. Furthermore, the rock guitar attained in metal a virtuosity, and a technical proficiency, previously unknown. Guitarists such as Yngwie Malmsteen and Ritche Blackmore studied and incorporated areas of Baroque music, and metal guitar has been extensively theorized, in the form of the professional magazines devoted to it.[40]

But metal has been demonized, particularly in America, as an evil influence on young people, causing them to take drugs, and even to commit murder and suicide. The Parents' Music Resource Center (PMRC) has attempted to censor certain types of music, particularly metal and rap, and court cases have been instigated against metal bands, arguing that the music has been harmful.[41]

It seems more than likely that what is being pursued in these campaigns is not the music per se, but the audiences, whose activities are seen as dangerously antithetical to normal American values. In fact, the accusations made against heavy metal don't stand up: the lyrics are not in fact full of violence and suicide, rather an intense romanticism and yearning.[42]

Furthermore, metal is not a monolithic music, nor does it have a monolithic audience: during the late 80s and the 90s, it has split into many different genres, for example, punk metal, soft metal, thrash, death metal, grunge, glam metal, rap metal, industrial, and so on. Three of the most significant developments have been a link with punk rock; the growth of rap metal (bringing together the two *bêtes noirs* of the PMRC); and the development of grunge, which in groups such as Pearl Jam, produces an intense emotional confessionalism. In fact, it is arguable that metal music, in its various fusions with other genres, has been at the radical cutting edge of contemporary music.

On the question of the racism, sexism and homophobia of which metal music is often accused, while there is no doubt that groups such as Guns N' Roses have produced songs that seem deeply reactionary, there are other bands well known for their radical political views, for example, Rage Against the Machine.[43] It is also noticeable that metal magazines are full of articles and correspondence attacking racism and homophobia. Indeed, the whole metal world seems to have been politicized since the mid-80s. In fact, there are massive political contradictions present: rap metal, for example, combines 'macho gangsterisms' and extreme misogyny with appeals for social justice and anti-racism.[44]

Something that strikes me about the whole heavy metal culture, including concerts, music videos, and magazines such as *Kerrang!*, is that the male sexual display is very much *for other males*. Thus *Kerrang!* often has a male centrefold picture: usually a metal group in poses of semi-naked menacing languor. The male torso is considerably exposed throughout the magazine, as it is in music videos and concerts. Here, as in action films, the spectacle of the male body is provided for other males.

This is a rather subtle spectacle, for the highly extrovert musicians in groups such as Guns N' Roses, Aerosmith and so on are presenting a very insistent image of male heterosexuality which may in fact be a kind of male hiding-place from women, and *a refuge from heterosexuality*.[45] Are the headbangers really celebrating their dominance of women? I am reminded of porn again – Simon Frith describes hard rock concerts as 'a masturbatory celebration of penis power', and the word 'masturbatory' is important here, for the focal point of such an erotics is not woman but oneself.[46]

I have also noticed that some teenage boys take to heavy metal enthusiastically, not as an excuse to demean women at all, but as a means of channelling their own sexuality, aggression and excitement. But even more interesting in recent years has been the surge in interest by teenage girls, which seems to show that metal's boundaries and meanings, contrary to the views of some critics, are extremely fluid and context-dependent.

CONCLUSION

This is an appropriate point to end this chapter, for the fragmentation and hybridization present in heavy metal in the 90s seems characteristic of popular music as a whole. In retrospect, this has probably been true of post-50s pop music in general. Innumerable kinds of fusions and mutual influences have taken place, some of them quite surprising. The funk of James Brown influenced jazz musicians such as Miles Davies; jazz in turn has influenced pop, and produced the 'acid jazz' groups such as Jamiroquai; at times, the more abstract kinds of house/techno music seem to approach a form of 'classical' music.

There have been short periods when a particular 'canon' has dominated, but with great speed it is overthrown, deconstructed or satirized. Those who have negative feelings about rock/pop might see this as a testament to the essential emptiness and transience of this music, but this view assumes that the canon of classical music, as we know it today, was itself Platonically pre-formed. This seems most unlikely: 'the hodge-podge of the classical canon – aristocratic and bourgeois music; academic, sacred and secular; music for public concerts, private soirées and dancing – has one thing in common: its function as the most prestigious culture of the twentieth century'.[47] Pop seems ephemeral, therefore, because we are living through the energetic revolts and fusions that characterize its developments.

The word that comes to mind is *experimentation*, but this word can also be applied to notions of gender and sexuality in rock and pop. The pop world is a world of fantasies, and men have been able to carry out fantastic experiments in terms of their own identity. There is no doubt that, as a patriarchal institution, popular music has witnessed many 'masculinist' images and narratives, but it has also encouraged transgression, inversion, fusion. It has granted homoerotic and feminine fantasies a safe place in which to exist; it has given fantasies of omnipotence to the powerless; and it has also allowed the subterranean misery and rage of men to rise to the surface.

One of the most haunting images in rock music in the 90s is the face of Kurt Cobain, which now stares down from innumerable posters and magazine covers. Cobain was the lead singer of Nirvana who, along with Pearl Jam and other rock bands, have revolutionized rock music in the 90s, with their songs full of emotional rawness, even anguish. Cobain's suicide in 1994 was yet another indication of how damaged young men are, and how rock music articulates some of their yearning and pain.

But rock and pop have not only lamented; above all, they have *celebrated*: from Elvis Presley to the Beatles, from Ray Charles to Michael Jackson, men have cast off their uniform of rational sobriety and have been intoxicated, and helped us to be intoxicated, by music and by life itself.

9 Male Sport

Sport is one of the most neglected areas of culture in academic studies, but cultural students and historians and sociologists of sport are now beginning to make up this deficit – this can be seen in the growth of journals specializing in sport.[1]

Sport has had a particularly opaque mystified quality. In this sense, it is part of 'everyday life', which as a whole has resisted political enquiry. Sport also fell victim to the elitist nature of academic study: it was not intellectual or refined enough to merit scholarly study.

However, the relatively new field of sports sociology is beginning to demonstrate that modern sport is an important carrier of ideological messages; in the words of one writer: 'a repository for dominant ideology in its celebration of ruthless nationalism, racism, militarism, imperialism and sexism'.[2]

THE INDUSTRIALIZATION OF SPORT

In the nineteenth century sport became an industrialized and socialized spectacle in both Britain and America, regulated according to the clock and formidable sets of rules. Furthermore, rules were administered by a referee or umpire, acting as the interpreter of law and the dispenser of punishment. Thus in many ways sport was like a mirror held up to a capitalist and industrialized society. Sport became a form of work – tightly controlled, organized according to a division of labour, and relying on corporate endeavour:

> Football, baseball and other games were transformed into 'scientific' extravaganzas with highly codified playing rules, special training regimens, authoritarian coaches and other hallmarks of bureaucratised sport.[3]

One can compare this process of 'bureaucratisation' with the conveyor belt methods introduced by Henry Ford and others in industry: sport is transformed from 'play' to 'work'.

Within this modern codification of sport, many interesting symbolic features arise: for example, there is a tension, exploited in all the mass sports, between the network of rules, and freedom within the rules. This might be called the paradox of improvisation within discipline. Thus in the rugby

147

codes, players cannot pass forward, can only kick into touch if the ball bounces, and so on. In Rugby League only 6 tackles are allowed before the ball is handed over to the other side.

The rules of certain games can become amazingly complex. For example in Rugby Union, the referee can pick out many infringements at the line-out or the scrum, and rugby commentators on TV discuss at length which rules have been broken. Players also take delight in breaking rules – in this respect there is an underground culture to sport. One can cite for example the famous 'hand-ball' by Maradona in the 1990 World Cup – the great Argentinian footballer scored against England apparently with his hand. Much indignation ensued from the British tabloid press, but of course most pro players would do the same!

Cheating and fouling in sport are equivalent to law-breaking in society at large: both are policed by authority figures, and watched by a partisan crowd, who are ambivalent towards 'crime'. Class differences are important here – for example, in Rugby Union (a more middle-class game) it is considered bad form to boo the goal-kicker from the opposing team; for football crowds, anything goes. Thus if a player from the other team is injured, one will often hear sections of the crowd shout or sing taunting insults: 'Get up you wanker!' Thus football crowds are much more abusive. But rugby is a much more violent game on the field – fights quickly develop, and go relatively unpunished. One might contrast here tennis – where throwing one's racket is severely punished, as is abuse of the umpire.

A complex interplay of gender and class seems to determine the way in which order and disorder are transmitted in various sports, and there seems little doubt that subliminal 'debates' go on in sport about the tensions between control and democracy, corporate endeavour and individual freedom, law and lawlessness.

ATHLETICISM

Athleticism came to acquire a formidable set of ideological meanings in the nineteenth century, and it is likely that these are still important today.

In the English public schools athleticism became a very powerful educational and moral vehicle, and direct parallels were frequently made between the rigours of the sports field and the requirements of empire. Both were seen as demanding self-discipline, unrelenting effort, and corporate endeavour in which the individual subsumed himself. The following comment, made in 1888, is typical of many:

Health, endurance, courage, judgement, and above all a sense of fair play, are gained upon the football field. A footballer must learn, and does learn, to play fairly in the thick and heat of a struggle. Such qualities are those which make a nation brave and great. The game is manly and fit for Englishmen; it puts a courage into their hearts to meet any enemy in the face.[4]

The degree to which sport was seen as an important training ground for boys by Victorian educationalists is astonishing. At its height, the cult of sport meant that in certain public schools and Oxbridge colleges, sport was more important than academic performance, and sporting prowess was given huge ideological significance. Here is a typical argument put forward by the Reverend J. E. C. Welldon, headmaster of Harrow School from 1881 to 1895, and foremost spokesman for Victorian headmasters:

When the athletic games of English Youth are considered in their reference not to physical energy but to moral worth, it would seem that they possess an even higher value than intellectual studies. For learning, however excellent in itself, does not afford such necessary virtues as promptitude, resource, honour, cooperation and unselfishness; but these are the soul of English games.[5]

And the 'games ethic' was exported to the British Empire: cricket, football, rowing, swimming and boxing were exported to all corners of the Empire, along with the underpinning ideology.[6] Furthermore, the British could pride themselves on playing such games better than anyone else: 'British athleticism – original, manly and pioneering – was but another illustration of the superiority of the British'.[7] Thus sporting prowess and racism became closely entwined in Britain.

It is interesting to consider the survival of these attitudes today. It can be found in government attempts to rekindle the spirit of competitive sport in schools. Thus the National Curriculum proposals, put forward by the British government in 1994, include compulsory competitive games, in the belief that playing games will foster the Victorian values: team-work, self-denial, patriotism. At the Conservative Party Conference in 1994, the Prime Minister, John Major, spoke very eloquently about team sport:

I don't regard sport – especially team sports – as a trivial add-on to education. It is part of the British instinct, part of our character. Of course, it can't supersede maths and English – but it must take its full place alongside them. We are therefore changing the national curriculum to put competitive games back at the heart of school life. Sport will be

played by children in every school from five to 16 and more time must
be devoted to team games.[8]

It is also noticeable how frequently John Major likes to be seen in sporting contexts. On a visit to South Africa in September 1994, Major was
televised practising in the cricket nets, throwing rugby balls and so on.

There is also an incredulity expressed today when British teams do
badly at international sport, for example at cricket or football. In relation
to cricket in particular, as the former colonies – India, Pakistan, West
Indies – regularly beat England, one can detect an undercover racism at
work: how can a white English team be beaten by black teams? One can
also cite the comments made by the Conservative politician Norman
Tebbitt, who suggested that one hallmark of 'Englishness' could be found
in support for the English cricket team. By implication, black people who
might support the West Indies or Indian or Pakistani teams would be
deemed 'unEnglish'. These comments show how sport is still used in the
late twentieth century as a hallmark of nationhood and patriotism.

THE MALE BODY

In the nineteenth century the male body became a supremely important
symbol, upon which were inscribed many meanings. In particular, the
body was to be subordinated to the 'discipline' and 'team-work' required
on the sports field. Sport was distinguished from spontaneous play – for
sport demanded internal discipline, stoicism in the face of discomfort, and
an ability to conform with strict rules. These are surely the requirements
that capitalism was now making on the labour force. Indeed, some
nineteenth-century educationalists commented negatively on the spontaneity and lack of competitiveness shown in children's play.[9]

This cult of the body focused on the *white* body, seen as genetically
superior. Black people receive massive projections: feelings forbidden to
the white male, such as sensuality and indolence, are imputed to the infe-
rior race. Sport has enshrined many myths about the differences between
white and black men, for example, that white men show intelligence, lead-
ership and emotional control, whereas black men exhibit strength, speed,
quickness, and good 'instincts'. Black men are seen as good at physical
not mental achievements.[10]

Athleticism was also seen as a sublimation of sexuality that kept white
Englishmen 'pure' and away from women. Thus, part of Victorian middle-
class masculinity is a fierce sexual repression, a constriction that drives

him out to the public world, away from the pleasures of the bedroom. The black male body is important therefore as the repository for such forbidden desires. Again, it is clear that these 'bodily meanings' are still in use today, and came into prominence in America during the trial of the black boxer, Mike Tyson, for rape.

The emphasis on the physical in the cult of manliness carries many meanings: for example, it also strikes an anti-intellectual and anti-spiritual note. Not for British men the theorizing of French or German philosophy: this was considered effete, when there was an Empire to be won and consolidated. This anti-intellectualism is of course not an innate 'English' characteristic, but probably emerged as part of the empirical and pragmatic way in which the industrial revolution happened, and the colonies were conquered. Theories had nothing to do with this: Englishmen relished the deed before the idea, since it was deeds that made England great. This also led to a pervasive philistinism which still haunts English masculinity today: how much more manly it is to take part in the rigours of the muddy sports field than read poetry or philosophy.

SPORT AS MALE HEGEMONY

I mentioned in an earlier chapter how sport played an important part in the elevation of men over women in the nineteenth century. Whereas men were encouraged to find fulfilment outside the home in industry, business or the Empire, women were consigned to domestic life, placed in extremely restrictive clothing, and described as frail creatures who easily fell ill. And part of the education of young males consisted in massive training on the sports field.

This image of sport as male, tough and 'unfeminine' survives to the present day. For example, only gradually have women been permitted to run long-distance races – the women's 1500 metres was only permitted in the Olympics in 1972; and women's cricket, rugby and boxing still cause surprise, humour or revulsion amongst men. Certain sports have been designated as female sports – netball, hockey and tennis being the most important in Britain – and women have had to fight to break into 'male' sports.

This split has encouraged feelings of superiority amongst men. No woman could 'take it' like a man can take it on the rugby field or the football field. Men continue to be seen as 'active', women as inert; men are proactive, women inactive. Michael Messner describes the 'toughness' of male sport in an American context:

For middle-class men, the 'tough guys' of the culture industry – the Rambos, the Ronnie Lotts who are 'fearsome hitters', who 'play hurt' – are the heroes who 'prove' that 'we men' are superior to women. At the same time, they play the role of the 'primitive other', against whom higher status men define themselves as 'modern' and 'civilized'.[11]

Men have also bonded together through sport: on the field and off, they have formed intense associations which have been completely segregated from women. In an interesting psychoanalytic study of rugby, Philip White and Anne Vagi argue that rugby provides men with intense physical intimacy of which they feel deprived.[12] Thus, arguably, a covert sexuality exists in male sport, providing contact between male bodies that is latent and deniable.

In relation to rugby, White and Vagi also show how the surrounding culture is full of erotic material: for example, rugby players are fond of doing strip-teases in bars. I remember these rituals from student days: the singing of the 'Zulu Warrior' song, the drunken crowd baying for more clothes to be taken off, the solitary 'stripper', who always stood on a table. One can also cite the intense embraces seen amongst professional footballers when a goal is scored.

This homoeroticism also links with the intense homophobia and misogyny which has existed in male sport. These attitudes express an unconscious ambivalence: as well as asserting the true 'manliness' of sportsmen, they also seek to bury the homoerotic and 'feminine' desires of men for each other.

But women have fought back against the masculinism of sport: the women's movement in the late nineteenth and early twentieth century campaigned on sport for women, and certain activities became intensely symbolic areas of contestation: for example, cycling, which focused much of the debate around physical exercise, decency and clothing.[13]

SPORT, VIOLENCE AND LAW-BREAKING

There is a huge ambivalence about law-breaking in male sport. This can be seen clearly in televised sport, when commentators often speak complacently of a football or rugby game being played in 'the best possible spirit'. Yet any aggressive clashes between players are focused on, replayed in slow motion, while pundits in the studio analyze it in detail. Clearly, everyone is thoroughly enjoying the misdemeanours,[14] just as in society at large, much cant is expended on the subject of crime, barely concealing a fascination and an identification with it – visible, for example, in the large number of TV programmes devoted to rehearsing details of major crimes, ostensibly with the aim of catching the criminal.

This ambivalence can be seen in the treatment of sportsmen in the media. While homage is paid to the gentlemanly player, the 'villain' is given bigger headlines. Footballers such as Vinnie Jones – notorious for his 'hard' tackling of other players – might be condemned at one level, but there is also a kind of glorification of them. What is more interesting is how football fans feel about such players: undoubtedly some fans revel in the behaviour of a tough player, but many others are interested in other things, such as skill, flair and grace.

But the former type of player – the 'gentleman' – is also used to construct a vision of a 'golden age', when footballers were honourable (and low-paid). The death of Bobby Moore – former England captain – in 1993 was the occasion of a massive outpouring in the press, lamenting not just the disappearance of players like Moore, but even seeing in his passing an emblem of the decline of Britain: 'Britain has lost, in Bobby Moore, a symbol of all that is good in life'.[15]

In fact, this image of Moore is heavily bowdlerized, ignoring, for example, his work as a sports editor at the *Sunday Sport*, the crudely sexist tabloid newspaper, and his attempts to leave his life-long club, West Ham.[16]

But the myth of the golden boy was required, not only to lament a long-lost England, but also to castigate the modern sportsmen, such as Paul Gascoigne, and also the contemporary working class, seen as ugly, brutish and yobbish. Moore seemed to symbolize an era when the working class was safely controlled, either by a sense of deference, or the new-found affluence of the 1960s, or by notions of good manners. Not so today, when Gazza belches and farts on camera, tells journalists to fuck off, and generally refuses to be disciplined by the unwritten codes of conduct prescribed for English players. Surely one of the hidden sub-texts in this debate is that the working class used to know its place, but today doesn't.

One of the common myths surrounding violence on the field, and amongst sporting crowds, is that 'things are getting worse', but this nostalgia is refuted by the historical evidence that sport has often been the occasion for violence. Indeed, the primitive ancestor of football and rugby – 'street football' – was played with savage violence, involving fatalities amongst players. Eric Dunning therefore states: 'present day football hooliganism may perhaps be understood as a kind of recurrently generated urban continuation of the old folk tradition'.[17] However, this argument begs the question as to why the 'folk tradition' is generated again: surely not out of sentimentality or habit?

Historical research has demonstrated that violence has been associated with sport for thousands of years. One can cite the Roman gladiatorial games, which involved not only the spectacle of violence, but violence amongst spectators. And as well as the long-established association of 'street football' with violence, soccer in Britain has aroused violence amongst crowds earlier in this century, particularly before the First World War.[18]

Male sport has always had violence built into it, and surrounding it, in the form of riots, crowd disorder and so on. In a British context, Rugby Union is probably the outstanding example of a popular game which institutionalizes a degree of physical violence between players. Although officially condemned, it is clear that violence is covertly condoned in rugby, and also that crowds respond with excitement to violence between the players. The same is true in football, yet here violence has probably lessened on the field since the 1960s. Tighter rules now make it more difficult to carry out really rough play, and players are likely to be sent off. This is partly because of the crack-down on violence amongst football supporters, which seems to be rarer among rugby supporters.

In America, American football has been the main repository of ritualized violence, clearly shown in the National Football League's self-advertisement: 'vicarious warfare nurtured by the technology that is this land's hallmark'.[19] Concern over the violence in football has surfaced periodically during this century, most notably during 1895–1915, when changes were made to the rules in an effort to curb violent plays.[20] But again, there is a fundamental hypocrisy at work, since part of the theatrical spectacle of gridiron football is the clash of male bodies against each other – a spectacle that is both violent and erotic.

Thus the attempts of commentators and legislators to find 'solutions' to the problem of crowd violence and violence amongst players have a massive flaw: one of the functions of male sport has been precisely to provide a ritualized form of violence. The ritualization does not preclude actual violence taking place on or off the 'field'.

One can relate the centrality of violence in male sport to the thesis of male hegemony, to notions of 'territoriality' amongst spectators, and to class conflict. That is, male sport provides a complex blend of violent self-assertion by men *qua* men, a battle over territories by mainly working-class youth, and also a subterranean kind of class war.

Furthermore, periods of anxiety and public debate about violence in sport seem connected with larger political issues, to do with a perceived instability in society:

Public recognition of and attention to what is deemed to be excessive violence in sport coincides with points in time when particular societies are undergoing fundamental socioeconomic upheavals and critical evaluations of their basic values.[21]

An example of this can be found in the anxiety in Britain over football hooliganism, which has formed part of a wide-ranging debate about 'youth culture', 'youth crime' and its possible causes and cures. Thus the 'hooligan' became for right-wing politicians a spectre used to frighten anxious middle-class voters, and to whip up enthusiasm for harsh punishments. Football hooliganism became a kind of coded emblem for the disoriented and disaffected British working class, and the problem of controlling them, as in the miners' strike of 1984–5. Sociologists have tended to see in the rise of hooliganism an indication of the 'dislocation', 'uncertainty' and 'erosion' suffered by working-class men with the onslaught of deindustrialization.[22]

But the relationship between 'hooliganism' and socio-political developments is probably extremely complex. It is interesting in this light that in England, violence among football crowds has waned considerably in the 1990s compared with the 1980s. No doubt, this is partly due to the changes made to grounds, the improved stewarding, the attention paid by clubs to racism and so on. But one can also suggest that crowd violence had a strange symbiotic relationship with the Thatcherite governments of the 1980s. I mean by this that in one sense the Conservative governments *needed* the myths about football hooligans, both as convenient targets and whipping boys, but also as covert representatives.

The hooligans are definitely working class, so that they could be portrayed as 'not one of us', to be excluded from Thatcher's vision of a prosperous, white, middle-class England.But at the same time, the hooligans were 'Thatcher's children', in some ways an eerie if distorted reflection of her own espousal of patriotism and gung-ho imperialism. For the hooligans were patriotic to a man, they waved the Union Jack, or more likely they wore it, they hated foreigners, and tried to take the fight on to foreign shores. Their racism, their fierce loyalty to club and country, their recourse to violence, has a surreal kind of mirror-image relationship to Thatcher herself, who was not averse to waving the racist flag and increasing her popularity by going to war and killing foreigners – witness the sinking of the Argentinian troop-ship, the 'Belgrano'. The famous *Sun* headline about that action – 'Gotcha!' – is both Thatcherite and hooligan.

SPORT AND ETHNICITY

I referred earlier to the 'primitivism' which has been particularly ascribed to black sportsmen in America, along with other qualities such as exceptional skill, beauty, grace, eroticism. This has led to various genetic myths about the natural propensity of black people for certain sports such as boxing and sprinting. On the other hand, it was believed for a long period that blacks could not excel at swimming, since they did not have a natural buoyancy.[23]

The same kind of myths existed in British football during the 1960s and 70s, when black players were beginning to emerge. The standard myth was that black men did not have natural stamina: they were graceful, artistic, but didn't have the 'bottle' for a tough game. Paradoxically, in America the myth operated in reverse: in American football the quarterback position – which demands most tactical intelligence – was forbidden to black men until recently. Black men were seen as huge hulks, who had brawn but no strategic ability.[24]

But for American blacks, sport has been one of the few areas of society – along with music – which has been open to them as a career. The plus side of this has been that sportsmen such as the basket-ball player Michael Jordan have fostered an improvisational and poetic style which has contributed to black culture and to a positive sense of identity for young black people. Unfortunately it has also produced a kind of ghettoization and stereotyping of black men.

Indeed, it can be argued that the notion of 'social mobility' for black people in sport and entertainment is actually a bulwark of institutionalized racism: 'the domination of certain sports by black males is more a sign of continued racism than a sign of progress'.[25]

Thus, black male youth pursue sports careers because they are barred from other avenues, and because their main black role models are athletes and entertainers: 'this partially reflects the lack of opportunities for blacks in traditional male positions involving authority, power and prestige'.[26]

In an eloquent article entitled 'Cool Pose', Richard Majors argues convincingly that the virtuosity and 'flair' demonstrated by such black sportsmen as Magic Johnson and Michael Jordan are not only a means of self-assertion, and an assertion of black identity, but also a covert testimony to a generalized political impotence for black males: 'the dominant goals of hegemonic masculinity have been sold to black males, but access to the legitimate means to achieve these goals have been largely denied black males'. Thus although one of the messages in black sport is 'White man, you can't copy me!', that is, a defiant assertion of superiority, this also operates against a background of political and economic impotence. Majors describes black men as 'men *manqué*'.[27]

However, these ideas strike me as relevant to whole areas of male culture, which can be seen both as helping to construct male hegemony, and also helping to bolster men who feel powerless and excluded from the magic circle of that hegemony. The Finnish sociologists, Laitinen and Tiihonen, make the interesting statement that 'an image of the male body is a *promise of power* in a society' [my emphasis].[28] The word 'promise' has a crucial ambiguity: for the promise is fulfilled for some men, but not for others, for whom such images are compensatory – for their lack of power.

But the increasing number of black sportsmen cannot simply be explained in terms of economic and social mobility and immobility, for that ignores the spectator's point of view. The black male has clearly become an important spectacle for white audiences, partly as an image of brutal strength and masculine prowess, as with Tyson and other boxers, but also as erotic objects.

This can be seen clearly with the British athlete Linford Christie. After his triumph at the Olympic games in 1992, the film of him winning the 100 metres was played frequently on television. Many comments and jokes were made on TV about his genitals, which were quite visible in the race, since Christie habitually wears skin tight Lycra. One female comedian, Jo Brand, spoke directly to Christie on a chat-show: 'get your shorts off, and let's look at your meat and 2 veg!'

Thus, Christie was seen as a kind of lithe sexual animal, displaying his genitals. This image is also fostered by TV advertising, which shows Christie rising from the starting blocks, filmed in slow motion. The effect is hypnotic; Christie stares into the camera with utter concentration; there is a charismatic beauty and eroticism about him which is startling, and often provokes comments from people watching. Thus the black male body is a container for sexual desire, beauty, grace, portrayed in a rather animal-like manner. It is difficult to think of white sportsmen being filmed in such an erotic and beautiful manner. Is this a subtle kind of racism? We are meant to admire the black sexual athlete, but is this not simply a mirror-image of the bigots who used to lynch him?

SPORT, POLITICS AND ETHNICITY: MUHAMMED ALI

Many of these images and ideas about ethnicity were brought together in the career of Muhammed Ali, who is probably the most famous sportsman of the twentieth century. Yet his career shows how a famous individual is often moulded and shaped by the political forces of the time, rather than the other way round. For Ali became world heavyweight champion just at a time when a constellation of political upheavals were going on in the United States, and to an extent world-wide. The Vietnam War was arousing increasing anti-war sentiment; black militancy was on a rising crescendo; and the 1960s counter-cultural movements were in full swing. Ali seemed to act as a lightning rod, first focusing the displeasure of the American Establishment, becoming a hero of black and anti-Vietnam radicals, but eventually finding acceptance again in middle America.

In fact, at first it seemed that the young Cassius Clay was going to be one of those favoured black sportsmen, such as Joe Louis, whom Americans have liked because of their cooperative manner: 'following the 1960 Olympics, Cassius Clay was perfectly positioned for a love-in with the American people: from the start of his career Clay had been regarded as a "good coloured boy" with which white America was comfortable'.[29] Significantly the syndicate that initially backed him financially was completely white.

The history of black boxing in America is a chronicle of racism: certain black boxers who ingratiated themselves were accepted, but those who refused to toe the line were treated with hatred and contempt. In 1910 Jack Johnson defeated the white man Jim Jeffries and triggered off national race riots. Johnson was also vilified during his life because he married three white women, thus playing on the fearful image of the black male as a sexual primitive. By contrast, Joe Louis projected a mild-mannered image, served in World War II, and became a national hero – the 'Brown Bomber'.[30]

Interestingly, Ali was to exploit these tensions throughout his career, sometimes taunting his opponents as 'Uncle Toms' – for example Floyd Paterson, and Joe Frazier, whom Ali scorned as the 'white people's champion'. On the other hand, Ali had opponents who were seen as the 'bad nigger', Sonny Liston being the most glaring example.[31] And Ali himself moved from category to category several times in his life.

Boxing has been one of the classic ways in which black men have been encouraged to channel their energies – the sports writer Robert Lipsyte has a fine passage in which he describes the sub-texts in the creation of the stereotypical black boxer:

> The heavyweight championship was a way for the white establishment to say to black America, 'You should channel your rage and energy into going out and being someone who fights to entertain us within very specific carefully bounded areas. You can go out, eat glass, get drunk,

get laid, do whatever you want as long as you stay within the parameters of what a member of the underclass is. Choke down your rage at how your people are getting screwed over, work very hard, make millions of dollars, have your pleasures in stereotypical ways, cars, women, wine, song, ultimately self-destruct, and keep our stereotypes in order'.[32]

To a degree, Ali broke down these stereotypes. In 1964 he joined the Nation of Islam (the 'Black Muslims'), and changed his name from Cassius Clay to Muhammed Ali. For years journalists and commentators refused to use his new name, for it symbolized a black separatist image they weren't interested in: they wanted to keep their stereotype, the clown who would recite poetry ('Float like a butterfly, sting like a bee'), dance round the ring, and entertain people safely. In other words, whites wanted a castrated black man to dance to their tune, which at first Ali refused to do.

In 1966 Ali was drafted for Vietnam, and made his celebrated utterance: 'Man, I ain't got no quarrel with them Vietcong'. He refused the draft, and one hour later his boxing license was rescinded, and Ali didn't fight for three years.

However, radical youth began to see in Ali a symbol of their own fight against Vietnam and against corrupt white America, and Ali began a process of rehabilitation amongst middle-class whites that was to culminate in him being invited to the White House by President Ford! Later in his life, in fact, Ali gave his political support to Reagan and Bush – he had come a long way from the black tiger who had terrified white America in the 1960s.

Ali also suffered brain damage, and Parkinson's disease, probably from too much boxing, became dull and slow in appearance and reactions, and showed the terrible toll that boxing takes. And Ali had had a beautiful physique in his prime; he seemed to stride the ring as the 'king of the world' he described himself as. His career is not only an extraordinary parable of political rebellion and acquiescence, but also of the physical destruction of the male body, which is offered up as a grisly offering for mass consumption.

Boxing has continued to provide complex images of masculinity: in the contemporary era, Mike Tyson has been the most prominent. Tyson's career has brought together many clichés about black boxers: the early career in crime, 'rescue' by a white guru figure, the early successes and a prowess in the ring often termed 'savage'. Tyson seemed to symbolize a black male primitive violence that was portrayed both as mindless and magnificent. But it has been Tyson's conviction for rape that brought his career to a nadir and a crescendo, for it seemed to confirm the racist stereotypes of the black rapist, who isn't safe to be let out.

SPORT AND CLASS

In Britain, sport has been shot through with class distinctions. The sport one followed or practised has often been a badge of class identification. Thus, few working-class people used to play tennis or polo or squash; few middle-class people played in the local darts team or played crown green bowling in the North of England. And even within particular sports, the class divide ran through like the Grand Canyon. For example, the very nature of county cricket matches – played from 11 am to 6 pm for three whole days – meant that working-class men weren't able to follow it. But the Lancashire League, played on Sundays, attracted a fanatical following from working-class crowds, and still does today.

Perhaps the most glaring example of a split caused through class is found in rugby, which has actually divided into two different codes, one played in the North of England as a professional game (Rugby League), and the other an amateur game for middle-class players and crowds (Rugby Union). This split began over payment to players for lost earnings, but became imbued with all manner of ideological oppositions. Yet in Wales, this distinction breaks down, for working-class men have played and watched Rugby Union rather than soccer, and Rugby League is a minor sport.

Cricket also had its own internal split between gentlemen amateurs and 'professionals', who were treated like servants. Thus, 'professionals were ... expected to look after the ground, clean the kit, serve the drinks, enter the ground by a separate entrance, and change in separate rooms'.[33] British sport frowned on commercial sport until recently: the true ideal was the man who played for honour, not money. Of course these ideals have wilted in the face of the intense commercialization of sport, but the conflict between amateurism and professionalism still rumbles on in Rugby Union, which has seen a number of financial scandals, as players are paid in secret.

Football was also divided by the issue of professionalism: the Football Association had been founded by public-school men, who looked askance at the northern teams who began to pay their players. But certain sports went even further, and actually banned working-class participation, for example rowing and athletics.[34]

SPORT, CLASS AND THE BODY: GAZZAMANIA

Perhaps nothing could seem further from the dramatic career of Muhammed Ali than that of Paul Gascoigne – 'Gazza' – the young English footballer who has fascinated the media during the 80s and 90s. Yet there are similarities: the media have desperately tried to create in Gazza a symbol of Englishness, yet the image has been ambivalent. There has also been a barely veiled contempt for him – the Fat Boy who trains on beer and Mars bars; the working class 'lad' who doesn't have the manners of a Bobby Moore or a Bobby Charlton.

The issue isn't Gascoigne's own personal foibles, but why the media should have chosen to hoist him up to the rank of icon, there to be adulated and reviled alternately. Nor is it particularly to do with his massive talents, for other greatly talented footballers – for example, Liam Brady, Bryan Robson, David Platt – have not excited such attention, nor have they courted it.

As with Ali, it is likely that Gascoigne is used by the mass media to articulate certain important social and psychological tensions in British society at the time. Here the issue of class seems paramount. Ian Hamilton, in his essay on Gazza, compares the Italian reaction to him with the reaction to him at home:

> In England, there was an essential hostility to Gazza: a class-fear, a culture-dread. Here he could be *placed*: on the terraces or on the rampage, down the pub or up before the beak. If we were to meet him, we'd be ill at ease – both awed and condescending, with the condescension somehow managing to win the day. When Gazza speaks on television, the English – or most of them – mock the *Auf Wiedersehn Pet* accent and his all-over-the-place syntax. But in Italy most people would think he's speaking proper Inglese, or that his dialect is interestingly regional ... And the Italians were not in the least disconcerted by other, to us, off-putting, aspects of his physicality: his huggings and kissings of colleagues, his pattings of bald heads, even his sniffing of opponents' arm-pits.[35]

These comments are fascinating on their own account, for the writer reveals as much about himself as Gascoigne. Who is the 'we' in this passage: 'if we were to meet him, we'd be ill at ease'? I doubt if working-class people would be ill at ease with Gazza – but Hamilton is surely articulating the anxiety of the middle class and the intelligentsia at this unlikely hero. Similarly with the comment about his 'all-over-the-place syntax'. What does this mean? Of course, Gascoigne has a marked regional dialect, which probably includes syntactic variations from Standard English. And I am not sure Gazza's 'physicality' would disconcert working-class people to the same extent as the writer indicates. My memory of working in factories is that such behaviour is common.

The really interesting thing about Gascoigne is that he has not moderated his behaviour for public consumption. He behaves as he would behave at home, or in the local pub, or down the factory. By contrast, many footballers who rise to eminence are aware that they should cultivate a polite and well-mannered manner. David Platt, already mentioned, springs to mind here. Now captain of the England football team, he has a decorous and well-spoken demeanour.

Some of Gascoigne's celebrated escapades are fascinating displays of 'physicality'. In the 1990 World Cup he burst into tears when England lost to Germany in the semi-finals. The photos of him crying were spread over the tabloid papers, and soon T-shirts were on sale with Gazza's tearful face on them and inscribed with the significant slogan: 'there'll always be an England'. What is interesting about this example, is that a type of behaviour normally condemned as unmasculine – crying – was turned into an emblem of manhood and patriotism. For Gazza, crucially, was crying over losing the chance of playing for his country. Yet how remarkable that a fiercely taboo activity should be 'iconised' in this way: the taboo turned into an asset, just as in other very restricted contexts, female apparel is permitted to men.

Later, Gazza attracted disapproval for belching into an interviewer's microphone (described as 'il commento gastrico' in the Italian press); on another occasion, when approached by a distinguished Italian journalist, he simply farted. On his triumphant reception back in Britain after the 1990 World Cup, he shocked people by appearing on the open-top bus wearing a huge plastic pair of breasts, complete with plastic beer belly.

Gascoigne also became famous for his diet, and his reputed predilection for beer, pizzas and Mars bars. What is interesting about all these details is their concentration on the body, indeed the *gross* body. This reminds me of some of the images I have highlighted earlier in this book: for example, the orificial body in pornography, the horrific body-in-pieces in horror films, the display of the male body in certain rock music genres, especially heavy metal.

Thus, Gazzamania conceals a complex sub-text about three things: gender; the white male body; and the British working class (and its relations with other classes). Gazza's proletarian male body excites devotion, contempt, adulation, but certainly fascination. He is both the artist and the clown, the athlete and the gross pudding of a man. In a sense, we peer at, and into, his body with fascination, and we watch its functions and its secretions with horror, dread and compulsive excitement. Look – he cries, he belches, he farts. Good God, what will he do next? He is like a twentieth-century Falstaff, although with less nobility.

Sometimes Gazza is seen as Our Boy, a national hero, really showing those foreigners how to play 'our' game. But in the next breath, he is reviled for his boorishness, his refusal to be castrated and refined.

But even more fascinating is the way certain intellectuals such as Ian Hamilton seem to have made such an emotional, indeed agonized identification with Gazza. Hamilton's essay is full of worry for Gazza: will he hurt his leg again if he plays? Will he 'do the business' and show his true artistry? Can he manage to lose weight this time? How's his beer consumption? Gazza is a kind of favourite son, loved with great anxiety and fear for the future. The middle class seems to see in him an icon of the working class, towards which it feels such ambivalence, such fondness and hatred.

Is there also a concealed homoeroticism in Gazzamania? There is certainly a fetishization of his body, towards which a complex mood of love and hate, envy and contempt seems to exist.

It is true that when Gascoigne plays well, he displays an astonishing grace and artistry. One of his moves was dubbed by the Italian press 'il passo doppio', and inspired writing of this kind:

> He has restored the magic of a tapestry. With beauty he has confounded the critics. He has given the game the dignity of the dance, and he has transformed the field into a drumskin.[36]

The ambivalent approach to Gascoigne reminds me of the central theme of Peter Shaffer's play and film *Amadeus*: how could God place such a divine talent in an idiot such as Mozart? That split between body and spirit that has haunted Christian cultures for millenia surfaces again here: how is it possible that the Fat Boy can go out and suddenly do something that is the footballing equivalent of Rudolf Nureyev? How can body and soul be joined together in a man such as this?

Thus the body/spirit split is mapped on to dualities within class and gender. The working-class male is seen as corporeal, gross, eructating; the middle class is more spiritual, more refined, but looks with envy and a certain excitement at the physical carnival enacted by men such as Gazza. Gazza's body and personality become a text, which is alienated from him, in fact becomes public property, upon which can be inscribed various messages.

EMOTIONAL INVOLVEMENT IN SPORT

Gazzamania gives an indication of the intense identifications made in male sport, and spectator sport can be a very emotional occasion, especially a big match, for example a Cup-tie in soccer or an international match in rugby. And for individuals, sport seems to offer a means of channelling intense feelings, for example, a sense of belonging, having a 'family'. During the game itself, spectators are able to go through violent swings of feeling, from love to hatred, adulation to obloquy. The opposing side has a particularly valuable function as target for one's hatred and contempt.

Nick Hornby's *Fever Pitch*, one of the most authentic books written on sport, gives us some inklings of these intense investments made in sport. He describes 'falling in love' with football at the age of eleven; and the intense sense of maleness that surrounded the game:

> Cigar and pipe smoke, foul language (words which I had heard before, but not from adults, not at that volume), and only years later did it occur to me that this was bound to have an effect on a boy who lived with his mother and his sister; and I remember looking at the crowd more than at the players ... My father told me that there were nearly as many people in the stadium as lived in my town, and I was suitably awed.[37]

Hornby's parents had separated by this time, and throughout the book one gets a haunting feeling that at the football games, he finds something that he has lost at home, perhaps a sense of completeness, and also a male connection. Hornby also writes brilliantly about the unhappiness that football causes, the misery when the team is losing, the hatred of the other team and the referee. Football provided him with a safe place to be miserable:

> I just didn't want to have fun at football. I had fun everywhere else, and I was sick of it. What I needed more than anything was a place where unfocused unhappiness could thrive, where I could be still and worry and mope; I had the blues, and when I watched my team I could unwrap them and let them breathe a little.[38]

There is so much else in this marvellous book, which is one of the few books on sport which gives an honest account of personal involvement, and also shows that the simplistic notion of 'entertainment', as applied to sport, is wide of the mark. As Hornby says, 'I go to football for loads of reasons, but I don't go for entertainment'.[39] This makes us realize perhaps how little we still know about sport and its significance for spectators and participants.

WEMBLEY: 10 APRIL 1994

By chance, while writing this chapter, I happened to go to a big football game at Wembley – an FA Cup semi-final. The two teams had particular resonance for me: one was Oldham, which was the town I had grown up in. The other was Manchester United, who had been the great glamour team in Manchester during the 1960s. As a school-boy I had gone to see George Best, Bobby Charlton and Dennis Law, and marvelled at the grace and power of these supreme athletes. In those days Oldham had languished in the lower divisions, but in the early 1990s they had been promoted into the top division. In any case, the FA Cup notoriously pitted teams of different qualities against each other, and gave them a sort of parity: anything could happen in the Cup!

On the way to the ground, I realized to my embarrassment that I felt tearful. We got on the Tube – I went with my son – and I could hear the Manchester fans – the famous 'Red Army' – roaring out some obscene diatribe against Manchester City, much despised local rivals. Why am I tearful? Partly because it makes me feel homesick for the North, and I feel homesick for 'the lads'. I wish I was part of the Red Army, roaring along without a care in the world.

From the Tube station at Wembley there is a long walk up Olympic Way, massed with fans from both teams. At intervals, groups would spontaneously gather around a flag or banner and strike up a chant or song. I saw some Oldham fans at the side holding out their caps to Manchester fans, saying sarcastically: 'Give us a player or two, we're only poor relatives'. Oldham fans bellowed out various ditties about the Manchester player, Eric Cantona, soon to be voted Player of the Year, but currently suspended. One song went: 'He's shit, shit, he's never on the pitch'. Manchester fans roared back a prosaic version of 'The Twelve Days of Christmas': 'Six Cantonas, five Cantonas, four Cantonas, three Cantonas, two Cantonas and an Eric Cantona'.

The sight of the Wembley pitch is awesome: so huge, so green, such a theatre promising great spectacle, drama, fear, triumph and tears. We sit in the middle of 20 000 Oldham fans, who fill the air with banter, songs, flags. This is Joe's 'barmy army' – Joe being the Oldham manager, Joe Royle. The cry of 'Viva Joe' echoes round – I wonder how these chants originate. One can sense the mixed feelings: inferiority – for Oldham are to Manchester United as cheese on toast is to caviar – and pride, that their team has made it to the semis. And a huge feeling of will-power – come on Oldham, put one over on the glamour boys.

The game is tense, defensive. Oldham neutralize the star Manchester players: Ryan Giggs – the amazing winger who has dazzled spectators for the past three years – Mark Hughes, Paul Ince. Manchester look unusually uncertain, nervous perhaps.

The second half sees a number of bad-tempered fouls, as both sides express their frustration. But the Oldham fans realize something: Oldham are holding their own without doubt. At the back of your mind there is the fantasy: if Oldham score, can they hang on? Around me people argue, families confer with each other: what's going to happen? There are plenty of kids, some of them looking totally bored. Behind me an old man keeps haranguing his grand-daughter: watch the game!

Ninety minutes go by with no goals: the match goes into extra time. By now the Oldham fans are buzzing like a vast blue and white bee-hive. Oldham have never been to an FA Cup Final. This could be it.

Sometimes you have a feeling that a goal is coming, and in the 107th minute, Oldham score. The United goal-keeper fumbles a cross, drops it, and an Oldham player wallops it into the net. Pandemonium. Around me everyone has punched the air, embraced each other. The noise is staggering. I can hear people screaming. Husbands and wives hug passionately. The grand-daughter is swept into the arms of grandad. I notice my son roaring out the Oldham songs – he, who was born and bred in Fulham! Oldham fans start singing the traditional victory taunts to the other fans: 'You're not singing any more'. And indeed the Manchester fans are very quiet. Then we sing the Monty Python song: 'Look on the bright side of life'. Middle-aged men dance in the aisles. There are only ten minutes left, and Oldham are nearly into the Final. A thought goes through my mind about Bakhtin's notion of carnival, then in the next breath I have to dismiss it. This *is* carnival, and one cannot stand back and think in this atmosphere. Isn't this one reason we all come: to cease thinking?

But with forty seconds to go, Manchester score. The score is level, and there will be a replay in three days' time. Everything changes round: the Manchester fans roar out their relief; the Oldham fans are stunned, silent. Everyone instinctively feels that Manchester will win the replay. The referee blows for time, and we stumble out, crushed, trying to console each other. Oldham played well. Curses for the other team: rich Manchester bastards!

That night and the next day I felt stunned, stupefied. Partly, disappointment that Oldham had had victory torn away in the last minute – the 120th minute! But also at the sheer emotionalism of the occasion. I felt I had gone through so many emotions in such a short space of time: boredom, anxiety, triumph, despair, my homesickness for the North.

It struck me that this is one of the functions of football: to provide a theatre where emotions can be experienced in safety. Of course in one sense it doesn't 'matter' if Oldham get in the Cup Final or not. Yet it does matter. I kept remembering Camus talking about football: 'All that I know about morality and the obligations of man, I know from football'. Was he serious? Yes.

But there is this searing embarrassment in me, as if I've been caught out in some shameful secret. Later that night I wept again and cursed the Manchester team, but I hide my feelings from my family. There is some kind of male shame here about the intensity of feeling, which can be safely released in the great ampitheatre along with sixty thousand other people, but then must be carefully put away when one gets home.

Football provides an arena, where one's view of life can be acted out, theatricalized, and contained. The containment is crucial: here one can go through hatred and love and loyalty and despair. Then the game is over, and the crowds slowly disperse. The catharsis is finished.

We can say this: we belong! For this moment, we belong together, to this team, to this town. Our loneliness and separation is transcended. It's not surprising football is a proletarian game. The have-nots have been able to indulge a fantasy: we have, we own, we are. It has also attracted the déraciné intellectuals, such as Camus, who find in it an organic and sensuous metaphor.

Several weeks later I watched a TV interview with the Manchester player, Eric Cantona, acclaimed by some as the one of the greatest players in the world. It's amusing to hear Cantona talk in such a non-English way about sport. A keen painter, enthusiast of the French poet Rimbaud, Cantona is rather different from the average English player. Asked about his obsession with football, he exclaims: 'le football, c'est le plus beau des arts!' He argues that football's spontaneity and passion raise it to the pinnacle of artistic expression: I wonder what the Stretford End (raucous section of the crowd at Manchester) make of this?

That same night, still sore from the semi-final, I exclaim in bitterness to the empty room: football is so unfair! This feeling is deeply satisfying. All my class resentment, my sense of inferiority and my omnipotent fantasies coalesce into a heated outrage: we should have won. Perhaps the joy of victory is only equalled by the virtuous despair of unjustified defeat. We was robbed!

But why am I ashamed of all these feelings? I hear a rational voice in me rather pompously pronounce that football is trivial, not worthy of so much fuss. Yet in a sense, that's the point. It's the essential *meaningless-ness* of football that allows us to project into this drama, and construct for ourselves such intense theatre. Yet somehow there is this deep embarrass-ment in me that I feel so intensely about a 'game'.

I also realize something quite bizarre and shocking: as I've got older, football has become too painful for me. Now I prefer not to watch it, even on TV, for I don't like the emotional ups and downs it induces in me. Or I will sometimes watch two teams who I don't care about. Sometimes I watch Italian football on TV on Sundays. This is far superior to British football – I marvel at the technical skill and the flair, but it doesn't excite me, for in that position, *I am not a fan*. Just as I no longer want to fall in love with anyone, and no longer want to watch Ingmar Bergman films, I no longer want to be a fan.

A RELATIONSHIP

It is astonishing how unconscious the influence of sport can be. I had been writing this book for over a year, when I had a realization about sport while standing in a sport shop, waiting to buy two hockey sticks! I should explain a little further.

When I go on holiday in summer to Norfolk with my family, my son and I play the following games in the garden: football, cricket, badminton, hockey, basketball. We also go fishing and play various unofficial games such as french cricket, 'leggy', and certain improvised games involving the dog! What is all this activity for?

In the case of my son, one might argue that all this activity helps him, as a teenager, actually inhabit his body and his gender and his sexuality. For myself, I am not so sure. I also inhabit my body – for me this is an intense relief after spending months working as a psychotherapist and writer. Somehow, sport takes me out of myself, back to nature one might say, back to something primitive. Interestingly, my partner spends many hours gardening, another form of back-to-nature maybe. Our games mainly bore her. Is this because she was not educated in sport, as boys undoubtedly are? Yet of course there are many women who do enjoy such games and sports.

But something else strikes me about this physical activity: it is the way my son and I relate to each other. Sport provides a medium through which our relationship can be conducted. In the culture I grew up in, mothers and daughters did this through going shopping, making clothes and so on. One might laugh at this picture of males frantically relating to each other through sport. Is it a prime example of male autism, an inability to speak? I would say not. Rather, it is a way of relating through the body, not the mind.

It releases our aggression, our companionship, our need for each other, in a safe and non-threatening way. We can inhabit our flesh and lose our ghostliness, that spectral insubstantiality that so many men have. That peculiar feeling of not really being in the world, of being non-corporeal, finds an antidote here, just as in the frantic games of football I played at school thirty years ago. It strikes me that men have a desperate hunger for such bodily grounding since they are so ungrounded in our culture, robbed of their physical, instinctual and emotional life.

10 Conclusions

One word that comes to mind, after surveying these images of men, and some images used by men, in a wide variety of genres and media, is *ambivalence*. Just as Superman hides the diffident figure of Clark Kent, so many other images of men are more complex than first meets the eye. Thus perhaps the most famous, or infamous, images of male depredation are found in pornography, yet I have argued that these images also reveal intense deprivation and infantile yearning.

Similarly, the western hero is not simply a white male conqueror: he also embodies a brooding sense of unease, mutilation, unwantedness. And the baroque image of the heavy metal singer – projecting a febrile animalism, with his gold chains, shaggy mane, and bare torso – may represent for the male spectator less a domineering attitude towards women, than a homoerotic connection that provides a comforting refuge from women.

The same ambivalence can be found in an action film such as *Die Hard* – at one level, an out and out assertion of male control and supremacy, as Bruce Willis lords it over foreign terrorists, police, the FBI and his own wife. Yet a film such as this also strikes me as a cry of male hysteria. The male body is shown as a bloody crucified one; and Willis is compelled to crawl through ventilation shafts and lift shafts, in his effort to be reborn. In her book *Spectacular Bodies*, Yvonne Tasker says of the 'muscular action cinema' that 'increasingly the powerful white hero is a figure who *operates in the margins*, while continuing to represent dominance' [my emphasis].[1]

Die Hard also illustrates a tendency for the male body to be increasingly presented as a spectacle. This extends across many media – cinema, pop music, advertising, sport. The male body has become objectified as a site of crisis and hysteria, but also as a place of beauty and strength.

To an extent, it is a *dumb body*, that cannot speak fluently in words, but must speak through its musculature and its actions. It is narcissistic, obsessed with itself, using itself as a bulwark against others: 'the body of the hero is the sole space that is safe'.[2]

The male body is a very complex sign today: at times it is also feminized and eroticized – for example in pop music and advertising – while there is also something desperate about its self-aggrandizement in the action cinema and in sport. It seems likely that the male body is being used to describe semi-conscious shifts in gender, sexuality and power.

MALE EXPERTISE AND DISINTEGRATION

There seems to have been an historical change in the depiction of masculinity in the twentieth century. Whereas the first half of the century presented countless images of the upright white male, in control, dominating women and non-white males, the second half of the century has seen an increasing destitution and dereliction in the male image. For example, the horror film began to show men, not as gallant rescuers of female victims, but as horrific monsters themselves, or alternatively, as the victims of female monsters. The western adopted a note of defeat: as Philip French says in his book *Westerns*:

> The most marked characteristic of the genre since the early fifties has been its increasing emphasis not upon victory and success, but upon losing – the suggestion that to remain true to oneself will almost certainly result in defeat.[3]

French's comments posit an interesting collision between authenticity and social acceptability, suggesting that whereas in earlier periods, such as the Victorian age, men were seen as upholders of the social order, and conventional masculinity as part of the cement that held it together, twentieth-century culture has begun to focus more on the damage done to men by society, and the struggle between conformism and personal integrity that goes on for the individual male.

This change can be seen in many genres. For example, whereas the pinnacle of Victorian boys' fiction is *Tom Brown's Schooldays*, with its proselytizing tone and its patriotic and conservative ethos, boys' fiction in the twentieth century became much more anarchic and rebellious. One can cite, for example, Richmal Crompton's superb series of stories about William Brown, who subverts all signs of social order, including vicars, 'swanky kids' and wing-commanders seeking his sister's attentions. Such fiction does not attempt to groom boys for their future role as experts and leaders, but celebrates their anti-social tendencies and their resistance to the adult world:

> He was an alien being – a clean little boy in a neat suit, with a fashionable mother and sister. He was beyond the pale, an outsider, a pariah, a creature to be mocked and jeered at. The position galled William. He was, by instinct, on the side of the lawless – the anti-respectable.[4]

One could argue that boy's fiction had simply become more realistic and less tendentious, but this in itself is a crucial shift.

In the same way, rock 'n' roll and rock music have represented rebellious and noisy explosions of energy, that tended to subvert British and American gentility and decorum. It is interesting that British rock music has been so influential throughout the world, and has had a much 'harder' edge than most European popular music.

Britain presents a fascinating case-study, since post-imperial history has subjected the male role to a fierce scrutiny. No longer 'monarch of all he surveys', the British male is prey to enormous confusion or tension. To some extent, popular music has helped to articulate some of these tensions. The cinema has been less available as a medium, since the British film industry has a vestigial existence , but one can cite the 1994 comedy, *Four Weddings and a Funeral*, as an expression of the 'useless male', Hugh Grant playing a man repeatedly struck by disaster, often self induced.

But American masculinity also seems crisis-torn in the post-war era, despite the political and economic dominance of the United States. One of the significant cultural developments in post-war America is the decline of the western, for in the post-Vietnam era the traditional western framework was simply too anachronistic and morally naive. The spaghetti western, imported from Europe, produced instead a vision of nihilism and self-parody.

The action cinema, dominant in the American popular cinema of the 80s, can be interpreted as a 'Reaganite' conservative expression, but I think this grants too much coherence to such films. Such male images as Rambo, the Terminator and RoboCop, or the stars of the 'muscular cinema' – Schwarzenegger, Bruce Willis, Stallone – can be seen partly as eruptions of 'macho fascism', but this ignores the massive crises which inhabit all of these films and their heroes, something Barbara Creed calls 'phallic panic'.[5] For example, in *Predator*, Schwarzenegger is confronted with a mysterious alien creature, who proves so elusive that eventually he asks plaintively: 'Who the hell are you?' One plausible answer is that this monstrous being is a mirror image of himself.

A MALE REFUGE?

I have already quoted Angela McRobbie's comment that some kinds of pop music may allow men a 'refuge from heterosexuality'.[6] I think this is a profound insight, not only into the music she was discussing, but to other cultural forms. If we think of sporting events, and certain film genres such as the western and the horror film, we can see a similar kind of hiding place.

Is it fanciful to relate this to the 'men's hut' commonly found in pre-industrial cultures, a place where men congregate, and where a variety of rituals takes place? Is the men's hut simply an emblem of male domination? No doubt it is partly that, but it is also a refuge.

I have argued that masculinity imposes many onerous burdens on men, and therefore these refuges permit some kind of escape from such responsibilities. For example in the western, men indulge in a myth concerned not with building towns, or raising families, but with a rough-hewn and minimalist culture, men against men, but also men with men. The western also involves a resistance to technology and a regression to pre-sexual identities, where a man's best friend may be his horse, and where women are a threat.

This argument suggests that machismo itself is not simply a monolithic male tyranny. It also represents a form of homoerotic refuge from women, and from heterosexuality. Machismo is deeply narcissistic, and in activities such as body-building, the male body becomes a home from home.

UTOPIA AND THE MALE WOUND

I have argued that popular culture partly shows a utopian restitution being made to men. In westerns, men live in the sensuous landscape of Eden, and are permitted a kind of homoerotic ecstasy of death and love. In rock music we see an orgiastic attempt to dissolve into a single experience that blurs the boundaries of mind and body. Pornography presents a sexual paradise, where repression is unknown, where desires and actions are one, and the masturbatory wish is father to the masturbatory (not the coital) deed. Pornography presents a messianic narcissism.

The action film has an almost hysterical recourse to the male body as a refuge from civilization. The pumped up pectorals of the muscular hero strike me as another utopian fantasy. The hero does not think, but flexes his muscles and becomes self-existent.[7] Thus in *Die Hard*, most forms of social existence seem to have failed – big business, the police, the FBI. Only the white male body stands between us and anarchy.

Men also seem to have a longing for death; a fascination with dismembered bodies (breasts, vaginas); a fascination mixed with horror about gender cross-over, and indeed a fascination with suicide. These are surely the result of masculinization itself, the process of becoming a man under patriarchy, which is deeply damaging.

GENDER LEAKAGE

'Official' masculinity is resolutely heterosexual and butch. However, there is plenty of evidence for a 'leakage' of homosexual and feminine attributes into the male image. This leakage can be found throughout popular culture: for example, in the male couple, one of the dominant structural forms in genres such as the western, the thriller, the police series. The male body has been foregrounded and eroticised in the last two decades, but there is more than a hint that such images are directed covertly at men. Furthermore, the exaggeration of the structure of the male body at times suggests an imitation of the female body, not a denial of it.

If we look in the reverse direction – that is, at how images of women have changed in the last twenty years – we can see the emergence of masculine traits. The female body is at times presented as a honed muscularity, rather than as the traditional feminine frills and curves. In narrative terms, the woman is able to occupy the place of hero, rather than heroine.

These remarks suggest that some degree of interpenetration between the sexes is going on. Popular culture permits an invaluable degree of experimentation in this respect: women can be given the role of doughty hero, as in *Silence of the Lambs*; men can be shown as moody and menstrual, as in the styles of acting derived from Brando, James Dean and Montgomery Clift.[8]

It is impossible to predict how far such interpenetration might go, but various cultural forms, such as drag, permit a complete blending of sexes and genders, and many popular films have also shown such fusions, for example, *The Crying Game*, *Farewell My Concubine*, *Mrs Doubtfire*.

SUBJECTS, OBJECTS AND OPPRESSION

Genres such as heavy metal rock music, the western and pornography, albeit very different from each other in content and style, have this in common: they appear to construct an image, or a position, of masculine prowess and virility. But how do we relate this to the psycho-social context? Do these genres simply help in the creation and consolidation of patriarchal hegemony? I have suggested something rather different in this study: that such genres also evoke a compensatory sense of power for those who are powerless. I suggest that some of the men who use such genres are not seeking a reinforcement of an established male position of strength, but are struggling to build islands amidst a crumbling landscape, where men feel useless and surplus to requirements.

In the immediate instance, one might relate this powerlessness to the economic crises that have plagued Western capitalism during the 80s and 90s, involving unemployment in the traditional heavy industries, a general sense of social disintegration and instability, and also a questioning of traditional masculine identities by women, gay men, and others.

But one can also suggest that this feeling of angst and despair is not at all new in popular culture: for example, it has constantly fertilized popular music, from the black blues to white country music. These are the musics that 'groan', that speak of oppression, suffering and stoicism. They also react against those conditions, and celebrate sexuality and pleasure.

To take a specific example, the fantasies embodied in western (cowboy) mythology can be related to the growth of an industrial, commercial and bureaucratic society: the fantasy is compensatory and utopian. There was a golden age, when freedom was available, when bureaucracy was unknown, when the land was open, when 'justice' was personal and honourable, not administrative and vicarious. But such a fantasy attains a high degree of intensity precisely when these conditions do not exist, just as Christianity, with its ecstatic promise of salvation, has flourished amongst those who are unfree and in chains. Thus Marx describes religion as 'the heart of a heartless world'.[9]

Another clear example can be found in sport, which, for American and British black youth, has become one of the avenues of self-assertion in societies which block many others for them. Black sport has become famous for its sense of style, virtuosity, 'cool pose', in the words of the sociologist Richard Majors, who argues that 'a black man may be impotent in the intellectual, political and corporate world, but he can nevertheless display a potent personal style from the pulpit, in entertainment, and in athletic competition'.[10]

But am I suggesting, via the argument that many heavily masculine genres are attempts to deal with modern alienation and a lack of power, that men have not oppressed women, but have been oppressed? That would be an undialectical view. Rather, men are both the subjects and objects of oppression: they oppress women, but are themselves oppressed by patriarchal capitalism. Indeed, one can suggest that part of their oppressiveness arises *because they feel so oppressed*. Surely, it is a psycho-political law in all cultures that the oppressed look around – not only to retaliate against the oppressor, but also for someone else to oppress.

Here it is worth considering the way Marx defines 'the inversion of subject into object and vice versa' as one of the defining traits of capitalism. This is not simply an ideological inversion (an appearance), but a material one.[11] Marx is referring to the paradox that the worker – who in one way is the object of capital – is actually its subject, since it is his labour which creates wealth. But alienation gives rise to the 'rule of the product over the producer'.[12]

We can relate this analysis to the contemporary attempt to define the male position in cinema, indeed in patriarchal culture as a whole, as a subject position, and the female as the object position. My argument is that the male is simultaneously an 'object' of oppression under patriarchal capitalism, and also someone in the position of 'subject' over women. That is, he is able to reduplicate and invert his own oppression by oppressing women. In a sense woman, as the victim of his own male ascendancy, provides him with a distorted image of his own victimhood.

This idea has fascinating consequences in relation to projection and identification in cultural works: for example, the image of the woman in pain, so common in Western culture, does not simply appeal to male sadistic power, but also to his own masochism, and his own secret knowledge that he is a victim. Similarly the images of dominance, seen in such genres as the action film, do not simply reduplicate the actualities of social existence, but also compensate for them.

FEAR AND LOATHING

One interesting aspect of some male genres is the distaste they arouse in certain critics and audiences. One can cite for example the way in which the action cinema is often reviewed patronizingly or disapprovingly – Yvonne Tasker quotes a review which describes Schwarzenegger as 'American Fascist Art exemplified', and another which describes *Dirty Harry* as a 'fascist love poem'.[13] Quite a number of Clint Eastwood's films have excited similar disapproval, and Paul Smith's book, *Clint Eastwood*, is palpably hostile to its subject. And the 'Rambo' films have probably provoked more critical excitement and dismay than any other group of films of the past twenty years.

In relation to sport, I noticed a piece in *Radio Times* which bemoaned the attention given to the World Cup on TV, and described it as a '*tidal wave of testosterone* engulfing us from the TV set' [my emphasis].[14] But many other male cultural forms – heavy metal rock, pornography, computer games, rap music – excite similar disapproval and fear.

Of course at one level these negative feelings are perfectly explicable, for it is arguable that some male genres do exhibit a supremacist and brutal tone that is repugnant both to feminists and to liberal audiences in general.

But I think there is more to it than this. The example of Elvis Presley sticks in my mind, for to begin with he aroused great hostility in Middle America through his exhibition of sexuality and working-class energy and confidence. It is particularly the working-class male and the black male who arouse fear and hatred, and their sexuality, combativity and refusal to be cowed make white middle-class people, including academics, very anxious.

The other point of interest is the dismay with which liberal critics view the audiences of such cultural products. Thus Derek Malcolm in the *Guardian* commented of *Rambo: First Blood Part II*, that 'only a fool would not be worried that an action movie of this banality should be received with such evident satisfaction'.[15]

These arguments take us back to the debate between pleasure and ideology, for some liberal critics have seemed to take delight in pointing out the 'bad' ideology in popular pleasures. The weak point in their argument is the assumption that the ideology is read off the text in a literal and linear fashion. This approach makes many assumptions about the meaning of texts, and tends to treat audiences as uncreative, passive receivers.

TEXT AND AUDIENCE

This book has presented some of my own interpretations of certain texts: in that sense, it is unashamedly subjective. But there is an important issue here: it is clear that interpretation is *always subjective*, since it flows from a relationship between text and audience. This book indicates the relationship between various texts and myself.

In this sense, the Lacanian view that texts help to create subjects can be reversed: audiences also help to create texts! The text on the printed page or in the film-can is inert, and only springs to life when someone experiences it. This is why it is impossible, for example, to define pornography, for the pornographic content does not reside in a particular image, but in a relationship between that image and someone's imagination.

These ideas have led me continually to interrogate the apparent coherence of masculine images in popular culture. The notion of 'multiple identification' has startling consequences for a theory of textual interpretation, since it dissolves any fixed notion that male viewers identify with fictional males, and so on. This rather monolithic view of interpretation has led to some very one-dimensional ideas – for example, that men look at images of women in order to 'possess' them, but look at images of men in order to 'be' them. I have argued that the reverse connections also go on.

In relation to the divisions between pleasure, aesthetics and ideology, it seems clear that a multi-level model of interpretation has to be constructed, that embraces the sensuous pleasures of the text, the various ideological meanings, the psychological symbolism, the contexts in which the text is produced and received, the nature of the audience, and so on. This would be a model of *textual (or semiotic) incoherence*, just as depth psychology is a model of psychological incoherence in the individual human being. So far from striving to arrive at a coherent view of a text as a semiotic homogeneity or uniformity, the task is to unpack it and arrive at a set of relationships between texts and audiences, relationships which by their nature are various and variable.

Notes

1 Introduction

1. Susan Faludi, *Backlash: The Undeclared War Against Women* (London: Chatto & Windus, 1992) Chapter 5; Lynne Segal, *Straight Sex: the Politics of Pleasure* (London: Virago, 1994) pp. 271–5.
2. Contradictions in Rambo are discussed by Yvonne Tasker, *Spectacular Bodies: Gender, Genre and the Action Cinema* (London and New York: Routledge, 1993) pp. 91–108; and by William Warner, 'Spectacular Action: Rambo and the Popular Pleasures of Pain', in Lawrence Grossberg, Cary Nelson and Paula Treichler (eds), *Cultural Studies* (New York and London: Routledge, 1992) pp. 672–88.
3. Dylan Thomas, *Collected Poems: 1934–1952* (London: Dent, 1952) p. vii: 'these poems ... are written for the love of Man and in praise of God, and I'd be a damn' fool if they weren't'.
4. See Lynda Nead, *The Female Nude: Art, Obscenity and Sexuality* (London and New York: Routledge, 1992); Marina Warner, *Monuments and Maidens: The Allegory of the Female Form* (London: Picador, 1987); S. R. Suleiman, *The Female Body in Western Culture: Contemporary Perspectives* (Cambridge, Mass.: Harvard University Press, 1986).
5. See Dick Hebdige, 'Towards a Cartography of Taste: 1935–1962', in B. Waites, T. Bennett and G. Martin (eds), *Popular Culture: Past and Present* (London and New York: Routledge, 1989) pp. 194–218.

2 Approaches to Gender

1. See H. L. Radtke and H. J. Stam (eds), *Gender and Power: Social Relations in Theory and Practice* (London: Sage, 1994).
2. See Stephanie L. Twin, 'Women and Sport', in D. Spivey (ed.), *Sport in America: New Historical Perspectives* (Westport: Greenwood Press, 1985) pp. 193–217.
3. Beatrix Campbell, *Goliath: Britain's Dangerous Places* (London: Methuen, 1993)
4. Ibid., p. 319.
5. Ibid., p. 324.
6. Lynne Segal, *Is the Future Female? Troubled Thoughts on Contemporary Feminism* (London: Virago, 1987) p. 17.
7. Lynne Segal, *Slow Motion: Changing Masculinities, Changing Men* (London: Virago, 1990) p. xiii.
8. *The Costs of Suicide: Ripples on the Pond* (Slough: The Samaritans, 1994) pp. 4–5.
9. Kate Millett, *Sexual Politics* (London: Sphere, 1972) p. 329.
10. Roger Horrocks, *Masculinity in Crisis: Myths, Fantasies and Realities* (Basingstoke: Macmillan, 1994) Chapter 6.

11. D. H. Lawrence, *Women in Love* (Harmondsworth: Penguin, 1963) pp. 389 and 224.

12. See Jeffrey Weeks, *Coming Out: Homosexual Politics in Britain from the Nineteenth Century to the Present* (London: Quartet, 1977).

13. Michel Foucault, *The History of Sexuality*, Volume I, *An Introduction* (Harmondsworth: Penguin, 1990) p. 103.

14. See L. Segal, *Straight Sex*, pp. 183–8.

15. Leslie Fiedler, *Love and Death in the American Novel* (London: Paladin, 1970).

16. Wayne Studer, *Rock on the Wild Side: Gay Male Images in Popular Music of the Rock Era* (San Francisco: Leyland, 1994); Mark Simpson, *Male Impersonators: Men Performing Masculinity* (London: Cassell, 1994); Marjorie Garber, *Vested Interests: Cross-Dressing and Cultural Anxiety* (Harmondsworth: Penguin, 1992).

17. Eve Kosofsky Sedgwick, *Between Men: English Literature and Male Homosocial Desire* (New York: Columbia University Press, 1985); and *Epistemology in the Closet* (London: Harvester Wheatsheaf, 1991).

18. E. Sedgwick, *Epistemology in the Closet*, p. 186.

19. Mark Simpson, *Male Impersonators*, p. 4.

20. S. Freud, *Three Essays on Sexuality*, in *On Sexuality*, The Pelican Freud Library, Volume 7 (Harmondsworth: Penguin, 1977) pp. 56–7.

21. See for example Michael Warner, 'Homo-narcissism; or Heterosexuality', in J. A. Boone and M. Cadden (eds), *Engendering Men: The Question of Male Feminist Criticism* (New York and London: Routledge, 1990) pp. 190–206.

22. S. Freud, *Three Essays on Sexuality*, p. 86; for a historical survey, see Kenneth Lewes, *The Psychoanalytic Theory of Male Homosexuality* (London and New York: Quartet Books, 1989).

23. For a description of a non-capitalist culture where sexuality is of great political importance, see Maurice Godelier, *The Making of Great Men: Male Domination and Power among the New Guinea Baruya* (Cambridge: CUP, 1986).

24. Jeffrey Weeks, *Sexuality and its Discontents* (London and New York: Routledge, 1989) pp. 13–14.

25. Louis Althusser, 'Ideology and Ideological State Apparatuses (Notes Towards an Investigation)', in *Lenin and Philosophy and other essays* (London: NLB, 1971) pp. 123–73.

26. R. W. Connell, *Gender and Power* (Cambridge: Polity Press, 1987) p. ix; Caroline Ramazanoglu, *Feminism and the Contradictions of Oppression* (London: Routledge, 1989) p. 14.

27. See L. Segal, *Is the Future Female?*, pp. 236–46.

28. See particularly David D. Gilmore, *Manhood in the Making* (London and New York: Yale University Press, 1990).

29. For an extended discussion of the relations between Marxism and anthropology, see Donald L. Donham, *History, Power, Ideology: Central Issues in Marxism and Anthropology* (Cambridge: CUP, 1990).

30 L. Hudson and B. Jacot, *The Way Men Think* (New Haven & London: Yale University Press, 1991) p. 49.

31. Ibid., Chapter 4. See also Robert Stoller, *Presentations of Gender* (New Haven and London: Yale University Press, 1985).

32. Erich Fromm, 'The Method and Function of an Analytic Social Psychology', *The Crisis of Psychoanalysis* (Harmondsworth: Penguin, 1973) p. 158.

33. Ibid., p. 155.

34. I am using an approach derived both from Jung, and from structuralist analysis: see C. G. Jung (ed.), *Man and his Symbols* (New York: Dell, 1973); Roland Barthes, *Mythologies* (London: Vintage, 1993); James J. Liszka, *The Semiotic of Myth: A Critical Study of the Symbol* (Bloomington: Indiana University Press, 1989).

35. Richard Dyer discusses this throughout *Stars* (London: BFI, 1979), particularly section 3, 'Stars as Images'.

36. See Chapter 4, section on 'Jungian Criticism'.

37. For an extended discussion of these aspects of myth, see J. J. Liszka, *The Semiotic of Myth*, pp. 164–202.

38. C. Geertz, 'Deep Play: Notes on the Balinese Cockfight', in *The Interpretation of Cultures* (London: Hutchinson, 1975) pp. 412–53; T. H. Breen, 'Horses and Gentlemen: The Cultural Significance of Gambling Among the Gentry of Virginia', in D. Spivey (ed.), *Sport in America* pp. 3–24.

39. On Roosevelt, see Edward Buscombe, *The BFI Companion to the Western* (London: André Deutsch, 1988) p. 214; on Reagan and the western, see Paul Smith, *Clint Eastwood: A Cultural Production* (London: UCL Press, 1993) pp. 192–3, 199–205.

40. See J. A. Hawkins (ed.), *Explaining Language Universals* (Oxford: Basil Blackwell, 1988).

41. Thomas Gregor, *Anxious Pleasures: the Sexual Life of an Amazonian People* (Chicago: University of Chicago Press, 1985), cited in D. Gilmore, *Manhood in the Making*, p. 10.

42. See Eve Sedgwick's discussion of the 'nature'/'nurture' opposition in *Epistemology in the Closet*, pp. 40–4.

43. See R. J. Stoller, 'Near Miss: "Sex Change" Treatment and its Evaluation', *Presentations of Gender*, pp. 152–70.

44. For further discussion of the relations between sex, gender and sexuality, see Lynne Segal, *Straight Sex*, pp. 245–53 and 267–74; Eve Sedgwick, *Epistemology in the Closet*, pp. 27–35; and the essays in *Sexuality: A Reader*, ed. Feminist Review (London: Virago, 1987).

3   Studying Popular Culture

1. See Antony Eastope, *Literary into Cultural Studies* (London and New York: Routledge, 1991).

2. Ien Eng, *Watching Dallas: Soap Opera and the Melodramatic Imagination* (London and New York: Methuen, 1985).

3. Allison James, 'Confections, Concoctions and Conceptions', in B. Waites, T. Bennett and G. Martin (eds), *Popular Culture: Past and Present*, pp. 294–307.

4. Dick Hebdige, *Subculture: The Meaning of Style* (London and New York: Routledge, 1979) p. 2.

5. See Dave Rimmer, *Like Punk Never Happened: Culture Club and the New Pop* (London: Faber and Faber, 1985).

6. F. de Saussure, *Course in General Linguistics* (New York: McGraw-Hill, 1966) p. 120.

7. Jonathan Culler, *Saussure* (Glasgow: Fontana, 1976) pp. 24–6.

8. F. de Saussure, *Course*, p. 113.

9. Pierre Bourdieu, 'The Historical Genesis of a Pure Aesthetic', in *The Field of Cultural Production: Essays on Art and Literature* (Cambridge: Polity Press, 1993) p. 259.

10. Ibid., pp. 259–61.

11. Janet Thumim, *Celluloid Sisters: Women and Popular Cinema* (Basingstoke: Macmillan, 1992) p. 148.

12. S. Faludi, *Backlash*, Chapter 5.

13. Sigmund Freud, *Jokes and their Relation to the Unconscious* (Harmondsworth: Penguin, 1976).

14. Graeme Turner, *British Cultural Studies: an Introduction* (New York: Routledge, 1992) p. 65; Turner summarizes hegemony, pp. 65–7.

15. Leon Trotsky, *Collected Writings and Speeches on Britain*, Volume One (London: New Park, 1974) p. 15.

16. See the chapter 'Big Tits!' in Mark Simpson's *Male Impersonators*, pp. 21–44.

17. Lucy Fischer, *Shot/Counter-Shot: Film Tradition and Women's Cinema* (Basingstoke: Macmillan, 1989).

18. Laura Mulvey, 'Afterthoughts on "Visual Pleasure and Narrative Cinema" inspired by *Duel in the Sun*', in E. Ann Kaplan (ed.), *Psychoanalysis and Cinema* (New York and London: Routledge, 1990) pp. 24–35.

19. This debate is summarized in G. Turner, *British Cultural Studies*, pp. 106–10. On soaps see Ien Eng, *Watching 'Dallas'*; also Tania Modleski, *Loving with a Vengeance: Mass-Produced Fantasies for Women* (New York and London: Routledge, 1990).

20. On gay fans of actions films, see Yvonne Tasker, *Spectacular Bodies*, pp. 127–8, 154–5, 162–4; on gay metal fans, see Robert Walser, *Running with the Devil: Power, Gender and Madness in Heavy Metal Music* (Hanover: Wesleyan University Press, 1993) pp. 115–16.

21. See Angela McRobbie (ed.), *Zoot Suits and Second-Hand Dresses: An Anthology of Fashion and Music* (Basingstoke: Macmillan, 1989) Part II, 'Transgressions', pp. 121–80.

22. See, for example, L. C. Knights, *An Approach to 'Hamlet'* (London: Chatto & Windus, 1964).

23. D. W. Winnicott, *Playing and Reality* (Harmondsworth: Penguin, 1986).

24. See, for example, M. Masud R. Khan, 'The Empty Headed', in *Hidden Selves: Between Theory and Practice in Psychoanalysis* (London: Maresfield, 1989) pp. 134–5.

25. D. W. Winnicott, 'Playing: Creative Activity and the Search for the Self' in *Playing and Reality*, pp. 62–75.

26. On rock music, see David Buxton, 'Rock Music, the Star System and the Rise of Consumerism', in Simon Frith and Andrew Goodwin (eds), *On Record: Rock, Pop and the Written Word* (London: Routledge, 1990) pp. 427–40; on leisure and capitalism, see John Clarke and Chas Critcher, *The Devil Makes Work: Leisure in Capitalist Britain* (Basingstoke: Macmillan, 1985).

27. Allan F. Moore, *Rock: The Primary Text: Developing a Musicology of Rock* (Buckingham: The Open University, 1993) p. 9.
28. T. W. Adorno, 'On Popular Music', in S. Frith and A. Goodwin (eds), *On Record*, p. 311.
29. Ibid., p. 311.
30. Susan McClary and Robert Walser, 'Start Making Sense! Musicology Wrestles with Rock', in S. Frith and A. Goodwin (eds), *On Record*, p. 283.
31. Robert Walser, *Running with the Devil*, p. 60; see also John Shepherd, *Music as Social Text* (Cambridge: Polity Press, 1991).
32. Simon Frith, *Sound Effects: Youth, Leisure and the Politics of Rock 'n Roll* (New York: Pantheon, 1981) p. 55.
33. S. McClary and R. Walser, 'Start Making Sense!' p. 287.
34. See, for example, Greil Marcus, *In the Fascist Bathroom: Writings on Punk 1977–1992* (Harmondsworth: Viking, 1993); Dick Hebdige, *Subculture*, pp. 62–70; 106–12.
35. S. McClary and R. Walser, 'Start Making Sense!', p. 287.
36. See Philip Tagg, 'From refrain to rave: the decline of figure and the rise of ground', *Popular Music* 13:2 (1994) pp. 209–22; Barbara Bradby, 'Sampling sexuality: gender, technology and the body in dance music', *Popular Music* 12:2 (1993) pp. 155–76; Tony Langois, 'Can You Feel It? DJs and the House Music Culture in the UK', *Popular Music* 11:2 (1992) pp. 229–38.
37. For example, Paul Smith's *Clint Eastwood: A Cultural Production*.
38. See, for example, on Hitchcock, Tania Modleski, *The Women Who Knew Too Much: Hitchcock and Feminist Film Theory* (New York and London: Methuen, 1988); on Eastwood, Amy Taubin, 'An Upright Man', *Sight and Sound* 3:9 (1993) pp. 9–10.

4 Psychological Approaches to Culture

1. Lionel Trilling, 'Freud and Literature', in David Lodge (ed.), *20th Century Literary Criticism: A Reader* (London: Longman, 1972) p. 279.
2. Ernest Jones, *Hamlet and Oedipus* (New York: W. W. Norton, 1949).
3. L. Trilling, 'Freud and Literature', p. 287.
4. D. W. Harding, 'Regulated Hatred: an aspect of the work of Jane Austen', in D. Lodge (ed.), *20th Century Literary Criticism*, p. 266.
5. Norman O. Brown, 'The Excremental Vision', in *20th Century Literary Criticism*, pp. 509–26.
6. Jacques Lacan, *Ecrits: A Selection* (London: Tavistock/Routledge, 1989) p. 128.
7. J. Lacan, 'The mirror stage as formative of the function of the I', *Ecrits*, pp. 1–7.
8. J. Lacan, 'Aggressivity in psychoanalysis', *Ecrits*, p. 28.
9. See, for example, D. T. Suzuki, *The Zen Doctrine of No Mind* (London: Rider, 1974).
10. See Mary Anne Doane, 'Remembering Women: Psychical and Historical Constructions in Film Theory', in E. A. Kaplan (ed.), *Psychoanalysis and Cinema*, pp. 45–8.

11. See Elizabeth Grosz, *Jacques Lacan: A Feminist Introduction* (London and New York: Routledge, 1990) p. 116–26; also Lynne Segal, *Straight Sex*, pp. 130–40.

12. Constance Penley, 'Introduction: The Lady Doesn't Vanish: Feminism and Film Theory', in C. Penley (ed.), *Feminism and Film Theory* (New York: Routledge, 1988) pp. 6–7.

13. S. Freud, *An Outline of Psycho-analysis* (London: The Hogarth Press, 1973) p. 11.

14. Karen Horney, 'The Dread of Woman', in *Feminine Psychology* (New York: W. W. Norton, 1973) p. 144.

15. K. Horney, 'On the Genesis of the Castration Complex in Women', in *Feminine Psychology*, p. 38.

16. Barbara Creed, *The Monstrous-Feminine: Film, Feminism and Psychoanalysis* (London and New York: Routledge, 1993) pp. 24ff.

17. Tania Modleski also discusses the 'devouring mother' in *The Women Who Knew Too Much*, pp. 106–8.

18. Amy Taubin, 'Invading Bodies: *Alien*[3] and the Trilogy', *Sight and Sound* 2:3 (July 1992).

19. Barbara Creed, *The Monstrous-Feminine*, pp. 20–1.

20. Ibid., p. 165; see also Barbara Creed, 'Phallic panic: male hysteria and *Dead Ringers*', *Screen* 31:2 (1990) pp. 125–46.

21. Edward F. Edinger, *Ego and Archetype: Individuation and the Religious Function of the Psyche* (Harmondsworth: Penguin, 1983) Chapter 2, 'The Alienated Ego'.

22. See C. G. Jung (ed.), *Man and his Symbols*.

23. On the Trickster, see Joseph Henderson, 'Ancients Myths and Modern Man', in *Man and his Symbols*, pp. 103ff. For a political analysis of the Bond stories, see T. Bennett and T. Woollacott, *Bond and Beyond: the Political Career of a Popular Hero* (London: Macmillan, 1988); for a structuralist analysis, see Umberto Eco, 'The Narrative Structure in Fleming', in B. Waites, T. Bennett and G. Martin (eds), *Popular Culture*, pp. 242–62.

24. Marie Louise von Franz, *Interpretation of Fairy Tales* (Dallas: Spring Publications, 1987).

25. See Greil Marcus, *Dead Elvis: A Chronicle of a Cultural Obsession* (Harmondsworth: Penguin, 1991).

26. Shorter Oxford English Dictionary.

27. Laura Mulvey, 'Visual Pleasure and Narrative Cinema', in C. Penley, *Feminism and Film Theory*, p. 57.

28. See the discussion in Jackie Byars, *All That Hollywood Allows: Re-reading Gender in 1950s Melodrama* (London: Routledge, 1991) Chapter 4; Janet Thumim, *Celluloid Sisters*, Chapter 6; Constance Penley, *Feminism and Film Theory*; and E. Ann Kaplan, *Psychoanalysis and Cinema*.

29. Laura Mulvey, 'Afterthoughts on "Visual Pleasure and Narrative Cinema" inspired by *Duel in the Sun*', in C. Penley, *Feminism and Film Theory*, p. 79.

30. See S. Cohan and Ina R. Hark (eds), *Screening the Male: Exploring Masculinities in the Hollywood Cinema* (London & New York: Routledge: 1993); and Pat Kirkham and Janet Thumim (eds), *You Tarzan: Masculinity, Movies and Men* (London: Lawrence & Wishart, 1993).

31. For an extensive illustration of this, see Mark Simpson's *Male Impersonators*.

32. Carol Clover, *Men, Women and Chainsaws: Gender in Modern Horror Film* (London: BFI, 1992) Chapter 1.

33. Donald Spoto, *The Life of Alfred Hitchcock: The Dark Side of Genius* (London: Collins, 1983) p. 419.

34. William Schoell, *Don't Go Into the Shower: The Shocker Film Phenomenon* (London: Robinson Publishing, 1988) p. 55; Carol Clover, *Men, Women and Chainsaws*, pp. 23 and 46.

35. Janet Thumim, *Celluloid Sisters*, p. 189.

36. See Warren Farrell, *The Myth of Male Power: Why Men are the Disposable Sex* (London: Fourth Estate, 1994) pp. 243–5.

37. A point made by Tania Modleski in *The Women Who Knew Too Much*, p. 4.

38. Jean Domarchi, 'Knife in the Wound', in Jim Hillier (ed.), *Cahiers du Cinema: Volume I, The 1950s: Neo-Realism, Hollywood, New Wave* (London: Routledge & Kegan Paul, 1985) p. 246.

39. Jackie Byars, *All That Hollywood Allows*, p. 141.

40. Francois Truffaut, *Hitchcock* (London: Panther, 1969) p. 376.

41. Tania Modleski highlights Hitchcock's ambivalence about femininity in *The Women Who Knew Too Much*, p. 3.

42. Laura Mulvey, 'Visual Pleasure and Narrative Cinema', p. 63.

43. Steve Neale, 'Masculinity as Spectacle: Reflections on Men and Mainstream Cinema', in S. Cohan and Ina R. Hark (eds), *Screening the Male*, pp. 9–20; see also Richard Dyer on the male pin-up, 'Don't Look Now', *Screen* **23**:3–4 (1982) pp. 61–73.

44. See Cynthia J. Fuchs, 'The Buddy Politic', in *Screening the Male*, pp. 194–210.

45. Both excerpts can be found on the video, *Elvis '56* (Elvis '56 Inc., 1987).

46. See Michael A. Messner, 'Masculinities and Athletic Careers', in J. Lorber and S. A. Farrell (eds), *The Social Construction of Gender* (Newbury Park: Sage, 1991) pp. 60–75.

5 Westerns

1. Leslie A. Fiedler, *Love and Death in the American Novel*, pp. 182, 198–9.

2. Jane Tompkins, *West of Everything: The Inner Life of Westerns* (New York: Oxford University Press, 1992).

3. This idea is amplified in Andrew Ross, 'Cowboys, Cadillacs and Cosmonauts: Families, Film Genres, and Technocultures', in J. A. Boone and M. Cadden (eds), *Engendering Men*, pp. 87–101; for an economic analysis of westerns see Will Wright, *Six Guns and Society* (Berkeley: University of California Press, 1975).

4. Edward Buscombe, *The BFI Companion to the Western*, p. 181.

5. Ibid., pp. 35 and 427.

6. On 'women's westerns', see B. Ruby Rich, 'At home on the range', *Sight and Sound* **3**:11 (1993) pp. 18–23.

7. *The BFI Companion*, pp. 36–43.

8. See for example, William K. Everson, *The Hollywood Western* (New York: Citadel Press, 1992).

9. *The BFI Companion*, pp. 46–8.

10. Will Wright extracts some of the basic plots and narrative functions in westerns in *Six Guns and Society*, pp. 32–3, 41–8.
11. Jane Tompkins, *West of Everything*, p. 41.
12. Ibid., p. 144.
13. See Mark Simpson's analysis of *Unforgiven* in *Male Impersonators*, pp. 253–65.
14. On the 'professional' western see Will Wright, *Six Guns and Society*, pp. 85–122.
15. See Kim Newman, *Wild West Movies* (London: Bloomsbury, 1990) p. 147.
16. *The BFI Companion*, p. 265; Phil Hardy, *The Western* (London: Aurum Press, 1991) p. 255.
17. Larry McMurtry, *Lonesome Dove* (London: Pan, 1990) p. 781.
18. Ibid., p. 83.
19. For a negative view, see W. K. Everson, *The Hollywood Western*, p. 242.
20. *The BFI Companion*, p. 63; a full examination of Remington as a western painter can be found in M. E. Shapiro and P. H. Hassrick (eds), *Frederic Remington: The Masterworks* (New York: Saint Louis Art Museum, 1991).
21. Louis L'Amour, *The Lonesome Gods* (London: Century Publishing, 1984) pp. 350–1.
22. Walter Van Tilburg Clark, *The Ox-Bow Incident* (London: Arrow Books, 1973) p. 7.
23. Ibid., p. 238.
24. See Paul Smith, *Clint Eastwood*, pp. 151–72, 207–23.
25. Ibid., pp. 90–119.
26. See Amy Taubin, 'An Upright Man', *Sight and Sound* **3**:9 (1993) pp. 9–10.
27. Paul Smith's *Clint Eastwood* mounts a fierce critique of it.
28. Jane Tompkins,*West of Everything*, pp. 229–33.
29. For a summary, see Paul Smith, *Clint Eastwood*, pp. 151–72.
30. See 'Chinese Poems of Enlightenment and Death' in Lucien Stryk and Takashi Ikemoto (eds), *The Penguin Book of Zen Poetry* (Harmondsworth: Penguin, 1981) pp. 41–61.
31. Robin Morgan, *The Demon Lover: On the Sexuality of Terrorism* (London: Mandarin, 1990) p. 100.
32. Paul Smith, *Clint Eastwood*, p. 46.

6 Horror Films

1. Carol Clover, *Men, Women and Chainsaws*, pp. 6–11, 41–47, 199–205.
2. James Twitchell, *Dreadful Pleasures: An Anatomy of Modern Horror* (New York: Oxford University Press, 1985) pp. 69ff.
3. See Mark Jancovich, *Horror* (London: Batsford, 1992) pp. 109–11.
4. 'Paranoid' horror is discussed by Andrew Tudor, *Monsters and Mad Scientists: A Cultural History of the Horror Movie* (Oxford: Basil Blackwell, 1989) pp. 103ff and pp. 220ff, and by Barbara Creed, *The Monstrous-Feminine*, pp. 154–5.
5. See Mark Jancovich, *Horror*, Chapters 2 and 3.
6. Barbara Creed, *The Monstrous-Feminine*, p. 29.
7. Stephen King, *Danse Macabre* (London: Warner Books, 1993) pp. 132ff.

8. Barbara Creed, *The Monstrous-Feminine*, Chapter 2; also Amy Taubin, 'Invading Bodies: *Alien*³ and the Trilogy', *Sight and Sound* **2**:3 (July 1992).

9. Stephen King, *Danse Macabre*, pp. 198–9.

10. See Chapter 4, section on Lacan.

11. Charles Dickens, *Bleak House* (Ware: Wordsworth, 1993) p. 674.

12. George Eliot, *Middlemarch* (Harmondsworth: Penguin, 1966) p. 185.

13. Phil Hardy (ed.), *The Aurum Film Encyclopedia: Horror* (London: Aurum Press, 1985) p. 113.

14. M. Jancovich, *Horror*, p. 27.

15. David Pirie discusses this film in *A Heritage of Horror: The English Gothic Cinema 1946–1972* (London: Gordon Fraser, 1973) pp. 38–42, 66–74.

16. See Joan Smith, 'He Knows He Can Make Money Out Of You', *Mythologies* (revised ed.) (London and Boston: Faber and Faber, 1993) pp. 31–45.

17. The problematization of masculinity in horror is discussed by M. Jancovich, *Horror*, pp. 104–9.

18. Robin Wood discusses *Psycho* in *Hitchcock's Films Revisited* (New York: Columbia University Press, 1989) pp. 142–51.

19. J. Twitchell, *Dreadful Pleasures*, pp. 69–71.

20. B. Creed, *The Monstrous-Feminine*, pp. 1–3.

21. E. Grosz, *Jacques Lacan*, p. 117.

7 Pornography

1. See Linda Williams, 'Pornographies on\scene, or diff'rent strokes for diff'rent folks', in L. Segal and M. McIntosh (eds), *Sex Exposed: Sexuality and the Pornography Debate* (London: Virago Press, 1992) pp. 233–65.

2. Andrea Dworkin, *Pornography: Men Possessing Women* (London: The Women's Press, 1990) pp. 23 and 69.

3. Ibid., p. 64.

4. See, for example, Lynne Segal and Mary McIntosh (eds), *Sex Exposed*; P. C. Gibson and R. Gibson (eds), *Dirty Looks: Women, Pornography, Power* (London: BFI, 1993); Laura Kipnis, '(Male) Desire and (Female) Disgust: Reading *Hustler*', in L. Grossberg, C. Nelson and P. Treichler (eds), *Cultural Studies*, pp. 373–91. For a discussion of women's porn see Constance Penley, 'Feminism, Psychoanalysis and the Study of Popular Culture', in *Cultural Studies* pp. 479–500.

5. See Kathy Myers, 'Fashion 'n' Passion', *Screen* **23**:4 (1982) pp. 89–97.

6. See Linda Williams, *Hard Core: Power, Pleasure and the 'Frenzy of the Visible'* (London: Pandora, 1990) pp. 218–9.

7. John Stoltenberg, 'Pornography, Homophobia and Male Supremacy', in Catherine Itzin (ed.), *Pornography: Women, Violence and Civil Liberties* (Oxford: OUP, 1993) p. 150.

8. See R. J. Stoller, *Perversion: The Erotic Form of Hatred* (London: Quartet Books, 1977) pp. 6–7, 33–4, 118–19.

9. See R. J. Stoller, *Sexual Excitement* (London: Karnac, 1986) pp. xii–xiii; R. Stoller, *Perversion*, pp. 128–31.

10. Nik Douglas and Penny Slinger, *The Pillow Book: The Erotic Sentiment and the Paintings of India, Nepal, China and Japan* (New York: Destiny Books, 1986) p. 7.

11. *Pornography: The Longford Report* (London: Coronet, 1972) p. 100.
12. See Lynda Nead, *The Female Nude*, pp. 91–2; also L. Williams, *Hard Core*, pp. 11–15.
13. Kenneth Clark, *The Nude: A Study of Ideal Art* (London: John Murray, 1956) p. 335.
14. See John Berger, *Ways of Seeing* (London: BBC, 1972) p. 63, for a comparison of Manet's *Olympia* with the Titian *Venus of Urbino*.
15. L. Kipnis, '(Male) Desire and (Female) Disgust: Reading *Hustler*', p. 376.
16. These paintings are discussed by Marina Warner in *Monuments and Maidens*, pp. 241ff.
17. L. Kipnis, '(Male) Desire and (Female) Disgust', p. 375.
18. Galatians **5**: 16–25, New Oxford Annotated Bible.
19. See Carole S. Vance, 'Negotiating sex and gender in the Attorney General's Commission on Pornography', in L. Segal and M. McIntosh (eds), *Sex Exposed*, pp. 29–49.
20. L. Williams, *Hard Core*, pp. 48–57.
21. M. Warner, *Monuments and Maidens*, p. 251.
22. C. G. Jung, 'The Psychology of the Unconscious', *Two Essays on Analytical Psychology*, The Collected Works, Vol. 7 (London and Henley: Routledge & Kegan Paul, 1977) p. 71.
23. See Anne McClintock, 'Maid to Order: Commercial S/M and Gender Power', in P. C. and R. Gibson (eds), *Dirty Looks*, pp. 207–31.
24. The texts used were: *Park Lane*, *Men's World*, *Mayfair*, *Raider*, *Open Door*, *Blue Climax*, *Deep Throat II*, *Fuckin' Superstars*.
25. R. Stoller, *Perversion*, pp. 96–110.
26. Ibid., p. 96.
27. See L. Williams, *Hard Core*, pp. 1–2.
28. *Park Lane*, No. 75 (1993) p. 77.
29. Anne McClintock, 'Maid to Order', pp. 217–19.
30. See Margaret R. Miles, 'The Virgin's One Bare Breast: Female Nudity and Religious Meaning in Tuscan Early Renaissance Culture', in S. R. Suleiman (ed.), *The Female Body in Western Culture*.
31. R. Stoller, *Perversion*, pp. 3–4.
32. L. Williams, *Hard Core*, Chapter 4.
33. Ibid., p. 48.
34. Paul Theroux, *The Happy Isles of Oceania: Paddling the Pacific* (London: Hamish Hamilton, 1992) pp. 499–500.
35. L. Williams, *Hard Core*, p. 113.
36. Ibid., pp. 259–60.
37. Ibid., pp. 246–50.
38. Emma Richmond, *Take Away the Pride* (Richmond: Mills and Boon, 1988) p. 147.
39. *The Best of Men's World* (1993) p. 79.
40. Carol Clover, *Men, Women and Chainsaws*, Chapter 1.
41. *The Best of Men's World* (1993) p. 78.
42. Ibid, p. 70.
43. The text is *Jeff Stryker's How to Enlarge Your Penis* (no publishing details); for an analysis of Stryker, see Mark Simpson, *Male Impersonators*, pp. 131–42.

44. L. Williams, 'Pornographies on\scene, or diff'rent strokes for diff'rent folks', in L. Segal and M. McIntosh (eds), *Sex Exposed*, pp. 233–65.
45. Constance Penley, 'Feminism, Psychoanalysis and the Study of Popular Culture', in L. Grossberg, C. Nelson and P. Treichler (eds), *Cultural Studies*, pp. 479–500.
46. See Janice Raymond, 'Pornography and the Politics of Lesbianism', in C. Itzin (ed.), *Pornography*, pp. 166–78.
47. A. Dworkin, *Pornography*, p. 45.
48. M. Simpson, *Male Impersonators*, pp. 134ff; L. Segal, *Straight Sex*, pp. 210–2.
49. See L. Kipnis, '(Male) Desire and (Female) Disgust', p. 388.
50. Harriet Gilbert, 'So long as it's not sex and violence: Andrea Dworkin's *Mercy*', in L. Segal and M. McIntosh (eds), *Sex Exposed*, p. 229.
51. Mary McIntosh, 'Liberalism and the Contradictions of Sexual Politics', in *Sex Exposed*, p. 167

8 Male Images in Rock and Pop Music

1. I am using the term 'rock 'n' roll' to mean the beat music of the 1950s; 'rock music' is the term developed in the mid-sixties to describe the music developing from rock 'n' roll; 'pop music' is used to describe the whole popular music business; but 'pop' is often used to refer to a style of music that is not like rock 'n' roll: something lighter, less driven by the beat. Further discussion of terminology can be found in Peter Gammond, *The Oxford Companion to Popular Music* (Oxford: Oxford University Press, 1993) under 'Pop' and 'Rock'; Peter Wicke, *Rock Music: Culture, Aesthetics and Sociology* (Cambridge: CUP, 1990) Chapter 1; Charlie Gillett, *Sounds of the City: The Rise of Rock and Roll* (London: Souvenir, 1983) p. 3.
2. See Gillian Gaar, *She's A Rebel: the History of Women in Rock & Roll* (London: Blandford, 1993); also John Potter, 'The Singer not the Song: Women Singers as Composer-poets', *Popular Music* **13**:2 (1994) pp. 191–9.
3. See Barbara Bradby, 'Sampling sexuality: gender, technology and the body in dance music', *Popular Music* **12**:2 (1993) pp. 167–8.
4. G. Gaar, *She's A Rebel*, pp. 412–7.
5. Ibid., pp. 418–25.
6. P. Gammond, *Oxford Companion to Popular Music*, p. 60.
7. Nelson George, *The Death of Rhythm & Blues* (London: Omnibus, 1988).
8. See Greil Marcus, *Mystery Train: Images of America in Rock 'n' Roll Music* (Harmondsworth: Penguin, 1991) pp. 65–95.
9. Allan F. Moore, *Rock: The Primary Text*, p. 65.
10. See Antony Marks, 'Young, Gifted and Black: Afro-American and Afro-Caribbean Music in Britain 1963–88', in Paul Oliver (ed.), *Black Music in Britain: Essays on the Afro-Asian Contribution to Popular Music* (Milton Keynes: OUP, 1990) pp. 102–17; Dick Hebdige, *Subculture*, pp. 47–70.
11. Nelson George, *The Death of Rhythm & Blues*, p. 174.
12. P. Gammond, *The Oxford Companion to Popular Music*, p. 134.
13. Burton W. Peretti, 'Caliban reheard: New Voices on Jazz and American Consciousness', *Popular Music* **13**:2 (1994) pp. 151–64.

14. See Philip Tagg, 'From refrain to rave: the decline of figure and the rise of ground', *Popular Music* **13**:2 (1994), pp. 209–22.
15. S. Sadie and A. Latham (eds), *The Cambridge Music Guide* (Cambridge: CUP, 1990) pp. 522–4.
16. Paul Willis, 'The Golden Age', in *On Record*, p. 54.
17. S. Frith, *Sound Effects*, p. 87.
18. Angela McRobbie, 'Settling Accounts with Subcultures: A Feminist Critique', in *On Record*, p. 70.
19. Nik Cohn, *Awopbopaloobopalopbamboom: Pop from the Beginning* (London: Paladin, 1970) p. 14.
20. See Greil Marcus, *Dead Elvis: A Chronicle of a Cultural Obsession*, p. 4.
21. C. Gillett, *Sounds of the City*, p. 80.
22. Alan Clayson, *Only the Lonely* (London: Pan Books, 1990) pp. 27–8.
23. S. Sadie and A. Latham (eds), *The Cambridge Music Guide* p. 523.
24. Greil Marcus, *Mystery Train*, p. 125.
25. Ibid., pp. 158–9.
26. Sue Wise, 'Sexing Elvis', in *On Record*, p. 395.
27. This is the description given by S. Frith, *Sound Effects*, pp. 23–7.
28. See Nelson George, *The Death of Rhythm & Blues*, pp. 92–3.
29. Nik Cohn, *Awopbopaloobopalopbamboom*, p. 32.
30. See Richard Goldstein, 'I Blew My Cool in *The New York Times*', in Clinton Heylin (ed.), *The Penguin Book of Rock & Roll Writing* (Harmondsworth: Viking, 1992) pp. 541–7.
31. Nik Cohn, *Awopbopaloobopalopbamboom*, pp. 150–1.
32. D. Clarke (ed.), *The Penguin Encyclopedia of Popular Music* (Harmondsworth: Penguin, 1990) p. 997.
33. See Jules Siegel, 'Goodbye Surfing! Hello God!', in *The Penguin Book of Rock & Roll Writing*, pp. 524–40.
34. Nelson George, *The Death of Rhythm & Blues*, pp. 86–7.
35. C. Gillett, *Sounds of the City*, p. 235.
36. See N. George, *The Death of Rhythm & Blues*, pp. 98–104.
37. See Kobena Mercer, 'Monster Metaphors: Notes on Michael Jackson's "Thriller"', in Angela McRobbie (ed.), *Zoot Suits and Second-Hand Dresses*, pp. 50–73.
38. Will Straw, 'Characterizing rock music culture: the case of heavy metal', in Simon During (ed.), *The Cultural Studies Reader* (London: Routledge, 1993) p. 379; R. Walser, *Running with the Devil*, p. 109.
39. P. Gammond, *The Oxford Companion to Popular Music*, p. 260.
40. See Robert Walser, 'Eruptions: heavy metal appropriations of classical virtuosity', *Popular Music* **11**:3 (1992) pp. 263–308.
41. R. Walser, *Running with the Devil*, Chapter 5.
42. Ibid., p. 139.
43. For a review of a notorious Guns N' Roses song, 'One in a Million', see W. Studer, *Rock on the Wild Side*, p. 101.
44. See the review of a Body Count concert in *Kerrang!*, No. 515, 8 October 1994, p. 19.
45. A point made by Angela McRobbie, 'Settling Accounts with Subcultures', p. 74.
46. Simon Frith, *Sound Effects*, p. 227.
47. R. Walser, *Running with the Devil*, p. 60.

9 Male Sport

1. See, for example, *International Review for the Sociology of Sport, Leisure Studies, Journal of Sports History*.
2. Jennifer A. Hargreaves, 'Gender on the Sports Agenda', *International Review for the Sociology of Sport*, 25:4 (1990) p. 295.
3. Roberta J. Park, 'Biological thought, athletics and the formation of a "man of character": 1830–1900', in J. A. Mangan and J. Walvin (eds), *Manliness and Morality: Middle-Class Masculinity in Britain and America, 1800–1940* (Manchester: Manchester University Press, 1987) pp. 17–18.
4. Montague Shearman, *Athletics and Football* (London: The Badminton Library, 1888) pp. 369–70, quoted in James Walvin, 'Symbols of moral superiority: slavery, sport and the changing world order, 1800–1950', in J. A. Mangan and J. Walvin (eds), *Manliness and Morality*, p. 242.
5. Quoted in J. A. Mangan, 'Publicists, Propagandists and Proselytizers: Ideals of Empire for Public Schoolboys', in J. A. Mangan, *The Games Ethic and Imperialism: Aspects of the Diffusion of an Ideal* (Harmondsworth: Penguin Viking, 1985) p. 41.
6. See the essays in J. A. Mangan, *The Games Ethic and Imperialism*.
7. Ibid., p. 250.
8. John Major, speech to Conservative Party Conference, Bournemouth, 14 October 1994, reported in the *Guardian*, 15 October 1994, p. 6.
9. See Benjamin G. Rader, 'The Recapitulation Theory of Play: Motor Behaviour, Moral Reflexes and Manly Attitudes in Urban America, 1880–1920', in *Manliness and Morality*, pp. 123–34.
10. See Joe Maguire, 'Sport, Racism and British Society: A Sociological Study of England's Elite Male Afro-Caribbean Soccer and Rugby Union Players', in G. Jarvie (ed.), *Sport, Racism and Ethnicity* (London: Falmer Press, 1991) pp. 99–103; Jose Parry and Noel Parry, 'Sport and the Black Experience', in the above, p. 155; and David K. Wiggins, '"Great Speed but Little Stamina": the Historical Debate over Black Athletic Superiority', *Journal of Sports History*, **16**:2 (1989) pp. 158–85.
11. Michael A. Messner, 'Masculinities and Athletic Careers', in J. Lorber and S. A. Farrell (eds), *The Social Construction of Gender* (Newbury Park: Sage, 1991) p. 67.
12. Philip G. White and Anne B. Vagi, 'Rugby in the 19th-Century Boarding School System: A Feminist Psychoanalytic Perspective', in M. Messner and D. Sabo (eds), *Sport, Men and the Gender Order: Critical Feminist Perspectives* (Champaign, Illinois: Human Kinetics, 1990) p. 76.
13. Richard Holt, *Sport and the British: A Modern History* (Oxford: Clarendon, 1989) pp. 122–4.
14. Described well by Nick Hornby, *Fever Pitch* (London: Victor Gollancz, 1992) p. 237.
15. Spoken by the MP Frank Field, quoted in John Williams and Rogan Taylor, 'Boys Keep Swinging: Masculinity and Football Culture in England', in T. Newburn and E. A. Stanko (eds), *Just Boys Doing Business? Men, Masculinities and Crime* (London: Routledge, 1994) p. 223.
16. Ibid., pp. 226–8.

17. Eric Dunning, 'Sociological Reflections on Sport, Violence and Civilization', *International Review for the Sociology of Sport*, **25**:1 (1990) p. 75; see also R. Holt, *Sport and the British*, pp. 327–8.
18. E. Dunning, 'Sociological Reflections on Sport', pp. 65–76.
19. Quoted in Peter Levine and Peter Vinten-Johansen, 'Sports Violence and Social Crisis', in Donald Spivey (ed.), *Sport in America*, p. 231.
20. Ibid., pp. 225–31.
21. Ibid., p. 220.
22. J. Williams and R. Taylor, 'Boys Keep Swinging', pp. 223–5.
23. 'Will To Win', Catalyst TV programme, broadcast 4.10.93 on Channel 4.
24. Ibid; also Joe Maguire, 'Sport, Racism and British Society', pp. 98–9; Ernest Cashmore, *Black Sportsmen* (London: Routledge & Kegan Paul, 1982) Chapter 3.
25. Richard Majors, 'Cool Pose: Black Masculinity and Sports', in M. Messner and D. Sabo (eds), *Sport, Men and the Gender Order*, p. 109.
26. Wilbert Marcellus Leonard, II, 'The Sports Experience of the Black College Athlete: Exploitation in the Academy', *International Review for the Sociology of Sport*, **21**:1 (1986) p. 36.
27. Richard Majors, 'Cool Pose', p. 110.
28. A. Laitinen and A. Tiihonen, 'Narratives of Men's Experiences in Sport', *International Review for the Sociology of Sport*, **25**:3 (1990) p. 189.
29. Thomas Hauser, *Muhammed Ali: His Life and Times* (London: Robson Books, 1991) pp. 28 and 63.
30. Frederic Cople Jaher, 'White America versus Jack Johnson, Joe Louis and Muhammed Ali', in Donald Spivey (ed.), *Sport in America*, pp. 145–92.
31. T. Hauser, *Muhammed Ali*, p. 231.
32. Quoted in Hauser, p. 84.
33. R. Holt, *Sport and the British*, p. 107.
34. Ibid., pp. 106 and 108–9.
35. Ian Hamilton, *Gazza Agonistes* (London: Granta, 1993) No. 45, pp. 114–15.
36. Ibid., p. 108.
37. Nick Hornby, *Fever Pitch*, p. 19.
38. Ibid., p. 43.
39. Ibid., p. 135.

10   Conclusions

1. Yvonne Tasker, *Spectacular Bodies*, p. 98.
2. Ibid., p. 65.
3. Philip French, *Westerns* (London: Secker and Warburg, 1977) p. 52.
4. Richmal Crompton, 'William's Evening Out', in *William the Fourth* (London: Macmillan, 1983) p. 98.
5. Barbara Creed, 'Phallic panic: male hysteria and *Dead Ringers*'.
6. Angela McRobbie, 'Settling Accounts with Subcultures: A Feminist Critique', p. 74.
7. See Yvonne Tasker's chapter, 'The Body in Crisis or the Body Triumphant?' in *Spectacular Bodies*, pp. 109–31.
8. Described in Graham McCann, *Rebel Males* (London: Hamish Hamilton, 1991).

9. K. Marx, 'A Contribution to the Critique of Hegel's Philosophy of Right. Introduction', in *Karl Marx: Early Writings* (Harmondsworth: Penguin, 1975) p. 244.

10. Richard Majors, 'Cool Pose: Black Masculinity and Sports', in M. Messner and D. Sabo (eds), *Sport, Men and the Gender Order*, p. 111.

11. K. Marx, *Capital: A Critique of Political Economy*, Volume I (Harmondsworth: Penguin, 1990) p. 990.

12. Ibid., p. 990. For a discussion of alienation and fetishism, see Geoffrey Pilling, *Marx's 'Capital': Philosophy and Political Economy* (London: Routledge & Kegan Paul, 1980) pp. 157–96.

13. Y. Tasker, *Spectacular Bodies*, pp. 81 and 70.

14. Polly Toynbee, *Radio Times*, 18–24 June 1994, p. 28.

15. Quoted in Y. Tasker, *Spectacular Bodies*, p. 108.

Index of Texts Cited

Literary Works

General Index